SHADES OF GRAY

Also by John Egerton

A Mind to Stay Here   1970

The Americanization of Dixie   1974

Visions of Utopia   1977

Nashville: The Faces of Two Centuries   1979

Generations   1983

Southern Food   1987

Side Orders   1990

SHADES OF GRAY

DISPATCHES FROM THE MODERN SOUTH

JOHN EGERTON

LOUISIANA STATE UNIVERSITY PRESS
Baton Rouge and London

First printing
00 99 98 97 96 95 94 93 92 91   5 4 3 2 1

Designer: Glynnis Phoebe
Typeface: Baskerville/Caslon Open
Typesetter: Graphic Composition
Printer and binder: Thomson-Shore, Inc.

Library of Congress Cataloging-in-Publication Data

Egerton, John.
  Shades of gray : dispatches from the modern South / John Egerton.
    p. cm.
  Includes index.
  ISBN 0-8071-1705-6 (cloth : alk. paper)
  1. Southern States—Civilization—20th century. I. Title.
F216.2.E36   1991
975'.043—dc20   91-12391
                                                                       CIP

Most of the material in this book first appeared in somewhat different form in the
following magazines: *American Heritage, Change, Foundation News, Motive, New Times,* the
New York Times Magazine, the *Progressive,* and *Southern Exposure.* Specific citations are
given at the beginning of each essay. In addition, material gathered on assignments for
several other magazines, including the *Chronicle of Higher Education, Race Relations Reporter, Saturday Review, Southern, Southern Education Report,* and *Southern Voices,* contributed directly to this collection. The author acknowledges with appreciation each magazine's part in the development and publication of the articles—and indirectly, of this
book.

In memory of some boon companions now departed:

Ephriam Barnes, Ewin Hille, J. A. ("Red") McCauley,
Tom Paine, Bernie Schweid,
W. O. Smith, Dick Weesner, Abner T. White

∾ CONTENTS

SHADES OF GRAY

✑ INTRODUCTION:
A DIFFERENT AND
FAMILIAR PLACE

Ah, the South, always the South. What is
there about it that fascinates us so? How does
it keep such a hold on us? Whether we love it
or hate it, this place is *in* us, and we can no
more escape it than we can get shed of our
blood and bones and flesh.

From some now-forgotten source, this
utterance of wonder and realization found its way into a file folder
labeled "Southern Notes," a grab bag of miscellaneous jottings and
clippings that I have been accumulating since the late 1950s. The
South, always the South—a comfort and a bane, a glory and a burden, a revelation and an impenetrable mystery.

Over the past thirty years or so, I have written hundreds of short
and long nonfiction pieces on a wide variety of subjects, but seldom
have any of them been far removed from some connection to this
land of my birth and abiding. It is as if I can't let go of it, or it of me.
One of the more telling ironies in this author-subject bond is the fact
that I have made a modest career out of writing about the imminent
demise of the South—and yet, the reports of its passing have all been
greatly exaggerated (to borrow Mark Twain's phrase), and its persist-
ent survival is all that has assured my own.

As much as it has changed in the last half of the twentieth century—and the changes have been truly revolutionary—the South still
clings to its own character and identity, its own quirky and eccentric
nature. It retains a seemingly infinite capacity to intrigue and fasci-
nate both residents and visitors, to seize their attention and hold it.
This magnetic power can be either positive or negative, can even be

1

both at once—unifying and isolating, inspiring and obsessive. The South is more complex than it generally appears; no matter what people see in it or think of it, there is usually more to it than meets the eye. For all its fusion with this nation of which it is a vital and now inseparable part, the South remains the most distinctive and identifiable region thereof and has been so since the earliest years of its colonial past.

Part and parcel of its complexity is its lack of a clearly marked geographical border. The South, some people say, comprises the eleven states of rebellion in the Civil War: Alabama, Arkansas, Georgia, Florida, Louisiana, Mississippi, North Carolina, South Carolina, Tennessee, Texas, and Virginia. But that excludes Kentucky, my home state, which is historically and stereotypically Southern to the bone, and Maryland, which has often aligned itself with the culture and politics of the South. And what about West Virginia, which was part of Virginia until the Civil War and certainly seems more Southern than Eastern or Northern? Then there is also Delaware, and the District of Columbia, and Missouri, and Oklahoma, all of which were aligned with the South in maintaining legally segregated schools up until the time when the U.S. Supreme Court overturned such laws in 1954. There is even Kansas, where the radical abolitionist John Brown first gained notoriety—and where, a century later, the Reverend Oliver Brown (no relation) brought suit against the segregated schools of Topeka and thus lent his name to the historic case (*Brown v. Board of Education*) that finally affirmed racial equality as the law of the land. Clearly, the South is many places to many people. Malcolm X, the charismatic black civil rights leader, had his own explicit definition of the region; the South, he said, "is anywhere south of the Canadian border."

Whatever its physical boundaries, the South of the mind and heart reaches far beyond them, and all who have been or continue to be touched by that South have known that its best and worst qualities are often on display in tandem, like a Jekyll-Hyde drama. Slavery, class consciousness, white supremacy, segregation, poverty, isolation, political demagoguery, religious fanaticism, and violence have all played a major part in shaping the history and character of the region; so too have music, food, speech, humor, manners, family continuity, friendliness, volunteerism, charity, and the blessings of nature.

In the South, irony and paradox and contradiction are not just isolated aberrations; they're well within the norm. Consider these examples:

•Beginning in the 1920s, when the Vanderbilt Fugitives and Mississippi's William Faulkner first gained national prominence in literature, and continuing without pause into the present generation, the South has produced a disproportionate plurality of the best American writers. But in defiance of that proud and positive tradition, there is also a Southern heritage of ignorance. The South has remained throughout this century the nation's least literate section; its population buys and reads fewer newspapers and magazines and books, builds and uses fewer libraries and bookstores, and generally possesses less mastery of or facility with the printed word. (The *spoken* word is another matter; political oratory, storytelling, and porch talk are among the South's great strengths.)

• The South has more churches per capita, and more of its residents attend religious services regularly, than elsewhere in the country. But if the region is known for its pious tendencies, it is also notorious for its aggressive ones. It has customarily led the nation in gun ownership, military service, police power, murders and killings (there's a difference, murder being between strangers), executions, and mob violence outside the law.

• The South leads the nation in the production of whiskey, both legal (bourbon) and illegal (moonshine); it also leads in abstinence and prohibition and even produces some of its legal whiskey in dry countries where the law prohibits its sale or public consumption.

A land of such pervasive paradox and inner conflict is almost certain to be filled to overflowing with great material for writers, or so it has seemed to me down through the years. It may be, in fact, that conflict itself is the single most plausible explanation for the South's abundance of twentieth-century literary talent. Whatever else its characters and places and events have been, they have never struck me as dull and uninteresting; on the contrary, their volatile and unpredictable nature alone is enough to make even the least appealing of them worth watching.

As a nonfiction writer throughout my career and a free lance for the past twenty years, I have had a continuing interest in one particular type of journalism: the long piece, five to ten thousand words or

3

more. Too long for most newspapers and many magazines, too short to be a book, these extended articles provide enough room for the development of characters and ideas while remaining within the focal range of single specific topics. Their main strength is depth, not breadth; more like a laser than a searchlight, they can be thorough and penetrating, even comprehensive, within narrow bounds of latitude.

Profiles of individuals lend themselves especially well to long articles; so do stories about particular places (a city, a university, an island) or about specific events (a trial, an election, a tornado). Flexibility of style is a hallmark of such writing; within the limits of the imperative to convey truth, the nonfiction writer can employ any device or technique available to the novelist. Tense and person, opinion and analysis, dialogue and descriptive narrative, historical and contemporary perspective—these and other elements of construction and style are free for the choosing. So many options, together with the freedom to "write long" (without severe space limitations), add up to an enormously appealing prospect for almost anyone interested in writing.

It is pieces such as these that make up the collection at hand—a baker's dozen true stories from the South of yesterday and today, all written between 1967 and 1988. The subjects range from race relations and education to law, crime, politics, and culture. Though several of the stories draw heavily on historical material, all have a direct connection to the time in which they were written. They are period pieces, to be read in the context of the time of composition rather than as products of the 1990s; each has a new introductory note and postscript, but the stories themselves remain substantially as they were originally written.

If there is a common denominator among them, it is this: All are about Southern people, places, events, or issues that have beneath their surface a deceptive complexity. What appear at first to be clear, simple, cut-and-dried tales in sharply etched images of black and white gradually reveal themselves to have deeper dimensions, subtle shades of gray. Like the South itself in its transformation from the old age to the new (the dividing line being the end of World War II), the subjects of these stories are harder to classify, categorize, and define than they may appear at first glance to be. Just as the South is

4

both an exotic and a familiar place, unique and yet recognizable, so are these people, these stories; in them, things we thought we understood turn out to be more complicated than we had imagined, even though a lingering familiarity surrounds them. Whether we identify with the characters or not, like them or not, believe them or not, we do still recognize them as being known quantities—and thoroughly Southern.

A shade of gray may also be the appropriate tone for a collection that touches on racial issues as frequently as these stories do. Race has been a constant preoccupation of the South—an obsession—throughout its history; inevitably, it has also been a dominant theme of the region's writers. In this instance, gray is not an allusion to Confederate gray, but rather a neutral tone that provides the background for a continuing series of studies in black and white.

In another dimension, several of the pieces in this set also bear a resemblance to detective stories—mysteries that gradually unravel to reveal some heretofore hidden or lost or forgotten detail of history. They may raise and leave unanswered new sets of questions, but to the extent that they answer any old ones, they also stir the problem-solving juices that are the lifeblood of every good mystery story.

Taken together, these thirteen pieces—examples of a particular type of magazine journalism and free-lance writing—are broadly reflective of the major social issues that have shaped the South in the twentieth century. Education, race relations, social activism, politics and public policy, crime and punishment, economic development, family history, and such specific concerns as aging, desegregation, strip mining, and censorship are addressed here in stories from the Deep South states of Alabama and Mississippi and South Carolina, from Florida and Virginia and Tennessee, and from the border states of West Virginia and Kentucky.

The perspective offered by this collection is of a South evolving, a different and familiar place in constant motion, like a painting in progress. The canvas is defined less by its boldly contrasting splashes of light and shadow, white and black, than by its more impressionistic tones, its gray hues. In a nation and a world grown decidedly more complex and inscrutable, the South with all its blendings of myth and reality finally seems to belong, to fit, to be a part of the whole.

5

∽ RACE AND CLASS IN HIGHER EDUCATION

For more than a decade beginning in 1965, I wrote regularly about racial issues in the schools for two Nashville-based magazines, Southern Education Report *and* Race Relations Reporter, *and also occasionally for such national education journals as* Change, Saturday Review, *and the* Chronicle of Higher Education. *On a tour of Southern state university campuses in January 1967, a group of education writers from around the country and I found that the desegregation trends that were then so much in evidence elsewhere in the South had not reached very far in higher education. Most of the essay below was based on that tour and was published in the November 1967 issue of* Motive, *a United Methodist Church magazine. The second part is a close-up look at one school, the University of Mississippi, based on a visit I made there in the spring of 1972. That story was published in the winter 1972–1973 issue of* Change.

The big state universities of the South are on the make. With great expectations, a sense of urgency, and more money than they have ever had before, they are seeking admission to the national arena of higher education. They are raising their academic standards, improving their faculties, strengthening their graduate programs, and plunging into research, in pursuit of the prestige and status that have escaped them for a hundred years. But those who make it into the big tent will pay a heavy price, for in the very process of their own improvement they are leaving virtually untouched the growing problem of race and class that plagues their states and that cannot be solved without their help.

6

Irony abounds in the story of the rise to prominence of these public institutions. The more they reach out for national recognition, the less they appear to be concentrating on the educational needs and problems closer to home. Even though their faculties and student bodies are more diversified than in the past, an increasing number of the ablest students and professors in their states—blacks in particular—are being recruited away by colleges and universities in the North, East, and West. And even as Southern blacks and low-income whites see the first glimmerings of opportunity beginning to dawn around them, their state universities remain virtually untouched as bastions of the white middle and upper classes.

The long and little-known history of black efforts to crack segregation in the colleges and universities of seventeen Southern and border states goes back at least as far as 1933, when the University of North Carolina used jim crow laws to deny a qualified black applicant admission to its pharmacy school. Later in the 1930s students trying to enroll at the University of Virginia and the University of Tennessee also were turned away. Finally, in 1936 an Amherst College graduate and Maryland resident named Donald Murray was admitted to the University of Maryland School of Law under a state court order, and he went on to graduate there.

West Virginia in 1938 became the first of the segregated states to voluntarily accept black students into its graduate and professional schools. Several other states, including Texas, Virginia, Louisiana, and Missouri, tried to avoid the issue by hastily creating graduate programs in their public black colleges. That tactic spawned a federal lawsuit in Missouri that was argued all the way to the U.S. Supreme Court.

By the late 1940s Arkansas had joined West Virginia in voluntary desegregation, and federal court rulings had opened universities in Missouri and Oklahoma as well as Maryland. Supreme Court decisions in cases from Oklahoma and Texas in 1950 finally established the legal principle of equal opportunity in higher education that the court then expanded and applied to elementary and secondary schools in its famous *Brown* v. *Board of Education* ruling four years later.

But *Brown* delivered no swift transformation; as the decade of the 1950s slipped away, the five Deep South states of Alabama, Georgia,

7

Louisiana, Mississippi, and South Carolina enrolled no black students at all in their historically all-white public colleges and universities, and only a token few were attending graduate and professional schools in the other states. (A young woman named Autherine Lucy had briefly entered the University of Alabama in 1956, but she was driven from the campus by rioting whites and then was expelled by the institution's trustees for accusing university officials of conspiring with the mob.)

Under heavy pressure from the federal government, the last of the segregationist universities yielded in the early 1960s. Hamilton Holmes and Charlayne Hunter were enrolled at the University of Georgia under a court order in 1961. James Meredith entered the University of Mississippi in the fall of 1962, but President John F. Kennedy had to override the authority of Governor Ross Barnett and federalize the state's National Guard to put down a riotous white reaction on the campus that left two men dead and over three hundred injured. Harvey B. Gantt was admitted to Clemson University without violent incident in 1963, but later that year President Kennedy took command of Alabama's National Guard to make Governor George Wallace step aside and allow James Hood and Vivian Malone to enroll at the University of Alabama.

Now, after several more years have passed, the senior universities of those last four desegregating states have moved grudgingly to accept a black enrollment of just over 1 percent (about six hundred students out of almost fifty thousand). And if that total seems minuscule, consider this: The senior universities of four other presumably more progressive Southern states—Arkansas, Florida, Kentucky, and Virginia—have only about four hundred black students among them, out of a combined enrollment of almost sixty thousand. Furthermore, the record is not much better outside the segregated South; in the combined enrollments of Penn State, Purdue, the University of Michigan, and the several campuses of the University of California, there are 180,000 students, of whom only 3,700—2 percent—are black Americans.

For the white educators of the South who have waited so long for their day in the sun, the emergence and persistence of the race/class issue is embarrassing, annoying, and frustrating. With some justification, these beleaguered public servants can—and do—offer a spirited defense of their actions. Their arguments run something like this:

"For all our history, we've had it thrown up to us that we were inferior institutions, and we have been self-conscious and defensive about it. We've tried to escape our provincialism by becoming more regional and national and even international in scope. We have become more selective in the students we accept, more cosmopolitan in our hiring of faculty, more sophisticated in the nature and level of our graduate programs and our research activities. At last, we can begin to take a little pride in our performance.

"But instead of praise for these accomplishments, what we are hearing are the same old impertinent and irrelevant questions about race and poverty. We've *had it* with civil rights. We've moved beyond the days of segregated drinking fountains and lunch counters. We no longer make any distinctions or keep any records by race, and any qualified student is welcome in our classrooms and our cafeterias and our dorms. You're beating us with a dead horse. Your questions are not only beside the point, they're harmful to the very cause of progress and improvement you've always criticized us for lacking. How about giving us a little credit for a change?"

It's a fair question. Certainly the universities are vastly improved in almost every way from what they were a generation ago. Furthermore, it would be grossly unfair to blame them for the pervasive race and class problems in their states, problems that are political and social and economic in origin—and older than the universities themselves.

But the problems are serious and growing, and they demand answers. The South has more blacks and poor people than the other regions of the country, and the question of what to do to improve their circumstances must be addressed. The universities, intentionally or not, are part of the problem—and willingly or not, they must be part of the solution.

The dilemma facing the universities (and it is primarily the large state universities to which this pertains, though not exclusively so) is this: As they become more specialized and fragmented, their interests and efforts—and money—turn more and more to graduate pro-

9

grams and research. The undergraduate student becomes less and less important, both to professors and to admissions officers, and standards for admission climb steadily higher. The universities, in the process, become preoccupied with status, with institutional advancement, and the flagship syndrome feeds on itself. In academics as in athletics, the burning desire among administrators and faculty is for more visibility, prestige, and national recognition.

Inevitably, the universities become less and less interested in or in touch with the masses of people in their states. The great motto of the past—"The borders of our campus are the borders of the state"— is seldom heard now. The state university is becoming the home of the elite, and the needs and problems of the average and the less able—social, political, economic, and especially educational needs— are being passed by default to the former colleges for teachers, the junior colleges, the vocational-technical schools, and other small institutions with limited means and fewer resources.

It is a curious anomaly that the medical, engineering, business, and agricultural schools of the big state universities contribute so much to the solution of public problems, yet the same universities seem unwilling or unable to mount an attack on discrimination, which most would acknowledge is the biggest domestic problem the nation now faces. The concept of service—historically one of the three main purposes of a state university—is the principle by which the institutions prove their worth and their usefulness to the taxpaying masses. Yet service in the nation's transition from a segregated to an integrated society has not drawn the interest, the funds, or the commitment of the academic community.

It should be noted that there is not a complete absence of activity in this area. A few universities are engaged in research or training programs in early childhood education, in cross-cultural teacher preparation, in precollege prep courses, and the like. But most of these projects are small-scale, inconspicuous, or coolly academic, and only a handful are strictly of local origin, without federal or philanthropic initiation. The crash program, the all-out effort, the clear evidence of local and state commitment—these signs of serious intent are seldom seen.

University educators say such visible and far-reaching efforts are too costly and too politically explosive to be undertaken at this time.

And there is the matter of priorities; the institutions, they say, cannot become top-quality universities and remain general-purpose centers of mass education at the same time.

It is in realizing the truth of this defense that the dimensions of the race/class problem in higher education come into clear focus. For the problem, at its roots, is political, and it is precisely here that the universities, for all their strengths, must lead instead of follow. In all the talk about priorities, what is left unsaid is the fact that universities do not grow in an orderly, logical, sequential way, from priority to priority, but rather in erratic response to the power and persuasion of individuals and groups within and without—which is to say they grow, or wither, politically.

Neither, it should be noted, are universities democratic institutions. In spite of their classic image as idyllic centers of unfettered inquiry and liberal thought and free expression, they are in reality tradition-bound citadels of conservatism ruled by unelected hierarchies that maintain a vertical pecking order from the boardroom to the mail room. In this caste system based on subjective standards of "excellence" or "merit," there is not much interest in unconventional programs or "high-risk" individuals.

Internal status is at stake here. There are no rewards for lifting up the least prepared. By far the most credit is given to those who take the cream of the crop and make of them clones of themselves. It is a self-fulfilling prophecy, like predicting that cream will rise to the top.

What is emerging, then, is not just a race/class conflict but a problem of such broad dimensions and deep seriousness that even the most preliminary suggestions of a way out seem premature at best. It is a problem not just for a few state universities, or for all those in the South, but for all the institutions of higher education in the nation, public and private. This is how one veteran educator, a native Southerner who has spent his life in the academic communities of the region, analyzes the dilemma:

"It's the same old story, and it's just as true in the North as here, if not more so: Educators theorize, preachers moralize, the affluent generalize and rationalize and hypothesize, but the poor—black and white—have to shift for themselves. There is no more real integration of races or classes in these universities than there is in the most middle- or upper-class neighborhood. All in all, it's a discouraging

11

picture, and there are no quick answers. You can't really fault a school for trying to improve its quality, but somehow there has to be a way to get at these other problems as well. If raising the level and quality of life among blacks and the poor isn't a responsibility of the best minds in a state, then pray God, whose responsibility is it? They can't do it alone, but they sure as hell ought to be giving some leadership. Or maybe the hard fact is that the state universities simply cannot get out in front of the political forces in power—and if that's the case, things aren't likely to get much better very soon."

Racial desegregation in the public schools of the South far outpaces that in the universities. All of the predominantly white universities visited by the education writers on their tour of Georgia, the Carolinas, and Virginia have more foreign students than black Americans in their student bodies, and most of the schools actually have fewer black students now than they had a couple of years ago. "At first," said one dean, "Negroes flocked to us for graduate work, but now we have only a few. Most of them are unprepared for the level of performance required here, because their college experience was limited by poor high schools, and that by poor elementary schools, and that in turn by years of preschool deprivation. I don't know the answer." Clearly, the answer will not come from doing business as usual.

The number of black faculty members teaching classes in formerly all-white Southern universities could almost be counted on the fingers of one hand. Here again, as with so many of the better black students, Northern institutions have sought and taken the best they could find—and the schools that suffer most from this brain drain are the historically black colleges.

In any consideration of race and education in the South, the plight of the black colleges is probably the most perplexing and emotion-ridden issue of all. What their future is in the context of a changing social system is undetermined, perhaps unfathomable—and, from a journalistic standpoint, largely unreported.

While desegregation moves forward in the larger society, the lives of most blacks and virtually all poor people, whatever their race, are still a world removed from the campuses of the big state universities. White academicians and administrators, even when their hearts are in the right place, still seem to be waiting for solutions that will not affect them adversely or require any real sacrifice on their part. In their preoccupation with growth and their striving for national ranking, they can only react with weary patience to the repeated questions about segregation and poverty.

Perhaps they are right. Perhaps the university is powerless in the absence of broader political and economic and social change. Certainly it cannot eliminate inequality of opportunity as effectively as its agriculturists have eliminated brucellosis in cattle, or its physicians have conquered polio. But eventually, when society reaches the bedrock problems of race and class discrimination, the universities will have to take a pivotal role in their solution, whether they are ready or not.

Ole Miss, 1972

The enrollment of James Meredith at the University of Mississippi ten years ago was one of those rare events in which protagonists on a collision course pass all the exits. It was like a shootout in the streets, like an all-or-nothing roll in a high-stakes dice game—in this case, Ross Barnett going for broke against the president of the United States. Orval Faubus had tried it five years earlier, and George Wallace gave it a shot in 1963. They, like Barnett, crapped out. Showdowns seldom come to such a dramatic climax.

Momentous dramas like the one at Ole Miss increase in significance as the stakes are raised. That one began as a matter of dispute between citizen-applicant James Meredith and the university admissions officer; before it ended, it pitted Governor Barnett against John and Robert Kennedy, drew thousands of individuals into armed conflict, and very nearly left Mississippi and its institutions in a state of war against the United States.

The fact that the side represented by Meredith prevailed is important enough to make of it a major milestone in the University of Mississippi's 128-year history. Ole Miss has an A.M. and a P.M.—ante-Meredith and post-Meredith—and the two are both literally and figuratively as clear as black and white.

It would be far too much to assert, however, that Ole Miss is an

13

institution totally transformed from its white racist past. The creation and refinement of white supremacy there consumed the first 118 years of its history. That was the A.M. Now, Ole Miss in the P.M. is a study in contrast. Ten years into its new life, it exhibits all of the paradox and confusion of a displaced transient in search of safe shelter. The most prestigious university in the poorest state in the nation wears its contradictions out in the open, like tattoos on a sailor.

"It takes us awhile, but we do eventually reflect the movements and changes of other college communities," an Ole Miss professor explained. "They're filtered and modified by the time they get here, but the movements do come—anti-war, anti-athletics, anti-fraternities, pro-blacks, pro-women, pro-youth." Indeed, the university seems to be locked in a slow-motion struggle between its reminiscences and its ambitions. It is still different enough to stand out in some particulars—most of them unfavorable—but it is also much more like universities elsewhere than it used to be, which is to say less overtly racist and more eager to join the club of American universities on the make.

The catalog of comparisons—Ole Miss pro and con, old and new, before and after—seems almost endless. A few examples:

• Black Mississippi politician Charles Evers, in his campaign for governor in 1971, drew turnaway crowds for two speeches he made on the campus—a major switch from 1968, when it took a court injunction to get him a platform to speak on behalf of Hubert Humphrey. The campus paper, the *Daily Mississippian*, devoted its entire front page to the Evers visit last fall, and when a professor named John R. Fawcett wrote in a letter of protest that Evers was "an acknowledge [*sic*] pimp," he was taken to task in subsequent letters and an editorial.

• Ole Miss in the fall of 1971 had between 250 and 300 black students in a total enrollment of about 8,000. It had a black basketball star but no black football players. It had one black faculty member, a female sociologist. And until last year, it required all applicants for admission to present written recommendations from five "responsible citizens of the same community"—preferably alumni—testifying "to the good moral character of the person making [the] application." How even a few hundred black students managed to get past that hurdle is not clear.

• James W. Silver, the Ole Miss historian who dared to lay out in the most explicit and critical terms his perception of the state in *Mississippi: The Closed Society* in 1964 and who was effectively forced out of the state a year after the book was published, left behind some colleagues who, though less outspoken than he, shared his assessment. One of them, Russell Barrett, later wrote a carefully balanced book, *Integration at Ole Miss,* that cost him pay raises and promotions and cast him as something of a pariah among his fellows. Barrett suffered the slights and rebuffs in polite silence, and now, finally, he seems to have outlasted them.

In many ways, Ole Miss is almost a mirror image of its more progressive sister institutions elsewhere in the country. Fraternities and sororities control student life on the shady, picturesque campus. There is no student union building as such, but there are almost forty Greek-society houses, and about half of the white students belong to the organizations. Prohibition of alcohol is seldom enforced in the houses, and although marijuana is riskier, it too is easily obtained. The contemporary accoutrements of America's youth are visible everywhere: lots of skirts and sweaters, and even coats and ties, but also hot pants and jump suits and blue jeans. Even a few bearded, long-haired hippie types can be seen among the bouffant hairdos and crew cuts. A column in the campus paper called "Lib and Let Lib" reports on the latest styles and fashions.

There is compulsory class attendance and the remnants of curfew, and *in loco parentis,* and there is also strong student sentiment for dorm visitation privileges; in a referendum, they favored it by almost ten to one. The *Daily Mississippian* made visitation its major editorial objective last year, and the paper has also favored open meetings of the university's trustees, an off-campus bookstore run by students, and a voter registration drive for newly franchised eighteen year olds.

All-female picket lines at the entrances to campus buildings last fall turned out not to be demonstrating for women's liberation but promoting the candidacy of a coed named Linda for homecoming queen. Linda eventually won the popularity contest, beating two other girls and a 250-pound stone dubbed Roxanna Boulder.

Ole Miss has more football coaches than English professors. Its athletic program is organized in a department that operates like an independent conglomerate, running the campus bookstore, vending

15

machines, and concessions at athletic events with no competition to hinder it and making no public accounting of its income and expenditures. Johnny Vaught, the legendary football coach, and Archie Manning, his superstar quarterback, are no longer on the scene, but Vaught's book, *Rebel Coach,* is promoted all over the state, and automobile bumper stickers proclaim "Archie is a Saint" (providing both the name of his National Football League team in New Orleans and a measure of his status among the mortal masses).

Friday night pep rallies are still major events, but they draw smaller crowds and less enthusiasm than they used to, and the football games are not always sellouts as they were in Archie's heyday. In the stadium, black students and townspeople sit together at a distance from the Rebel-yelling, "Dixie"-singing, Confederate flag–waving whites; sometimes, as if to make a mildly rebellious statement of their own, they cheer for the black players on the visiting teams.

Downtown Oxford, the university's hometown, offers similar contrasts. You can get a mixed drink at the only bar in town and a half-pint or a fifth of liquor (no pints, though) at one of the several package stores, but the sale of beer is illegal. Housing is segregated and employment is very nearly so, but the public schools have managed to desegregate more effectively and more fairly than those in most Mississippi communities. The town's two movie houses and two motels have black customers, but the churches are segregated and so, of course, is the country club, about half of whose members belong to the Ole Miss faculty and administration.

All in all, it's a mixed bag, a collage of shifting images. Ole Miss clearly ain't what it used to be, but it's impossible to say with any preciseness what it is or what it is becoming.

If that blurred image fits the university as a whole, it may be less applicable to some of its individual units. There is, for example, the Law School, which seems to operate by its own clock and calendar. Ahead of the modest changes that are here and there in evidence elsewhere on the campus now, the Law School in the mid-1960s was, in the eyes of the state's legal and political power structure, a hotbed of revolution. It had been taken over by "traitors" and "radicals" and "outsiders." The coup was as swift as it was unexpected. It began just as James Silver branded the state a "closed society" and ended five or six years later. Things are more or less back to normal at the Law School now.

It would be difficult to overestimate the importance of the Ole Miss Law School in the legal and political scheme of things in Mississippi. It is the state's only accredited law school, and its graduates are automatically licensed to practice there, without the bother of taking a bar examination. A majority of Mississippi's three thousand lawyers are alumni of the Law School, and they dominate the state legislature, the state supreme court, and the federal judiciary in Mississippi—and, for more than twenty years now, the governor's mansion. *Time* magazine once called the Ole Miss Law School "the prep school for political power in Mississippi."

In 1962, the year federal force finally succeeded in getting James Meredith enrolled as an Ole Miss undergraduate, a law professor named William P. Murphy resigned after a five-year fight against pressure to fire him. Murphy had been teaching his students that the 1954 *Brown* decision was the law of the land, and he was a card-carrying member of the American Civil Liberties Union; for those "crimes" it was decided that he had to go. One of his defenders was Dean Robert J. Farley; later, when Farley offered to testify in favor of Meredith's legal right to an Ole Miss education, he too was ousted.

Murphy and Farley were the house liberals on a law faculty of Old South patricians who were comfortably ensconced in a feudal utopia. For the most part, the faculty's interests were strictly local—Mississippi law, drinks on the veranda, and such spectator sports as state and local politics and Ole Miss football. As much as possible, they avoided scholarship, administrative work, committee assignments, and students, the more to enjoy the splendid isolation and anonymity of academia in Oxford. It was not so much that they disliked and resented Murphy and Farley, or even disagreed with them—it was just that their two colleagues were a little too active and outspoken, too involved, too visible, and that complicated things.

A newcomer to the Law School faculty in 1962 was Joshua Morse III, a forty-year-old lawyer from Poplarville. He looked safe: his daddy once shared a law office with master racist Theodore G. Bilbo, and the Morse family was Old Mississippi through and through; furthermore, the young professor was a personal friend of M. M.

17

Roberts, the Ross Barnett ally who served as president of the all-powerful board of trustees that governed Ole Miss and the rest of the state's public colleges and universities. When Farley was turned out, a faculty committee tapped Morse for the deanship.

Instead of beginning his new duties in the fall of 1963, Morse took a year's leave to do graduate work in the Yale University Law School. Whether he was somehow transformed by that experience or slyly used it to prepare for a palace revolt is a matter of some continuing dispute; whatever the case, when he came back to Ole Miss in 1964 he brought with him two new professors (Yale graduates Ken Vinson and Bill Holder), foundation money to recruit black students and finance other daring innovations, and some unarticulated plans for further changes a bit later on. The next year he recruited Mike Horowitz, another Yale alumnus.

The first black students enrolled without incident. Then Morse got more philanthropic support—including $500,000 from the Ford Foundation—and the reconstruction rolled into high gear. Bobby Kennedy, the *bête noire* of Mississippi segregationists, was brought in for a speech (he drew a rousing ovation from the students and screams of outrage from the alumni), and a steady stream of controversial speakers followed. Fifteen of Yale's and Harvard's most illustrious faculty, followed by others from Columbia and New York universities, flew in for lectures on constitutional law, and new courses were offered on such theretofore taboo subjects as civil rights law and legal services for the indigent.

It was enough to alarm the most placid of the Law School's patricians, not to mention the Mississippi establishment, but it was only the beginning. In 1966 Morse added five more newly graduated Yale lawyers to his faculty (making eight out of a total of twenty-one), and about a dozen black students were enrolled. They made up only 3 percent of the school's enrollment of 360, but in a state that had no more than five or six black lawyers, the number was significant.

The Yale corps got busy in a hurry. They initiated federal lawsuits on malapportionment, civil liberties, and the justice of the peace fee system. Morse got a grant from the federal Office of Economic Opportunity (OEO) to start a legal services program for the poor. The young professors spent most of their time in the classroom, in late-night rap sessions, and in their active pursuit of legal and social reforms. Through their efforts, law school admissions requirements were rewritten, changes were made in the curriculum, and recruitment of black students continued apace. The white students were by no means unaffected by it all; they fell into factions that ranged from ardent disciples to implacable enemies.

"Josh's concept of administration was dreaming up good ideas and throwing them into someone's lap to implement," George Strickler recalls. Strickler and Mike Trister, two of the Yale recruits in 1966, took a special interest in the OEO-funded programs, and eventually they had a free hand. The older faculty members were deeply disturbed by what they saw happening around them, but they seemed not to know what to do about it, and Morse remained easygoing, relaxed, and benign.

"He's a strange and unpredictable man," Mike Horowitz reflected later. "He's no screaming liberal—he hired us because he liked us, not because of any ideological motive. He likes to go bird-watching and fishing. He likes parties, he's a great storyteller, and he's an incurable jock—he used to draw plays on scraps of paper and give them to the football coaches who were his friends. He's no scholar, but he's a hell of a fund-raiser, and a politician. We were all over the place, into everything, and he loved to see all that activity. It was as if there wasn't anything he couldn't solve over a bottle of bourbon with his friends down at the Capitol in Jackson."

Horowitz and a couple of the other young faculty members left for greener pastures before the 1967 fall term, and Morse didn't turn to Yale for more replacements. By then the rumbling of discontent had grown loud enough that it could no longer be ignored. The black enrollment was up to about twenty students—more than any other predominantly white law school in the nation was thought to have at that time—and Reuben Anderson, the first black graduate in the school's history, had gone out to begin changing the complexion of the state's legal fraternity. The legal services program was everywhere—into school desegregation suits, challenging welfare residency requirements, giving poor people their long-denied day in court—and the Yalies were out making speeches, involving students in a variety of off-campus activities, and generally making themselves heard.

The Jackson newspapers, the legislature, the university's trustees, and alumni all over the state finally galvanized in opposition to this whirlwind of activism. Morse was called down twice to appear before legislative committees, there was talk of opening another law school in one of the other state universities, and the inevitable charges of Communist subversion were thrown in. A collision was unavoidable.

It came in the spring of 1968. Ole Miss chancellor Porter Fortune, under pressure from the trustees and the legislature, told Morse that the Law School would have to give up its OEO legal services program. Strickler and Trister and a third professor, Luther McDougal, then succeeded in getting the program shifted to Mary Holmes Junior College, a black church-supported institution nearby, and Morse told them they could teach half-time and continue working in the program.

They did, until late summer. The pressure was still intense, and by then it was clear that the three faculty members would be forced to choose between their teaching posts and the OEO program. Morse had lost control, and though he took the position that employing part-time faculty was a common and acceptable practice—a position supported by a vote of his faculty—he couldn't make it stick. Mc-Dougal chose to leave the legal services program, but Strickler and Trister refused, and they were promptly fired. They then filed suit against the university to block the dismissal.

When the case came up in federal district court, Strickler and Trister argued that the firing was politically motivated. Judge Orma Smith, after a half-hour recess following the brief hearing, ruled in favor of the university. The two men appealed. A few months later, Strickler moved to New Orleans; Trister stayed with the legal services program at Mary Holmes Junior College.

In October 1969 the Fifth Circuit Court of Appeals reversed the dismissal ruling and ordered both men reinstated. Meanwhile, the American Association of Law Schools (AALS) had opened an investigation on the Ole Miss campus. The departure of Strickler and Trister had not brought peace to the Law School, and neither had the court decision ordering their reinstatement. By fall Morse himself was out of his job—whether he jumped or was pushed is not clear—and the palace revolt was over.

The AALS voted censure on the law school. Joel W. Bunkley, Morse's replacement, was eager to satisfy the association without having to reinstate the two professors, and he wanted out of the court battle that was then on appeal to the U.S. Supreme Court. He didn't worry much about Strickler, who was by then in a new job in New Orleans, but Trister was still around and apparently intent on rejoining the faculty. Bunkley, with the approval of Chancellor Fortune and M. M. Roberts, the trustees' president, offered Trister twenty thousand dollars to drop the entire matter and go away. He refused the money, and in the spring semester of 1970 he was reinstated. That summer, having made his point, Trister resigned, taking a job in Washington. He was the last of the Yale men to leave.

The Ole Miss Law School's six-year orbit into activism was a spectacular aberration, a reversal of form that briefly turned a conservative institution into one of the most progressive and experimental in the nation. Realistically, it never could have lasted. Mississippi's only law school—its "prep school for political power"—would not have survived the permanent transplant of a legal philosophy so alien to its history. Looking back, it is easy to see mistakes: Morse was too lax, the Yalies were too free-wheeling, there was too much unnecessary antagonism of the establishment and too little diplomacy. But more tact and more finesse, while it might have delayed the reaction, could not have averted it. Mississippi has not yet shown that it is ready for sweeping social reforms, any more than Michigan or Illinois or Pennsylvania have; institutional reformation of this magnitude is not on the agenda.

So the Ole Miss Law School has reverted to form. The patricians are back in control of the faculty, the curriculum has been purged of its "new" courses, the foundation- and OEO-funded programs are gone. "There's a uniformity of political beliefs in the faculty now," observed a senior law student. "The pendulum has swung back. You used to get some theory, some perspective of what the law is in the broader social and political context. Now you get technical training in how to be a successful Mississippi lawyer."

Between fifteen and twenty blacks have graduated from the Law School since 1967, and almost all of them are still in Mississippi, either in private practice or in civil rights and social action programs. One of them is Alex Sanders, who is now the director of the OEO-supported legal services program, which has offices in several north Mississippi towns.

"There are twenty or twenty-five black students in the Law School now," Sanders says, "but the only recruiting that's going on is being done by students, and they're having to raise the money themselves. The school isn't helping any." Furthermore, he says, other schools are now recruiting black students, and many of them have scholarships to offer. With federal and privately funded legal aid programs facing an uncertain future, the opportunities for a legal career in Mississippi appear to be diminishing for blacks.

The Law School's return to pre-Morse tranquility is thus complete. It is not as if nothing ever happened, though. There are the new black lawyers in the state, as well as white lawyers who also profited from the "Yale era." And the current crop of students, though most of them were not present then, are beneficiaries too. "We had an activist faculty and an apathetic student body back then," a senior declared, "and now I'd say the reverse is true. The relationship between black and white students is better, too—more relaxed, more honest, less self-conscious."

Yale alumnus Ken Vinson, who left Ole Miss the same year Josh Morse did (and who, with another colleague, John Robin Bradley, went with Morse to Florida State University's law school), looks back on his five years there as a great experience—and a worthwhile one for Ole Miss. "There has been a temporary setback," he says, "but the Ole Miss Law School and the entire university will be better in the long run because of what happened there."

The six-year tenure of Joshua Morse as dean of the University of Mississippi Law School in the 1960s coincided with the admission of the first black student there (in 1964) and the desegregation of the Mississippi bar (in 1967) by the first black law school graduate in the history of the university. By 1990 about 120 African-American students had graduated from the law school. Blacks now make up about 6 percent of the total enrollment in law at Ole Miss, about 9 percent of the university's overall enrollment (in round numbers, one thousand of eleven thousand), and slightly more than half of the Ole Miss Rebel football team.

WEST VIRGINIA'S BATTLE OF THE BOOKS

This story was researched and written in the late winter of 1975 and published in the June 1975 issue of the Progressive.

For more than a year now, the people of Charleston, West Virginia, and surrounding Kanawha County have been engaged in an emotional and sometimes violent struggle over what on the surface seems like a relatively trivial matter: the content of public school textbooks. No other issue—not the resignation of Richard M. Nixon, his pardon by President Gerald Ford, the Watergate trial, inflation, recession, the energy crisis, not even the locally crucial United Mine Workers strike—has generated as much heat or as much hostility in the West Virginia capital as a seemingly harmless collection of language arts books with such innocuous titles as *Communicating, Dynamics of Language,* and *Man in Literature.*While the nation has been preoccupied with the battle of the budget, the burning obsession in Kanawha County has been the battle of the books.

Public protest has become such a routine part of our national life that it has almost attained the status of an art form. A dispute arises; leaders emerge; there are mass meetings and marches and boycotts. Demands are made and rejected. Press conferences are called, charges and countercharges are tossed about, pressure grows. There is violence, and the national media come in. A compromise is sought; some change takes place, and the intensity of the conflict diminishes. Uninvolved viewers and readers begin to lose interest. The reporters and cameramen leave. The issue once again becomes local and isolated as other events in other places command attention. The protest, whether over or not, is forgotten by all but the most directly affected participants.

To a predictable degree, the West Virginia book controversy has followed that pattern, and the general impression it has created leans heavily toward stereotyped simplicity. Observers, and occasionally the press, have summoned straw figures to explain the conflict, and participants have often encouraged that practice by using it themselves. It is, some say, a clash between book-burners and defenders of academic freedom, or between fundamentalists and atheists, or between know-nothings and intellectuals, or between hillbillies and city slickers, or between patriots and traitors, or between prudes and libertines, or between populists and elitists, or between traditionalists and progressives.

But such one-dimensional labels are deceiving. The Kanawha County conflict is not a civil Super Bowl from which a clear-cut victor will emerge at the appointed hour, nor is it an isolated local dispute of only passing concern to the rest of the nation. It is in part a class war, a cultural war, a religious war. It is a struggle for power and authority that has sundered a peaceful community into rigid and fearful factions. And it is a complex and profoundly disturbing reflection of the deep fissures that crisscross American society. The surface calm in Charleston at midwinter concealed an ongoing crisis that few people there believe can be satisfactorily resolved, and its implications for other school systems and other communities are too serious to be ignored.

It is hard to know just where to begin sorting out the multiplicity of issues and ideologies that have attached themselves to the textbook dispute. A review of the chronology of events may be as good a place as any.

The first open sign of trouble appeared in April 1974 when Mrs. Alice Moore, a member of the Kanawha County School Board, objected to the procedure followed in adopting new textbooks. A five-member committee made up of language arts teachers from various schools and grade levels had recommended the adoption of more than 330 different titles—basic texts, supplementary materials, hardbound and softbound sets—to replace the grammar, reading, English, and literature books then in use. Mrs. Moore complained that whereas in the past a larger advisory committee had been used in the selection process, no such group had been called upon in this instance.

Furthermore, she asserted, her own preliminary inspection of the recommended materials had led her to the conclusion that many of the books on the language arts list contained material that was disrespectful of authority and religion, destructive of social and cultural values, obscene, pornographic, unpatriotic, or in violation of individual and familial rights of privacy. She moved that the board delay a decision to purchase the books, and when the motion passed, the Kanawha book war formally opened.

In the ensuing two months, the battle lines were formed. The executive committee of the county parent-teacher association sided with Mrs. Moore, and in many churches and public meetings there was a groundswell of protest against immoral, obscene, unpatriotic, and antireligious reading material. Representatives of other churches, of the textbook publishers, of the local chapter of the National Association for the Advancement of Colored People and the state human rights commission all endorsed the books in question, praising their multiracial and multicultural content and their overall quality.

On June 27, after hearing three hours of testimony from supporters and critics, the school board dropped eight of the most severely faulted supplementary paperbacks and then adopted, by a vote of three to two, all of the remaining 325 titles. Between then and the beginning of the fall term, the protest gathered momentum. Antitext committees were formed, principally in small towns and rural communities outside Charleston, and they joined in calling for a boycott of the schools. On September 3, the first day of school, 20 percent of the anticipated enrollment of 45,000 students were absent; the following day, an estimated 3,500 coal miners staged a wildcat strike in sympathy with the book protesters. Picket lines went up around many businesses and industrial plants in the county in an effort to muster sympathy for the book protest, and marching parents disrupted school operations.

There followed a flurry of court injunctions, arrests, shutdowns, and strategy sessions, and on September 11 the school board agreed to remove the new books from the schools and submit them to review by a representative citizens' committee. The action came too late to stop violence on both sides of the picket lines. Two men were wounded by gunshots, another was badly beaten, the schools were closed, politicians at every level exchanged charges of failure to maintain law and order, eleven men (including three ministers) were arrested for contempt of court, rallies were held on the steps of the state capitol, and demands were made for the resignation of Superintendent Kenneth Underwood and three members of the school board.

A full-page advertisement in the Charleston *Gazette,* paid for by a protest faction called the Business and Professional People's Alliance for Better Textbooks, listed several hundred items that the protesters found objectionable in the books. Among them were some "dirty words" and profanity, such as *goddam, bastard, son of a bitch, tits, piss,* and *whore.*

In addition, the ad said, some of the books contained "depressing stories . . . disregard for governmental authorities, stealing, beating, shooting, hate, and lying." Another of the criticized stories was said to portray a "bully [who] speaks of doing God's dirty work." Still another contained a passage saying, "The most dangerous threat in the modern world is based on the 'either or' fallacy, namely: that we must choose between 'capitalism' and 'communism.'"

By late September an eighteen-member textbook review committee had been appointed by the individual members of the school board, but the protest seemed beyond defusing. A Baptist minister, the Reverend Charles Quigley, prayed publicly for God to strike dead the three protextbook members of the board. A second boycott of the schools was advocated, and there were more arrests, including that of the Reverend Ezra Graley, a protest leader, who was subsequently jailed and fined for contempt of court.

The tension mounted. Early in October three schools were vandalized, three thousand miners were off the job in a continuing sympathy protest, six members of the review committee withdrew to prepare a minority report opposing the books, and the school board president, Albert Anson, resigned in protest against the removal of the books from the schools. Another school building was damaged, this time by a Molotov cocktail, a janitor was assaulted, the car of a jailed protester was set ablaze, shots were fired at a school bus as its driver returned from his rounds, school attendance dropped to 70 percent, an empty school was dynamited, and both the pros and the antis organized marches in the streets of Charleston. After the twelve remaining members of the review committee issued a report favorable to the textbooks, a dynamite blast damaged the school system's central office building, and Superintendent Underwood announced that he was looking for another job.

On November 8 the school board voted four to one to return all of the books to the schools. A few of the books were ordered to be placed in school libraries as supplementary material to be used only with parental permission. The board further decided that parents objecting to any book on moral or religious grounds could have their children excused from using it. Still, the violence continued—sniping, fire-bombing, phone threats—and the superintendent and three board members were arrested on warrants charging them with contributing to the delinquency of minors. (They were quickly released.)

Finally, late in November the beleaguered school board adopted new guidelines for future textbook selection and set up a procedure by which a committee of five teachers and fifteen parents would screen all prospective new books to eliminate those not in conformity with the guidelines. It was, by all accounts, a victory for the protesters. Said Alice Moore, the school board member who had started it all: "This doesn't get rid of the language arts books we're opposed to, but if they were up for adoption now, they couldn't be approved." The National Education Association, on the other hand, said the new procedures allowed parents to act as censors, in violation of West Virginia law.

The school board action signaled the beginning of a shaky truce. After three months on a continuous emotional binge, Kanawha Countians staggered into the holiday season in a state of shock. There was quiet, but no real peace. The schools remained a topic of conversation, but talk was subdued and dispirited. The people of Charleston, both the pro- and antibook advocates, were like Londoners between bombings during the Blitz.

The period of relative calm offered an opportunity for reflection. What had brought such grief to this seemingly placid community? Why had something so routine as a textbook adoption generated so much anger? Was it just a battle over books, or were the books a symbol of larger problems, deeper dissatisfactions?

Almost twenty years earlier, in the mid-1950s, Kanawha County had voluntarily abandoned racial segregation in its schools; now the textbook controversy had brought some disturbing manifestations of latent racism to the surface. Just a year before the book dispute erupted, the voters of the county had approved an increase in the tax levy for school operations by an overwhelming nine-to-one margin; now a public opinion poll showed six people in every ten opposed to the language arts textbooks—and, by implication, lacking confidence in the school board and administration. What could have caused such a dramatic turnaround in public satisfaction in such a short time?

Around Charleston, the search for answers to those questions is painful and agonizing. The Kanawha County school system, like schools everywhere, is a reflection—almost a mirror image—of the community it serves. Charleston is a compact city of 70,000 people in a sprawling nine-hundred-square-mile county with a total population of 230,000, and the contrasts between urban and rural life are pronounced and pervasive. As the seat of both state and county government and the headquarters of much industry and commerce, Charleston has long dominated the region, exercising minority rule over a rural majority that has been isolated and almost voiceless. Within the city, there is a small black population—10 percent or less—and the combined proportion of Catholics, Jews, and other religious and ethnic minorities is also quite small. It is a predominantly white, Protestant, middle-class city, an urban valley enclave surrounded by mineral-rich mountains that shelter a large and overwhelmingly white population of rural Appalachian people.

Charleston's minorities appear to live fairly compatibly in the urban environment. School desegregation was accomplished in a relatively smooth and uneventful manner, and while housing patterns still keep a high proportion of blacks in a few school zones, race has not been the stormy issue there that it has been in so many other cities. This is the South, but not the Deep South; of all the Southern and border states, West Virginia probably is the least burdened by racial inequity.

The great division in Kanawha County is not between whites and blacks, or Protestants and Catholics; it is between cultures and economic classes, between urbanites and country people. Urbane Charlestonians—smarting, perhaps, from the remarks of sophisticated Easterners, who often treat *West Virginia* as a synonym for *hillbilly*—tend to put the greatest possible distance between themselves and the mountain folk around them. At best, the rural, hill-and-hollow residents of Kanawha County have been ignored; at worst, they have been ridiculed, scorned, and exploited. They are, in local parlance, "the creekers"—coal miners, truck drivers, factory workers, sectarian preachers, perpetuators of a mountain culture that many upper-class residents of suburban South Hills ("the hillers") would just as soon forget.

And there the root of Kanawha County's bush of thorns is buried. Charleston rules, and the people who live in places like Campbell's Creek and Cabin Creek and Coal Fork and Nitro are subjects. Charleston is Episcopalian, Methodist, Presbyterian; the churches in the narrow hollows are Free-Will Baptist, Pentecostal, Church of God of Prophecy. Charleston is wool and double knit, sports cars, cocktail parties; rural Kanawha is jeans and khakis, coal trucks, white lightning, and abstention. Charleston aspires to a modern, affluent future; Cabin Creek struggles against heavy odds to preserve a hard but often heroic past.

Seldom do the twain meet, and long years of separate existence have allowed mutual ignorance and suspicion to flourish. There has been, under the circumstances, surprisingly little open conflict along class lines in the past, however, and a tenuous coexistence between town and country has prevailed. The one institution that embraces the entire county is the school system—a potential arena of conflict even in the best of settings. Perhaps it is inevitable that the schools have become Kanawha's theater of war.

Traditionally the school system has operated more like a closed shop than a public institution. The school board, whose members are elected countywide to staggered six-year terms, has been dominated by the Charleston power structure, and the system's administrators and teachers have been no more inclined to encourage community participation and parental involvement than professional educators elsewhere. Such citizen activity as there has been in the internal operation of the schools, moreover, has been heavily weighted in favor of affluent townspeople, accentuating the split between urban and rural interests. It has been customary for the board and administration to conduct business in private, for teachers to provide instruction behind closed doors, and for parents to serve—if allowed to serve at all—on advisory committees that have little influence and no authority.

Alice Moore, the wife of a fundamentalist minister, was elected to the board in 1970 on an anti–sex education platform, and an experimental program to incorporate sex education into the curriculum of a few schools was abandoned, largely because of her efforts. Her reputation as a hardworking and conservative member of the board has grown steadily, and although she is a native Mississippian and lives now in the town of St. Albans, rural Kanawha County has become her adopted turf, and its people have responded to her leadership as if she were one of their own. What she feels and says—about the books, the schools, the society—apparently reflects what most of them believe but have been unable to express with such clarity, force, and authority. Mrs. Moore has become the voice of the county's silent majority—and in the process, she has tapped a potent source of "creeker" power.

There can be no doubt that schoolbooks today are not what they used to be. The waspy blandness of *Ben and Alice* and *Run, Spot, Run* has given way to material that contains more realism, more variety, and more pertinence to contemporary life in the society at large. West Virginia, like many other states, now requires by state directive that the content of instructional materials be multiracial and multicultural. The growing emphasis on individualized instruction requires greater diversity in the tools of teaching, and educational technology has produced an array of multimedia materials to meet the needs of students with differing backgrounds and differing levels of achievement.

Those changes have been welcomed by many people—by minority groups whose culture is getting some long overdue recognition, by educators in need of more effective ways to reach the diversity of learners, and by students who found the traditional materials sterile and uninspiring. But a sizable segment of Americans has reacted with alarm and anger to books that seem to challenge the values and moral absolutes they were taught to respect.

The West Virginia controversy is not an isolated outburst; Charleston is no special case, no singular aberration. What it is experiencing can be seen as an indicator of the current state of education and social relations in the nation. Angry parents have reacted in recent months against books in schools in more than a dozen states, and while the protests have been similar in some ways, they appear generally to be not an organized conspiracy but a spontaneous chain reaction. To be sure, there are individuals and organizations eager to exploit the unrest, but they range across the spectrum from right to left, and the only thing they seem to have in common is a deep distrust of existing authority. During the height of the Charleston crisis, the book protesters were offered support by such groups as the John Birch Society, the Ku Klux Klan, the Heritage Foundation, and the pro-Communist International Workers Party.

What makes this phenomenon so disturbing is the conflict it produces between some of the most fundamental of American ideals and principles. On one side, it can be argued that the protesters are following a tradition as old as the Boston Tea Party and as recent as the civil rights movement. They seek redress of deeply felt grievances. They belong with the advocates of community control, power to the people, consumer protection. They have adopted many of the same tactics that blacks, Chicanos, Indians, and women have used to assert their rights—tactics that have produced, among other things, a more honest and equitable portrayal of those groups in school textbooks. In the name of majority rule, freedom of religion, the right to privacy, patriotism, and free enterprise—all hallowed phrases in American history—the petitioners have risked their jobs and their security to challenge a government and a social system they feel has abused them.

But there is another side. The advocacy of censorship and bookburning conjures up images of authoritarian control that are abhorrent in a society pledged to freedom of expression. The protesters have sought to keep books not only from those who object to them but also from all other students in the school system. The right of teachers to teach and students to learn has been threatened by informers in the classroom and by intimidating pressure groups outside the schools. In the belief that they do in fact represent a majority of Kanawha County citizens, the protesters are attempting to gain control of the educational system in order to impose their authority— and in the process to silence the ruling minority that has so effectively silenced them. Patriotism, nationalism, democracy, and their own brand of the Christian faith have been amalgamated by the antibook advocates into a vivid and frightening expression of civil religion that leaves no room for compromise and encourages totalitarian extremism.

The schools, already beset with problems enough, are caught in this withering cross fire. The decline of authority and effectiveness that has eroded public confidence in American institutions is especially apparent in the schools. Fairly or not, they are widely viewed as antiquated institutions in need of major renovation and restoration, as an unresponsive and self-protective bureaucracy that rewards mediocrity and resists openness and accountability. With each passing year, the squeeze on schools tightens: costs escalate, and government at every level seems less able to pay the bills; students drop out, or even graduate, without the ability to read and write; teachers, fearing a loss of jobs as a result of declining enrollment, move closer to a national union more concerned with pay and fringe benefits than with productivity or quality of service. Lacking any coherent theory of what they should be doing or how it should be done, the public schools have been unable to resist the steadily increasing demands made on them. Called upon to do far more than they have the ability or the resources to accomplish, they have spread themselves too thin and invited the wrath of those they are unable to serve effectively.

In an earlier time, the schools were primarily expected to build basic skills (reading, spelling, ciphering) and to indoctrinate students in the widely accepted values of the American way of life—patriotism, obedience to authority, free enterprise, and all the rest. Now schools are expected to select advantaged students and prepare them for college, to provide occupational training and career education, and to reconcile somehow the conflicting beliefs and values and ideals of a society that no longer accepts a consensus definition of the American way of life. Furthermore, schools are legal repositories—compulsory day-care centers—for more than forty million children between the ages of five and sixteen, and they are expected to provide social finishing for young people who at the age of eighteen officially become adults. Every time the society perceives an external deficiency, it looks to the schools for a remedy, and new programs are added on: driver education, sex education, drug education, human relations training, and such.

It is little wonder that the schools cannot cope with this multiplicity of expectations. Public education is at heart a political enterprise, directed by elected and appointed officials who preside over enormous sums of tax funds and huge bureaucracies. Like all American institutions, the schools tend to move ever closer to consolidation and centralization of power—and in such places, efficient and impersonal interests are more dominant than individual ones.

The public schools are generally ill equipped to bridge the cultural gaps in American life. The educators who rise in the bureaucratic pyramid are on the whole poorly chosen, poorly trained, and poorly prepared for the complex and demanding jobs they face. Many of the best leave early, and many of the worst lean on tenure and seniority to protect them until they can retire. And the task the survivors face becomes more difficult as affluent adults buy private education for their children, leaving the public schools with the poor, the working class, the marginal middle class—young Americans who lack the financial strength to purchase their own freedom of choice. When the problems of society show up in the schools—racism, drug abuse, depression, disruption, violence—adult society tends to fault the young people or school authorities, or both, rather than seeking the cause and the cure in the society itself.

This dismal litany of woes is being sung in communities all over the United States, and not least in Charleston, where the few private schools are too small and too marginal to offer a realistic alternative to public education. Kanawha County educators, eager to lift their schools into the main currents of American education, have made an effort to conform with contemporary national trends and priorities. They have begun to emphasize individualized instruction, to recognize cultural diversity, to replace single textbooks with multiple learn-

33

ing materials, to be concerned with what and how their students think and feel as well as with the facts they accumulate and the basic skills they acquire. For their trouble, and to their utter dismay, they are now being accused of promoting communism, atheism, and thought control, of undermining the authority of the home and church, and of exposing students to the harsh and seamy side of life.

Ironies abound in this conflict. A confused, frustrated, and hitherto voiceless segment of the population lashes out against changes intended to strengthen individualism, diversity, and cultural identity and insists on a return to the narrow and rigid kind of instruction that has contributed so much to its own subordinate status in the community. Contemporary instructional materials give a more favorable and representative portrayal of blacks, women, Indians, and other groups, but the mountain culture to which so many Kanawha Countians belong is stereotyped and distorted in the materials (when it is presented at all). The political superstructure that so effectively limits and controls the Kanawha County school system—the elected board, the city and county governments, the state department of education, the legislature, the governor—strikes a collective pose of powerless impotence in response to the storm of public protest. Angry citizens debate the use of four-letter words and the proper treatment of ethical and moral questions in school, and all the while, the most effective instruments of instruction—television, movies, magazines, newspapers, records and tapes, and the daily experiences of people—make the debate meaningless. And while the controversy continues, most of the new language arts books remain on the shelves, an upcoming adoption of social studies materials is in jeopardy, and the dominant impression around Charleston is that no effective teaching and learning of any kind is taking place in the schools.

So Kanawha County, a house divided, has turned to its educational institutions for relief from its social and cultural and religious ills, and the schools have not been—could not be—equal to the task. The breach remains as wide as ever. Even the most avid supporters of the textbooks acknowledge that a majority of the county's population disapproves of most of the adopted materials. Many people apparently share the view of a supporter who said, "I like the books, and will defend them—but I feel uncomfortable defending the school board. They've been notoriously cautious, secretive, conservative, inaccessible, and arrogant." Another probook person added, "If you had told me a year ago that I would be standing up to defend this system of public education, I'd have said you were crazy."

Among the book protesters, there is talk of a continuing attempt to get the books before a jury for a final determination of their suitability, and there is also a confident expectation that the school system will never again be able to approve new books over their protest, no matter what is finally done about the language arts books. The Reverend Marvin Horan, a minister and truck driver who has been in the forefront of the protest movement, vows that there is "no way we'll ever stop" until the books are removed. Horan is facing trial in federal court on a conspiracy charge in connection with the bombing of a school. He denies the charge and asserts: "If they put me in the pen, there'll be ten more behind me to take up the fight against anarchy, atheism, and disrespect for the law. I won't break the law, but I'll never give up."

In a calmer voice, Alice Moore expresses the same determination. Demure and articulate, she is a persuasive exponent of a conservative point of view that she confidently believes is the majority view in Kanawha County. "From our own assessment," she says, "we believe that 80 percent of the people are against this adoption. No more than half of the 325 books would ever get majority support, if they were put to a vote. All of this has come about because parents no longer buy their children's books, and they no longer know what's going on. I'm the only board member who ever paid any attention to the curriculum, and because I did, we have been able to see for the first time what is being done in the name of education. Crude language, lax morals, crime and conflict and violence, atheism, situation ethics, and the so-called new morality—it's all there. We believe in moral absolutes—in respect for the family and the church, in patriotism, in the basics. And so do most of the people in this county."

She is undoubtedly correct. It is less certain that most of the people of Kanawha County also believe that textbooks should be chosen by popular vote, or by jury, or by committees of parents, but that is what could happen. Alice Moore has almost single-handedly stirred up a people's revolt, and if she fears losing control of it, she gives no hint of that concern. Sitting in the living room of her modest brick home while her husband, Darrell, a Church of Christ minister, pours coffee for visitors, she seems too shy and soft-spoken to be the charismatic leader of a protest movement. One wonders what Gloria Steinem or Betty Friedan would make of her—wonders why they have not, in fact, made anything of her.

One of her local opponents, a woman who is protextbook in Charleston and pro–women's movement nationally, seemed to be grappling with the same question when she paid Alice Moore a high compliment. "She's a genius," the woman said. "She never went to college, but she is the true leader of the protesters and the feared adversary of the book defenders. I have a lot of respect for her."

The Reverend James Lewis, an Episcopal minister in Charleston and one of the leading advocates of the language arts books, doesn't question the sincerity of the protesters; what bothers him is the sort of narrow and unyielding certitude that allows no self-doubt and no respect for the views of others. "I got into this," he says, "because I was horrified that they would line up kids at school and take their books away from them. People were afraid—they're still afraid—and the churches, when they have spoken out at all, have either been on the other side or on the fence. So I have defended the books with some other people—teachers, parents, individuals instead of organizations. One of the things that has bothered me, though, is that middle-class, middle-age, supposedly liberal people like us have been mindlessly and routinely discriminating against the working class and the poor people right here. We've contributed to their political disfranchisement. Charleston doesn't have a black-white problem; it has a creeker-hiller problem. Liberal Christians can't muster the zeal, the devotion, the fervor of the fundamentalists. It's almost impossible to rally middle-class America for anything more than a cocktail party. We're just very late—maybe too late—to be waking up to this class problem, to be realizing that our ignorance of them is a major contributing factor in all this."

Recently Mrs. Moore gained school board approval for the opening next fall of three or four "basic education" elementary schools as alternatives to which students may go if they choose. The schools presumably will be based on a number of traditional features: dress codes, letter grades, rote learning, single-teacher classes, tight discipline, and the like. But on the resolution of the present dispute, she is not hopeful. "I think we could have had an agreement at one time," she says, "but now we're to the point where it's very difficult to find acceptable textbooks, and people on both sides are afraid to lose face."

The National Education Association, at the invitation of its local affiliate in Charleston, conducted a three-day inquiry in Kanawha County last October. The report of that investigation acknowledged numerous mistakes and examples of bad judgment on all sides but came ultimately to the conclusion that professional educators and school boards must, by law and by logic, be the ones who make the final decisions about curriculum and materials of instruction. If parents are allowed to determine the content of public education in order to ensure against violation of prevailing community and parental values, the report said, "which parents and whose values shall prevail?"

It is fruitless to argue whether or not schools should teach values; the fact is that they do and always have. For a long time they transmitted the white Anglo-Saxon Protestant value system of the majority—a narrow, rigid, monolithic set of beliefs and ideals that were held to be self-evident truths. The awakening of nonwhites and so many other groups to the inequities in that system of values has led, over the past twenty years, to the beginning of a new appreciation for individualism and cultural diversity. It is profoundly ironic that educators would treat what should be a liberating manifestation of pluralism as simply another educational dogma, as if they had learned nothing from the blacks and others who forced them to discover pluralism in the first place.

In West Virginia, a major decision on new textbooks was made, in the words of a staunch supporter of the books, "in an arbitrary, unilateral, dictatorial fashion," and a group of white Anglo-Saxon Protestants who had been ridiculed and rejected by the value system of old turned out to be the last true believers in that discredited system.

The book protesters surely are wrong in insisting that they be judge and jury not only of their own children's educational programs but also of the entire community's.

But trite as it may be to say it, education is too important to be left to educators. And it is precisely that cleavage—between experts, authorities, technicians, and bureaucrats on the one hand and the multitudes of culturally diverse and pluralistic people on the other—that threatens not just the peace and freedom of West Virginians but the future of public education and the achievement of true democracy in America.

In the late 1970s Alice Moore moved to Columbus, Ohio, leaving the Kanawha County Board of Education and its network of public schools to work out their problems without her. There is now a countywide sex education program in the schools, but neither it nor the textbook selection process has stirred up much controversy. An advisory committee of parents and other local citizens is still involved in previewing new texts, and parents who object to any book in use may ask the teacher to find an alternative for their children. Few such requests are made. The principal concerns of school patrons in Charleston in the 1990s are declining enrollment, consolidation and closing of schools, pupil achievement, and the perpetual quest for adequate revenue to fund school programs.

⟪ ALEX HALEY'S
TENNESSEE ROOTS

Henning, Tennessee, the hometown of Roots *author Alex Haley, was thrust into the national spotlight in 1977 in the wake of his book's spectacular success. Before, during, and after Haley's return there for a celebration in his honor, I gathered material in Henning for an article about the man, the town, and the times. It was published in the July 8, 1977, issue of* New Times.

Wednesday, May 11:

Three elderly gentlemen—two whites and a black—are sitting in the dappled shade of the courthouse square in Ripley, Tennessee, whittling and talking.

"I hear tell there's gonna be ten thousand people over there next week," one of them remarks.

"In Henning?" comes the response. "Where they gonna stand? It ain't as big as my shirttail."

"They're coming for the colored fellow. Seen him on TV."

"You going?"

"Naw, not me. But I think it's nice, real nice. I think people feels pretty good about it. I don't see no hate showing. Wasn't always so. No sir."

Five miles down the road, Fred Montgomery, Jr., stands outside his plumbing supply business on Henning's Main Street and ponders the task he faces. "We've got a week to get ready," he says earnestly. "But we'll make it. It's gonna be a big day for Henning, the biggest day this town ever had."

Montgomery, a master plumber and a lifelong resident of the town, is the only black member of its board of aldermen. He is also the local chairman of the Welcome Home Alex Haley Committee, a statewide body planning a three-day tribute to the celebrated author of *Roots*. The tribute will begin here in Henning eight days from to-day. There will be a parade, celebrities, politicians, speeches, lots of people. The highlight, of course, will be Haley himself—the now-famous native son, the returning hero, the hometown kid made good.

At the age of sixty, Fred Montgomery is a few years older than Alex Haley, but they have been friends since boyhood. "Palmer is mature for his age," he explains. "We always called him Palmer—that's his middle name. Nobody knew him as Alex. He was a serious boy, a reader, a dreamer."

Around the corner from the main entrance to Montgomery's place of business, a large expanse of the brick building's outside wall is being painted by the plumber's brother, Eddie Montgomery. His handiwork displays a white background with bold black letters and red trim. The words welcome one and all to HENNING, TENNESSEE, HOME OF ALEX HALEY. In the upper right-hand corner of the wall, Eddie Montgomery has painted a fierce, proud fighting cock in vivid shades of red and brown. Beneath the bird is a single word, a name: GEORGE.

Fred Montgomery, surveying his brother's artistry, shows his pleasure with the slightest trace of a smile. "I told Eddie to put old Chicken George on there, just for fun," he says.

The American roots of Alex Palmer Haley are sunk deep in the fertile soil of this quiet farming community forty-eight miles northeast of Memphis. Henning is his hometown—not his birthplace, but his growing-up place—and four generations on his mother's side of the family are represented in the town cemetery. Haley hasn't lived here in almost forty years, and he has no close relatives left in the town, but the extraordinary success of *Roots* and the author's frequent references to his Tennessee childhood have led the people of Henning and surrounding Lauderdale County—the blacks quickly, the whites gradually—to show pride and a certain possessiveness in their long-ago fellow townsman.

Haley may be the nearest thing to a national hero that Tennessee has had since Sergeant Alvin York returned from World War I. When Haley addressed a joint session of the Tennessee General Assembly early last month, he was introduced by Governor Ray Blanton as "the author of the social statement of the century." The impact of his work has been compared with that of Harriet Beecher Stowe's *Uncle Tom's*

Cabin. Hardcover sales of *Roots* have long since zoomed past the million mark, and they continue to soar. The television adaptation of the book drew the largest viewing audience in history, and eighty million people—almost 40 percent of the nation's population—watched the final episode.

In the wake of that stunning reception, celebrity and controversy have swirled about Haley incessantly. He has been honored with a Pulitzer Prize and a National Book Award. Novelists and historians have alternately praised and criticized both the quality and the authenticity of his book. He has been accused by two other black novelists, Margaret Walker and Harold Courlander, of plagiarizing portions of their books, and Haley himself has sued Doubleday and Company, his publisher, over a contract dispute. The attention, favorable and unfavorable, has only served to swell the *Roots* phenomenon into a publishing/media event of unprecedented proportions.

The instant-superstar status thus attached to Haley has not gone unnoticed by the people of Henning. Not many of them remember him, but those who do are quick to point out that not only he but also his parents, his grandparents, his great-grandfather Tom Murray, and his great-great-grandfather Chicken George Lea (the latter two given posthumous fame by the power of television) lived in the community. From a distance, the townspeople have basked in the reflected glow of Haley's comet; next week, that sparkling light, and whatever else goes with it, will be beamed direct and unfiltered upon Henning itself.

Two hundred ten years after Kunta Kinte, Haley's now-famous African ancestor, left the Gambian village of Juffure in chains, and 105 years after Chicken George led a wagon train of black families out of North Carolina to Henning, the author of *Roots* is about to lead an entourage of dignitaries and a crowd of who knows how many back to his Tennessee connection, to the place he proudly and repeatedly refers to as "my home." Henning—like Juffure, like Plains, Georgia—is about to receive an unaccustomed jolt of public exposure. How long it will last, and what effect it will have, no one can say.

For the moment, though, the town has about it a tranquil look of timelessness, of casually preserved antiquity, like a thousand dusty villages on the rural backroads of the American South. It could be a movie-set Southern town, one of the myriad and anonymous country communities where time has wrought changes both vast and imperceptible, a place at once transformed and untouched by the twentieth century. Without knowing what to expect, the people of Henning are preparing for and awaiting the coming event, wondering—hoping, fearing, doubting—if the place will ever be the same again.

Under the watchful eyes of armed guards, a crew of inmate laborers from a nearby state prison farm is cutting and burning fifteen years of undergrowth from the black section of Bethlehem Cemetery. Bethlehem dates back to 1862, to the Civil War period prior to Henning's founding and the arrival of Chicken George's wagon train. Approached from the highway, the cemetery displays a broad expanse of manicured green under leafy oaks and walnuts and cedars. At the crest of a knoll running the length of the burial ground, a rusty barbed-wire fence marks the dividing line between the white and black deceased of Henning.

The prisoners are working on the back side, cutting to the bare earth, uncovering simple stone markers long hidden from the light. Fred Montgomery walks among the graves, identifying those connected with "Palmer" Haley: "Palmer's mother, Bertha Palmer Haley. Died in 1931 at the age of thirty-five. His daddy is buried in Arkansas. His grandfather, Will Palmer. Died in 1926. His Grandma Cynthia is here too, but there is no stone for her. I doubt if they could afford one when she died in 1948. Here's his great-grandparents, Tom and Irene Murray. Tom was a blacksmith, and Cynthia was their baby girl. They were all in the wagon train with Chicken George."

The Palmers and Murrays are together in a plot next to the barbed-wire fence. Nearest the fence is a bare space, an unmarked grave. "Best we can tell," says Montgomery, "this is where Chicken George is buried."

A few paces away, one of the inmates has unearthed another stone. It bears the name of George W. Palmer, born 1859, died 1915. "Must be Will Palmer's daddy," Montgomery concludes. "Didn't know he was in here. Everywhere you dig, you find a grave. This place is full of forgotten people."

The televised version of *Roots* concluded with the arrival of Chicken George and his followers in Henning. Filmed on location somewhere in the bare brown hills of California, the scene bore no resemblance to the real Henning, which is situated on low, rolling terrain near the edge of the saucer-flat delta plain of the Mississippi River. In his book Haley deals directly if briefly with the Tennessee phase of his family's odyssey, and in his subsequent public appearances he has often expressed a mellow remembrance of his own boyhood days. In his grandmother's house in Henning, he told the state legislature, he was blessed with the benefits of a small-town Southern upbringing, where "you learn more about faith, about the work ethic, about the so-called old-fashioned things—and in the final analysis, they're the things that count."

Henning still exhibits some of the old virtues—and, in more muted tones, the old vices—of its past. In the beginning it was a railroad town, founded in 1873—the year Haley's ancestors arrived—by D. M. Henning, the man whose name it bears. It was also a cotton town, surrounded by endless summer fields of snow-white fiber, and very nearly a river town, being just sixteen miles east of the Mississippi. It counted a population of four hundred in 1885, and the supposition is that between a fourth and half of the residents were black.

Just as the river missed Henning, so now, in a sense, does the railroad, and the highway. Illinois Central freight trains still ply the double tracks that parallel Main Street, but passenger trains haven't stopped regularly in more than twenty-five years; Amtrak's Panama Limited, running between Chicago and New Orleans, makes a once-daily pass in each direction without so much as a whistle. Main Street also used to be U.S. Highway 51, but a bypass a mile west of town ended that. Five miles up the road in Ripley, the Lauderdale County seat, shopping centers and fast-food outlets and other signs of the modern age are evident in abundance, but Henning has joined its colorfully named sister villages on the outlying landscape—Glimp, Arp, Golddust, Nankipoo—in isolation and obscurity.

The present population of about five hundred whites and one hundred blacks is changed from the citizenry of a century ago primarily in the sense that it is older. ("We have become," says one senior resident, "a town full of widows and old maids.") Although timber-cutting and farming remain the principal sources of personal employment and income, the methods of production have changed. Mechanized corporate farmers have replaced sharecroppers and small-acreage family farmers; $55,000 four-wheel-drive tractors with air-conditioned cabs have replaced mules and plows in the fields, and soybeans have replaced cotton as the top crop. Race relations have changed too, but an unspoken attitudinal separation still exists between blacks and whites. The Henning of old is no more—and evermore.

In his many public reminiscences about life in Henning, Alex Haley has seldom alluded to segregation, perhaps because his family struggled so hard—and, for the most part, successfully—to prevail against it. They were craftsmen, businessmen, farmers, teachers—solid middle-class citizens—and they were respected members of the community. Still, segregation and discrimination were inescapable realities in the schools and stores and churches of Henning, as they were all over the South, and Haley, when asked, readily acknowledges that.

Whites now outnumber blacks by about three to two in the desegregated public schools of Lauderdale County. Blacks work in the shops and stores and factories in Ripley. Many black adults claim never to have been denied the right to register and vote. A new public housing project in Henning is desegregated, and older housing in the town reflects a patternless black and white proximity, as it always has; only in the newer subdivisions is there apparent racial separation, and there the result is attributed to economics more than race.

Henning and the rest of Lauderdale County didn't experience the more abrasive confrontations of the civil rights movement, as nearby Haywood and Fayette counties did, or as Memphis and Shelby County did. "We get by," a white school official in Ripley says. "Our county has handled desegregation as well as or better than any other in this area. But there's really not much desegregation outside the schools even now. The schools are required to be the conscience of the community, to do what the adult population won't do. Prejudice has diminished somewhat—but I'd say the adult white community as a whole is still segregationist at heart."

The Lauderdale County *Enterprise,* a weekly newspaper published in Ripley, carried a story on Haley and his book-in-progress back in 1974. Now, a week before the Henning celebration, it has returned to the subject with a four-inch story at the top of page one. The editor, William A. Klutts, refers a visitor's inquiry about Henning to his assistant, Terry Ford. Ford says the local reaction to Haley's prominence has been "mixed, low-key, pro and con. Ask out on the street—you'll see what I mean." He pauses and then adds with a smile: "Better wear a catcher's mask—for the ones who don't like the question."

Protection seems unnecessary; not even a man who asserts that Haley "made the whole thing up" objects to being asked. Most reactions, in fact, are favorable. "I think it's great," a middle-aged white woman says. "I hope it's a big success." A young white man says he is "very happy for Alex Haley, for this county, for us all. His achievement has brought credit to everybody here." A black woman who teaches in the school system expresses pride in Haley and adds: "*Roots* is fine—but I'm worried about all these twigs and branches around here, these kids who can't read and write."

In the Wal-Mart Discount City Shopping Center, just past the Pizza Hut and the Dairy Queen, a black clerk says T-shirts imprinted with the word KUNTA and tentacular tree roots that extend to the armpits are "selling real good—better than that Farrah What's-Her-Name."

At the public library, a block from the courthouse square, librarian Jennie Forsberg says there is a waiting list for the three copies of *Roots* in the collection. "People who are interested in genealogy are tremendously complimentary of the book," she adds. "They say it's a great thing Haley has done, and I agree. The book and the TV series have let the black people know they have a heritage. It's a beautiful thing for them—not only around here, but everywhere."

Mrs. Forsberg retrieves a copy of *Lauderdale from Earliest Times,* a county history published in 1957, and turns to the chapter on Henning. There it states that the town was destroyed by fire in 1886 and quickly rebuilt, that it got TVA electric power in 1939, that its streets were first paved in 1944. Only the last paragraph mentions Henning's black community, noting the existence of the New Hope Colored Methodist Episcopal Church and the Palmer-Turner School, a consolidated rural elementary school with a 1956 enrollment of 455.

Like Alex Haley, Mrs. Forsberg is interested in genealogy. In the

1880 census, which she has on microfilm, she searches through the Third Civil District of Lauderdale County for George W. Palmer, hoping to establish that he was in fact the father of Will Palmer. She doesn't find him—but she finds Thomas Murray, blacksmith, age forty-seven, born in North Carolina, and his wife, Renie (Irene), and four of their children, including Cynthia, age nine. And in the household of William P. Posey, white, she finds listed a black woman named Kizzie Morris, age thirty-four, a domestic servant—a sister of Tom Murray and a namesake of the first Kizzy, who was the only child of Kunta Kinte and his wife, Bell.

The census lists one more name in William P. Posey's household: George Lea, age seventy-four, black, a servant, born in North Carolina—and the Tennessee patriarch of Alex Haley's family.

"Chicken George!" Mrs. Forsberg exclaims. "There's the proof!"

Minna Crutcher, the widow of Major John Flowers Crutcher, lives in a rambling white-frame, green-shuttered house on the east side of Henning. Now seventy-eight years old, she is "a Mississippi girl who came up in the good old days." Her husband has been dead for twenty-five years. She keeps herself "busy and happy with hobbies, sunshine jobs, rainy day jobs"—and with Granny's Antiques, a business she operates out of what used to be a turkey brooder house in the side yard of her home.

The cool, high-ceilinged interior of her residence is an antique museum, a wondrous menagerie of walnut and mahogany, bone china and cranberry glass, crystal and sterling. Her four-poster bed once belonged to General P. G. T. Beauregard, who ordered the firing of the first shot of the Civil War at Fort Sumter. She also owns a walnut pump organ that she bought from Cis Palmer—Alex Haley's Grandma Cynthia.

"This little town used to be such a lively place," Granny Crutcher says. "I remember when the train used to stop here, and there would be a band there to meet it. But the town has been dying on the vine for a long time. Maybe this Haley thing will revive it—it's real good to have a little spark."

Even so, she is not altogether pleased with the prospect. "The town as a whole doesn't want to be upset," she says. "We're a happy people. We don't know what this thing's gonna do to Henning. I start worrying about having another Plains. There's really nothing to see here. I hope after next week things will settle down again."

About *Roots*, Mrs. Crutcher is also somewhat ambivalent: "I watched it on TV, and I thought the acting was superb, but I don't think it was entirely true. I'm no historian, and I wasn't there, and I haven't read the book, so I won't express an opinion. But I will say this: I know slaves were mistreated by landowners, but Alex seems to be saying that every white man was a sonofabitch and every colored man was a perfect gentleman, and that's just not so."

The relationship between whites and blacks in Henning, she says, is good: "I couldn't get along without the colored people. They're my neighbors—I help them, and they help me. Fred Montgomery, my plumber, lives right behind me. He's the number one colored man in this town—black man, I believe he wants to be called. He's a very intelligent person, and very diplomatic—he says the right thing at the right time. But the colored people and the white people here are like redbirds and robins—we don't fraternize."

Mrs. Crutcher is fearful that a crowd of ten thousand people at the Haley celebration could mean trouble for Henning. She says she doesn't plan to attend. But for that day's visitors at her antique shop, she has a bonus: out by the turkey house, there is a wheelbarrow heaped with assorted scraps of native wood and, atop it, a sign. It says, FREE ROOTS FROM HENNING.

Across town, in a neat clapboard house two blocks off Main Street and not far from the Palmer place, lives Virginia Alston Tuholski. She was born in Henning in 1900. She met her husband-to-be on a trip to Europe in 1923, and they lived in New Jersey until he retired from teaching in 1952. They moved to Henning after that, and Mrs. Tuholski, now a widow, has remained.

"I grew up in a house that was right in front of where Bertha Palmer lived as a child," she recalls. "She was about four years older than I, but we played together a lot. She was still a young woman when she died—she had TB. I didn't know Alex very well—I was gone during most of the years he was here—but his grandmother Cis Palmer, Ber-

47

tha's mother, was a very fine person. When I came back here to visit in the late 1940s, she came to see me. It must have been just before she died."

Mrs. Tuholski says she didn't read *Roots* or watch much of it on television. "To me it was so terrible when they captured the Ancestor in Africa," she says. "And that trip over on the ship—I just couldn't stand to read it or watch it. It was horrible—and it was true. I read somewhere that nine million slaves perished on those ships. They were worse than cattle ships. For some, it was terrible after they reached this country, too. Not all of the slave owners were Simon Legrees, though. My great-grandfather owned a slave, but before the Civil War he realized that slavery was wicked, wrong, sinful, and he freed that Negro man, who continued to live with him and make a crop with him. Some people say Alex didn't really paint a fair and true picture of white slave owners, that he should have said something about those who were kind."

Haley's success with *Roots* and his approaching visit to Henning, Mrs. Tuholski says, have caused some to fear that the town will be flooded with people, "and maybe not all the right kind of people." Are the townsfolk proud of him? She pauses for a moment and then replies: "I would say the Negro people are very proud of him. The white people are also pleased and proud, in a way—but to them, he's still a Negro. Some people have said to me it's all a hoax. I tell them I don't believe that. I think what he's done is great, and I'm proud of him. I know what a struggle it was for him to write the book. He's been discriminated against, subjected to slights and insults. I'm glad he's so successful now, and I hope his book and his visit here will do a lot of good."

In 1974, when she first heard of Haley's forthcoming book, she wrote him a letter of congratulations and got back from him a warm response, which she has kept. Next week, her church—and all the others in town—will have a refreshment booth on Main Street to accommodate the visitors. Mrs. Tuholski plans to be there, selling cookies. "I just hope there aren't too many people," she says.

Back up on Main Street, just before closing time, Fred Montgomery pauses in his shop to go over the homecoming plans once again. Near the front window, his wife, Earnestine, is busy making decorations on her sewing machine. There will be a parade, says Montgomery, with bands and floats moving up the street from the south. At the Palmer home, a ten-room frame house where Alex Haley first heard the story of Kunta Kinte and those who followed him, there will be speeches by the governor and other dignitaries and a commemoration of the house as a national landmark and historic site. After that, there will be more ceremonies at the New Hope Colored Methodist Episcopal Church, which was founded a century ago by Haley's forebears, and an African granite monument honoring Haley and *Roots* will be unveiled there. After a luncheon at the church, the party of visiting politicians and others, including Haley, will leave for Memphis and more ceremonies elsewhere in the state. The celebration in Henning won't end then, however; at three in the afternoon and again at seven in the evening, there will be a Hallelujah Jubilee at the church.

How many people does Montgomery expect will attend the day's festivities? "They're saying ten thousand, but I can't hardly dream of that many," he replies. "I don't want to guess how many. But we'll be ready. We've had great support from the white race and the black race. Everybody in town is painting up, fixing up. The churches will have food booths. There'll be souvenirs—bumper stickers, key rings, pens. Most everybody is making some move to capitalize on this, and I can understand that. This has been considered a dead town for years, but recently we've seemed to have more enthusiasm. Next Thursday is gonna be a great day for Henning."

Montgomery pauses, choosing his words. "I think all over, *Roots* has been a happening that's done something for all races," he says finally. "All of the people in America, except maybe the Indians, came here from across the water. This story started everybody to thinking where they came from. Every American's ancestors made that trip. When you think of it, that's really something. That's why this is such a big thing."

❧

Writers are like sharecroppers. We writers work to produce the crop, deliver it to someone else, and they give us what they decide is right. They run the land, they own the cotton gin and the company store.

—Alex Haley

Thursday, May 19:

Alex Haley would know about sharecropping: it was the standard arrangement on the land around Henning when he was a youngster growing up here in the 1920s and 1930s. Now it is as if the sharecropper, the supplicant, has bought out the cotton gin and the company store. After twelve years of unremitting stoop labor, the bumper crop finally came and kept coming. *Roots* lifted Haley out of tenancy and into the tall cotton.

But the harvest exacts its own heavy price, and in this case, the price is fame. It is wealth and renown and honor—and it is also publishers, movie producers, agents, attorneys, accountants, politicians. With the satisfaction of an arresting achievement has come name and face recognition—and a loss of privacy, of control. As surely as he has been attacked by some who, for their own reasons, do not like his work, Haley has been smothered by others who do, and especially by those who covet a share of the *Roots* harvest.

"You'll find that the people who celebrate you will kill you," the weary author was quoted as saying during his recent return trip to Juffure. "They forget you are blood and flesh and bone. I have had days and weeks and months of schedules where everything from my breakfast to my last waking moment was planned for me. . . . Someone has you by the arm and is moving you from room to room. Then people *grab* you! You're actually pummeled—hit with books—and you ask yourself, 'My God, what *is* this?'"

The questions linger: Is Haley the writer still Haley the figurative sharecropper? Has he bought the cotton gin and the company store—or is the retinue at his coattails devouring the crop piece by piece, like boll weevils on a cotton tuft? Finally—and more to the point of this day—what will Henning reap from Alex Haley's return?

It was well past midnight when he and his entourage arrived in Memphis. Now, barely six hours later, people are stirring in the slanted shadows of early morning on Henning's Main Street. Church women and others are setting up their concession stands. State and military policemen are everywhere, calling one another on walkie-talkies. In Memphis, Haley should be just about finishing breakfast by now; he's due here at 9:00 A.M.

In a shady corner of the New Hope CME Church parking lot, Ionie Geater, the mother of Fred Montgomery, responds softly to a question. "A big day, yes," she says. "To my way of knowing, the biggest day Henning has ever had." She is eighty-two years old, a slight woman with clear, probing eyes. "Looks like this might pull Henning out. It was kinda going down. Maybe this'll make a difference. It's kinda hard to tell, though. You don't just get up on a bank and jump off too quick. Better take your time."

Mrs. Geater remembers when she couldn't vote in Henning, "years back." Of the community now, she says this: "It's better than it used to be, better than when I picked cotton for forty cents a hundred. Yes, it's better—but there's room for more improvement."

At the former home of Haley's grandparents, two short blocks from the church, microphones are being set up on a platform in the front yard. Nearby, the official marker designating the house as a historic site has been installed. Official-looking people are rushing about, making last-minute preparations. Overhead, the *whup-whup-whup* of a helicopter sends throbbing vibrations down through the trees. Drumbeats and brass echo up from the direction of Main Street. It's nine o'clock, and the parade is beginning right on schedule.

A Girl Scout troop leads the way, followed by the Ripley High School marching band and, after it, a string of convertibles. Politicians, pretty women, the usual parade characters—and then, there comes Alex Haley, waving from a white Lincoln. At the intersection of Main and McFarlin streets, the car stops, and Haley steps out, shaking hands with the waiting dignitaries. The crowd and the rest of the procession follow them toward the Palmer house. Haley is wearing a tan suit and a stunned smile. People are thrusting copies of *Roots* into his hands; he struggles to sign them as he walks.

On the platform, there is some confusion; the microphones don't work very well. The crowd is drawn in close, buzzing, waiting. It is not ten thousand people, not even five thousand; nonetheless, it seems like a large throng, and it seems curiously out of place here in this usually empty street. Maybe two thousand—and that would be

51

more than three times the town's population. The mix of whites and blacks appears to be about even.

The bishop of the CME Church prays. There are brief remarks by Fred Montgomery and Teddy Withers, a black member of the Tennessee General Assembly. Congressman Ed Jones, home from Washington for the occasion, says Haley's book "not only brought credit to him but enriched us all." Governor Ray Blanton says Haley "roamed the world to find his way home" and opened "a new era of mutual understanding and respect."

Now it is Alex Haley's turn to speak. His manner is gentle, even self-effacing. "What I say is coming from my heart," he begins, and what he says are words of thanks to the assembled crowd, gratitude for his forebears, and praise for Henning and the South. "The South is on its way to being reborn," he declares. "As a son of the South, I like to think this occasion symbolizes that new beginning."

After he is presented with a key to the city by Henning's mayor, B. G. Graves, Haley and the platform guests move on to the church, where more people are waiting. At a brief press conference inside before the unveiling of the monument honoring him, Haley appears calm, almost serene—and tired. He is asked if he attaches any significance to the fact that he has come to Henning on the birthday of Malcolm X, whose autobiography he helped to write. No, he says, after a pause, "just an interesting coincidence." Then, comparing his journey to Juffure with his return here, he says this experience is "much more sheerly emotional, because I *know* here."

Does he feel that what has happened to him was somehow predestined? "When I look back over the whole of my life," he replies, "it seems to me that I was in fact being prepared, one way or another, to meet the challenges of *Roots* when they came later down the line. I can see no explanation for it, other than that it was meant to be."

Does Haley think the barbed-wire fence separating the graves of whites and blacks at Bethlehem Cemetery will be removed? "It may or may not be," he says. "I don't think there would be an ounce of reaction one way or the other. That was a tradition that went way back, decades back, and I honestly don't think that tradition still exists any more. The best proof I have of that is what's happening here today."

The unveiling of the monument in front of the church follows, and then there is a luncheon for invited guests back inside the building. Events have moved swiftly and on schedule. The crowd disperses and mills about in the shady streets and downtown stores, as if awaiting the next event. And then, as suddenly as he appeared in the town at the stroke of nine, Alex Haley is whisked away after lunch, accompanied by the politicians, the planners, and the press. There will be an afternoon ceremony in Memphis, followed by a flight to Knoxville for more activities tonight, and then another flight to Nashville for breakfast with the chamber of commerce at 7:30 in the morning.

Haley had said it: Every waking moment is planned, and the people who celebrate you will kill you. His long-awaited Henning homecoming has lasted four hours.

Not many of the townspeople got a chance to speak to Haley. But they saw him pass, they waved, they watched and listened and applauded, and they have drawn from the occasion a variety of impressions, most of them favorable.

Kenya De Souza, a black woman and professional singer from Louisville, Kentucky, whose parents grew up in Lauderdale County, describes the day as "a beautiful experience. It's not a black thing, it's a people thing—and I think it'll last from now on."

Brenda Hansbrough and Thelma Boyd, watching from in front of the dry-cleaning shop on Main Street, agree that "the publicity has already done us a lot of good, whether or not it lingers," because the prospect of it prompted a lot of painting and renovation in the town.

Edith Lunn, a white schoolteacher who has lived all her life in Henning, says she is "quite honored to have grown up in the same town with a famous person like Alex Haley," but she expresses the opinion that most of her white neighbors don't share her sense of pride, and she doesn't expect them to change very much. "This is today," she says. "Tomorrow will be like yesterday. Henning will still be Henning."

A black man sitting in front of the café and pool hall on McFarlin Street (an establishment described by one disapproving black woman as "that colored tavern that looks a little frail") asserts happily that Haley's presence, however brief, will bring big changes to Henning.

53

"We're gonna be like Plains," he says, "and that's all right with me, 'cause that means money."

Three middle-aged black women on the lawn of the Palmer house draw a different conclusion. They are proud of Haley but less than hopeful about Henning, which they say is in dire need of better housing, jobs, and wages for low-income people.

Jim Hickman is here, too, having watched the festivities from the Texaco station at the corner of Main and McFarlin. Until Alex Haley gained world renown, Hickman was Henning's most famous native son. A faded sign on the edge of town identifies him as a star performer for the Chicago Cubs, and he also played for the New York Mets and other major-league teams. Retired from baseball now, he lives in Henning and farms in the county. He is pleased to see the town gain recognition because of Haley and *Roots*: "It's a great thing for Henning. It'll liven things up. The town has been slowly dying. This interest in the place is bound to help us. We won't be like Plains, though. Jimmy Carter still has his home there, but Haley has been gone from here for a long time."

By midafternoon, Henning is beginning to return to normal. The church women and others whose concession stands have been stocked to serve a multitude are disappointed that no multitude came. There is an abundance of leftover food, drink, and souvenirs. One woman is irate. "This was supposed to be Alex Haley Day in Henning," she complains, "but it wasn't. We hardly even saw him. They rushed him in and rushed him out, pushed the poor man from one place to another. I think the politicians have got hold of this thing, and they're milking it for all it's worth."

Mrs. Tuholski and Mrs. Forsberg were there, but they have gone home to escape the heat, which is rising now in shimmering waves from the downtown pavement. Mrs. Crutcher is at home too, having stayed there throughout. She is relieved. "I feel better about it, now that it's over," she says. "It's not gonna change anything much."

Only at the New Hope CME Church are people still gathered. It is time for the afternoon Hallelujah Jubilee. A few dozen well-dressed people are there, all of them black, most of them members of the congregation. There will be gospel singing, preaching, and thanksgiving for this day and for Alex Haley.

Fred and Earnestine Montgomery are here, in the fellowship room behind the sanctuary. They have worked long and hard to make the homecoming a success, and they are numb with weariness.

"The crowd was about what I expected," Montgomery says slowly. "I was happy with it. It was a peaceful crowd—the way we are peaceful people. We never expected any trouble. The good effect will be permanent. Having all this attention focused here—with Haley, with the governor—will make it easier for everybody to share, and for Henning to progress." He says he is sorry Haley didn't get to visit the cemetery, "but he'll be back soon." Haley and his brothers want to buy the Palmer house and restore it, he says, "and I hope that can be done. It's a matter of satisfying Mrs. Reid, the present owner."

Emma Lee Reid has lived in the Palmer house since she and her husband bought it from the Haley brothers in 1959. She is sitting alone now in a rocking chair on the front porch. The yard is littered with paper cups, sandwich wrappers, empty film boxes. Mrs. Reid's husband died just two weeks ago; her face bespeaks her grief.

"I heard they wanted to buy my house," she volunteers, "but nobody has said anything to me. I'm not anxious to sell." She looks out at the historical marker freshly planted in the yard. "I don't like that sign where it is. It impresses people that this place is his. I want the sign moved."

Mrs. Reid is not critical of Haley, though. A former schoolteacher, she says *Roots* "brought out Negro history so plainly for me. And today—I thought it was just grand to have this day. Whites are beginning to realize that people are just people. The older heads have still got some pull-back in them, but the young ones, they don't have that problem. Things are improving, and today helped a whole lot."

Mayor Graves is back at the town hall, glad that the celebration is over and certain that it won't change Henning. "We won't attract a lot of tourists," he says. "Maybe three or four a week will come by. Everything will be back just like it was—and that's fine with me."

Now that Haley is gone, the mayor indicates that he never thought too much of the homecoming idea in the first place. He is seventy years old now, a former state trooper, and he is still in the habit of saying "nigger."

"It wasn't because of Haley Day that the town got spruced up," he declares. "One family started painting and fixing, and the rest just fell in with them. We got their cemetery cleaned up thanks to Haley, but it'll be back like it was, 'cause there's nobody left around here to take care of it." And the fence? "It'll stay there."

Late in the day, there is a peaceful stillness at Bethlehem Cemetery. Charles Echels, a black man from Memphis, has stopped to look around. His mother is with him. She was born in Henning.

"Today was a shot in the arm for Henning," Echels says. "I think it'll pick up around here now. People will start coming back from up North. The black/white thing, it's already changed, it's pretty good. If I didn't have my job in Memphis, I'd come here too. This place reminds you of the way it used to be—in all the good ways."

There is a new headstone in the cemetery, placed there just last week. It stands next to the markers of the Murrays and Will Palmer, beside the rusty fence. Engraved in the smooth granite are these words: FINAL RESTING PLACE OF CHICKEN GEORGE.

Friday, May 27:
Newspapers in Memphis and Nashville played the story of Alex Haley's Henning homecoming on their front pages the next day. The New York *Times* gave it nineteen lines in the B Section. The Lauderdale County *Enterprise* ran a picture but no story. There was nothing in the next week's *Time* or *Newsweek*.

Fred Montgomery was sick for two days after the celebration. "He was just worn out," his wife says, "and I was too. We're okay now, though. Things have kind of settled down. You don't hear too much talk about it. I guess people are just resting up."

It has been announced that there will be a televised sequel to *Roots*, dealing with the Tennessee years of Haley's forebears. A film crew from Hollywood was on hand to observe the homecoming. Presumably some of the new series will be filmed on location in Henning.

There is a new restaurant on Main Street, and some people say property values have risen sharply. A federal grant has been received to extend sanitary sewers to about a hundred families, most of them black, living just outside the corporate limits of the town. Many blacks say the section—commonly referred to as "the colored property"—should be annexed. Many whites, including Mayor Graves, are opposed to that. "If we brought them in," the mayor says, "they'd have as many votes in this town as the whites. It's gonna stay the way it is—as long as I'm mayor, as long as I'm on the board of aldermen, as long as I'm able to mark a ballot."

A regular election for all city offices is imminent. Graves is not a candidate for reelection, but he is running for an aldermanic post. Fred Montgomery is seeking reelection to the board. He is the only black candidate for any office. There are 358 registered white voters in Henning and 92 blacks.

Yesterday, just one week after the big event, Emma Lee Reid died suddenly of a heart attack in the old Palmer house. The consensus around town seems to be that her heirs will offer the property for sale to Haley and his brothers, or to the state of Tennessee, and the place will be restored as a museum and historic site.

Haley has returned to California, where he now lives. For a little while, the curse of fame that is now his constant companion was visited upon his hometown. Like him, Henning reacted with ambivalence. It was stunned, appalled, fascinated, exhilarated. Its exposure was brief and relatively mild. It will recover. With a heightened consciousness of the possibilities it has, Henning may even find itself free at last to change, to be whatever it wants to be, on its own terms.

Alex Haley, a good and gentle man, should be so lucky.

Alex Haley now lives and writes most of the time in east Tennessee, where he restored a nineteenth-century farmhouse in the 1980s. The Henning home of Will and Cynthia Palmer, his maternal grandparents, where Haley heard as a youth the generational stories that inspired Roots, *is now a state-owned historic site. Haley bought the house from the heirs of Emma Lee Reid and then deeded it to the state. It was restored and opened to the public in 1986 as the Alex Haley Boyhood Home, administered by the Tennessee Historical Commission. Fred Montgomery, Haley's closest friend and companion in the days when they were children, was elected mayor of Henning in 1989. Now in his midseventies and retired from his plumbing business, he works part-time as host/interpreter at the Haley homeplace.*

THE TRIAL OF
HIGHLANDER
FOLK SCHOOL

Of all the organizations ever formed to combat dis-
crimination against minorities and the poor in the
South, none has been more durable than High-
lander. Since its founding in 1932 it has survived
numerous assaults, not least of which was the ordeal
described here. This article was prepared in the fall
of 1977 and published in the spring 1978 issue of
Southern Exposure.

For more than a year, the pressure
had been building: Southern public officials seeking evidence of
Communist subversion in the civil rights movement had been zeroing
in on the Highlander Folk School, a racially integrated adult education center on the Cumberland Plateau near Monteagle, Tennessee.
An undercover agent sent there by the governor of Georgia had returned with photographs of whites and blacks dancing and swimming
together and with a group picture showing Martin Luther King, Jr.,
in the company of a writer for the Communist *Daily Worker*. The attorney general of Arkansas had charged that Highlander was "flying
in formation" with the National Association for the Advancement of
Colored People, which he denounced as an "agent of a Communist
conspiracy designed to set up a 'Black Republic' in the South." Mississippi and Alabama officials, likewise given to equating integration
with communism, were also urging the governor and the legislature
of Tennessee to eliminate what many archsegregationists in the region were calling "a Communist training school teaching methods
and tactics of racial strife."

The year was 1959. For more than a quarter of a century, the Highlander Folk School had held firmly to its small base in Grundy County. Occasionally it had received substantial support from among "the common folks" in the area but more frequently it had been a controversial presence resented and opposed by the county's power holders. The school could boast not merely that it had survived but also that it had been an effective voice for unionism, integration, and the rights of the poor. But in the climate of fear and defiance that was sweeping the South in reaction to the movement for racial equality, an irresistible consensus was forming in Grundy County and elsewhere across Tennessee and the South: Highlander was a troublesome symbol of radicalism and discord. It would have to go.

First, a resolution was introduced in the Tennessee General Assembly "to investigate the Subversive Activities of the Highlander Folk School." It passed both houses with scant opposition and was signed by Governor Buford Ellington.

Then, five members of the legislature appointed by the governor held closed and open hearings in Tracy City, near Monteagle, and in Nashville, the state capital. They heard an outpouring of allegations against the folk school and a few voices in defense of it.

Next, the committee presented a condemnatory report to the state house and senate and urged them to direct the district attorney general to bring suit against Highlander for the revocation of its state charter. The legislature quickly passed a resolution to that effect without debate, and again, Governor Ellington added his signature.

There followed a raid on the school by state and local police and agents of the district attorney, the arrest of four persons for possession of whiskey and interference with police officers, a court hearing on whether the school should be padlocked as a public nuisance, a jury trial to determine whether its charter should be voided, a conviction, and two futile appeals. Finally, in the pre-Christmas gloom of 1961, a court-appointed receiver sold the holdings of the Highlander Folk School at public auction.

The investigation, raid, hearing, trial, and conviction all happened swiftly, between February and November of 1959. The appeals required almost two years. The forced sale was over in a matter of hours. Twenty-nine years after its founding, Highlander was finally gone from Grundy County.

59

Myles Horton remembers. He was Highlander's first and only director during all the years of its existence in Grundy County—and
for a while after it was "reborn" as the Highlander Research and Education Center in Knoxville. Now seventy-two years old, he lives in
semiretirement as director emeritus of the "new" Highlander Center
at its mountaintop location in Jefferson County, farther east in the
Tennessee countryside of southern Appalachia.

"I was in Europe when they staged the raid," he recalls. "They
arrested Septima Clark and Guy Carawan and a couple of others,
charged them with illegal possession and sale of alcohol and resisting
arrest. When the cops threatened to break down the door of my
home with axes, they were given a key. They found a little gin in
there, and down in the basement they found an empty ten-gallon keg
with an open bunghole. It smelled like whiskey to them, so they
poured a little water in it and sloshed it around, and then they got
one of the highway patrolmen to taste it. At the hearing, he testified
that it tasted like liquor, said it was god-awful. So I went home and
checked that old barrel, and found out it had mouse droppings in it.
When I saw that cop the next day, I said, 'You know what you drank?
You drank mouse turd soup.' He turned pale."

Horton chuckles at the recollection. He is a garrulous man, given
to easy laughter, and he nourishes a Southerner's penchant for anec-
dotes and storytelling. He looks considerably younger than his years.
It is hard to imagine him as a radical of the 1930s.

"We had a little bit of trouble in our early history," he says, "but the
first twenty-five years were relatively noncontroversial compared to
what happened in the late 1950s. It was the temper of the times—to
be specific, it was the race issue—that brought on all the trouble.
Ironically, it was outside agitators from the state governments of
Georgia and Arkansas who applied the pressure. Governor Ellington,
in my opinion, didn't have enough sense or ability or energy to lead
an attack on Highlander. He was a neuter—a racist, but not an en-
ergetic one, like Marvin Griffin of Georgia or Orval Faubus of Arkansas. I think Ellington agreed to the Highlander purge because he was
under pressure, not because he believed the charges against us."

Time may have mellowed Horton's memory of the folk school's early years. Hulan Glyn Thomas, who wrote about them in a Vanderbilt University master's thesis in 1964, recorded numerous examples of hostile opposition to Highlander from its origin until the beginning of World War II. The school's commitments to the laboring classes and to the trade union movement in the South incited the wrath of courthouse power blocs, antiunion industrialists, some religious leaders (including evangelist Billy Sunday), the American Legion, and the Ku Klux Klan.

Myles Horton was a Tennessee sharecropper's son who managed by a stroke of luck to study at Union Theological Seminary in New York and at the University of Chicago. In the midst of the Great Depression, he returned home with the intention of applying adult education methods he had learned in the Danish folk school movement to the needs of unemployed miners and timber-cutters in the mountains. Such noted figures as Socialist leader Norman Thomas and "social gospel" theologian Reinhold Niebuhr had given him encouragement and support; labor union leaders such as John L. Lewis also welcomed his determination to develop an outpost on the frontier of the labor movement in the South. With Don West, another young Southerner interested in transplanting the Danish folk school idea in the mountains, Horton secured the use of a Grundy County farm owned by Lillian Johnson of Memphis. From the start, their attempts at participatory democracy were controversial.

They set up evening classes, music lessons, a library, and other programs for adults in the Monteagle community, but their union organizing activities and general support for unemployed and unrepresented working people drew such fierce opposition that Lillian Johnson was put under heavy pressure to evict them from her land. (After a few years she deeded the property to Highlander, but in 1934, after Don West had departed, Horton was offered an alternative site in Fentress County, one hundred miles northeast of Monteagle, and he actually chartered the school in that county because he anticipated losing the Grundy County site.)

In the waning years of the Depression an organization called the Grundy County Crusaders launched a campaign of harassment and intimidation to drive Highlander out of the area, and others who saw liberalism, unionism, socialism, and communism as one and the same—and racial integration as the proof of the pudding—kept Highlander in a state of uncertainty throughout the 1930s. Even the liberally inclined Nashville *Tennessean* saw fit in 1939 to infiltrate the school with an investigative reporter and subsequently to publish a series of articles purporting to expose a hotbed of Communist activity there. According to the Hulan Thomas thesis, Highlander probably survived its first decade only because the prolabor Roosevelt administration was in office—and because "the profound shock of Pearl Harbor . . . destroyed much of the remaining opposition to the radical left, and Highlander was no exception."

If Horton's remembrance of the distant thirties has softened, his recollection of more recent years—and particularly of 1959—seems much more detailed and precise. In a matter-of-fact manner, without apparent bitterness, he talks about Highlander's year of crisis:

"The whole thing was a put-up job. The legislative investigating committee admitted it could find no proof of Communist activity—it couldn't, of course, because there wasn't any—but they told A. F. Sloan, the district attorney general, to sue us for the revocation of our charter anyway, because we were in technical violation of some state laws. That was in March, as I recall. It took Ab Sloan until the end of July to move against us. That's when they staged the raid, during a workshop on school desegregation, and arrested Septima Clark and the others. She was our director of education, a black woman from South Carolina, a marvelous person. They were arrested and jailed, but never brought to trial. Sloan got what he was after—that little bit of alcohol they found in my house—and that was all the excuse he needed to take us to court.

"There was a preliminary hearing, and then in September, at the Grundy County courthouse in Altamont, there was a three-day hearing in circuit court after Sloan had asked for an injunction closing us down as a public nuisance. That was the so-called padlock hearing, before Circuit Judge Chester C. Chattin. We had a young lawyer from Nashville named Cecil Branstetter representing us. The state had Sloan and three or four other lawyers."

Sloan had given a revealing quote to the press after the raid. "The members of the legislative committee gave me information mostly on integration and communism," he said, "and I wasn't satisfied I could be successful on that. I thought maybe this [raid to find whiskey] was the best shot, and I think now I'll be successful." In the files of Nashville and Chattanooga newspapers, in a book on Highlander by Frank Adams (*Unearthing Seeds of Fire*), in another Vanderbilt master's thesis by Joan Hobbs, and in the voluminous record of court proceedings, the full picture of Sloan's successful prosecution is preserved in great detail.

The state's primary strategy in the padlock hearing appeared to be to present Highlander as a place where illegal and immoral behavior between whites and blacks went on routinely. A parade of witnesses, most of whom were shown on cross-examination to have police records or reputations of unreliability in the community, testified to having witnessed wild parties, drunkenness, and open sexual intercourse between whites and blacks at the school. One man said Highlander had a reputation in the community as "an integrated whorehouse." Another, edging closer to the truth, said "people don't like it" that Highlander was integrated. "Don't allow them [black people] on this mountain," he added. (Although the folk school had included blacks in its program from the beginning, none lived in Grundy County.)

John Clark, one of only a handful of local people to testify for Highlander, said he had never witnessed any immoral behavior at the school; it was opposed, he said, because people in the community "don't like the colored folks. That is the main burning issue."

Defense attorney Branstetter called about twenty witnesses, all of whom denied categorically the charges that had been made. They were treated roughly on cross-examination by Sloan and his prosecution team, who drew repeated protests from Branstetter and an occasional admonition from Judge Chattin.

In closing arguments, prosecutor A. A. Kelley asserted that "there is proof here, abundance of it, that [Highlander] is a place where moonshine whiskey was kept and stored. Great quantities, and where bonded whiskey exists. Rums. Gins. Vodkas. And the whole range and gamut of the fancy, fine drinks." Attorney General Sloan, repeating the testimony that Highlander was thought of in the community as "an integrated whorehouse," said in his closing statement: "I don't care if it is integrated or not. I am after it. It is against the law to have one of them in Grundy County. . . . We are not interested in that school for what it teaches. We are not interested in that school for the type of students that it has. . . . I filed this [complaint] to try to stop it before they trained the youth of this country to follow the footsteps of those people that were caught in sexual intercourse out of wedlock. That is the kind of practice that I am against . . . not what they teach."

In the testimony, there had been an admission by Myles Horton and others that beer was made available at cost to participants in the school's workshops and programs who wanted it. In effect, a refrigerator containing beer was placed where the adults could take from it and pay on the honor system during their leisure hours. Sloan charged that the practice amounted to selling beer without a license and likened the school to the sort of "roadside honky-tonks" he was pledged to eliminate.

At the conclusion of the hearing, Judge Chattin issued a ruling from the bench. "I don't see anything at all to the charge of immorality," he said. "I don't think the state has made out its case at all on that point. As to the charges of fighting, quarreling, and drunkenness, and boisterous crowds, no proof at all whatever about that. Just not there. The only thing I see wrong is the sale of beer. . . . I think that the proof shows by great preponderance that they have been selling beer out there. . . . That is a nuisance, to permit the sale of beer without a license." He issued a temporary padlock order on the school's main building, allowed continuation of its programs elsewhere on the grounds, and set an early November trial date to determine whether there was sufficient evidence to justify the revocation of Highlander's state charter.

The original cause for the attack on Highlander—the allegation that it was tainted by communism—had receded from view. But the climate of hostility and outrage against the school was, if anything, more intense than ever. The state was determined to carry out its purge.

May Justus remembers. She is eighty years old now, living alone in a small house near the old Highlander property. A native of the Tennessee mountains, she came to Grundy County in 1925 with Vera McCampbell, a colleague of hers at a Presbyterian mission school in

Kentucky. They taught in the local schools—Miss Justus until 1938, when she turned her talents to writing books for children (she has now written over sixty), and Miss McCampbell until 1958, when she was fired from her teaching job for attending a Highlander event at which Eleanor Roosevelt and Harry Golden spoke. In 1959 May Justus was Highlander's secretary-treasurer. She testified in defense of the school during the legislative investigation and in court. When one interrogator suggested that she might have come under "suspicion" because of her involvement with the folk school, she replied: "Sir, a person must live by his Christian principles regardless of what human beings think about him. As long as I can lie down and sleep at night, knowing that I have lived right, people can think what they want to about me."

She has remained in the community, holding steadfastly to her belief in Highlander and her own commitment to its purposes. "I'm surrounded by a great deal of love," she says serenely. "My children from the days when I taught school never were against me. They know me, and we understand each other's feelings. These people have come to be my family, the only children God ever gave me. I'm devoted to them, and they to me. Some of them are in their sixties now."

May Justus recalls: "I offered to resign from my church, but not from the Kingdom of God. Many people were shocked and angered at my association with 'niggers,' but an eighty-year-old elder in the church told me, 'I know a lady and a Christian when I see one. Don't leave.' So I never did. I harbor no bitterness. I had none at the time. Those who hated Highlander—they are what they are, and can't help it. There are reasons why, scars they didn't cause. I was never threatened, and I was never afraid. I had been here so long, I was confident they wouldn't harm me, even though they didn't approve."

The people of Grundy County haven't changed their views about Highlander or about integration, Miss Justus says: "The trial didn't have anything to do with beer, or with Myles Horton's personal gain—those were just excuses, ridiculous charges. No, it was about racism. People here just couldn't think of blacks as human beings. 'We don't want them niggers in our county, even going through our town,' they would say. The first thing I learned when I came here was, no blacks.

Total segregation. It went deep—a feeling of superiority, of 'White is right.' Not even one black family lives in the county today, and never has. That's what it was about, and that view hasn't changed.

"If the trial was being held here now, and you picked a jury at random, it would end up the same way. It was not just the unlettered and illiterate of Grundy County who were against Highlander, though. It was also the upper class, the rulers—lawyers, doctors, politicians, here and in places like Nashville. They were wrong. In the long and shameful history of human bondage and slow emancipation, Highlander will someday have a bright chapter."

Septima Clark remembers, too. She is also nearing eighty, living now in her native Charleston, South Carolina, where in 1956 she was dismissed from her teaching job for being a member of the NAACP. "I had forty-one years of service," she says quietly. "They took my pension. But I have recently received $7,200 from the state—10 percent of what they owed me—and next year, I'm supposed to get my pension. There are thirteen black members of the legislature now, and one of them got it for me."

The Citizenship Education Program that Mrs. Clark developed for Highlander became the model for future black voter registration training programs in the South. "Many of the achievements of the civil rights movement started with that Highlander program," she says. "You can see the results everywhere—in black elected officials, in voters, and now in the efforts of Indians and Appalachian whites to get their rights. The segregationists were scared of Highlander. They said Myles Horton was taking money from the school, but integration was what really worried them. Myles didn't profit—he was doing people a favor, helping people. They just wanted to get rid of him and the school."

Mrs. Clark is now a member of the same school board that dismissed her more than twenty years ago. "It just goes to show," she says, "that we *can* get something done nonviolently."

The trial opened in Altamont on November 3 and lasted four days. The state's opening claim was that Highlander's charter should be revoked for three reasons: it sold beer and other items without a commercial license; Horton had received property and money from the school—in other words, had realized personal gain—in violation of the charter; and the school had permitted whites and blacks to attend together, in violation of a 1901 state law. (The U.S. Supreme Court's 1954 *Brown* decision had voided that law, but the state claimed that the court's ruling affected only public schools, not private ones such as Highlander.)

Cecil Branstetter, for the defense, conceded to the third charge and invited conviction on it. Highlander had always been integrated, he said, and welcomed an opportunity to defend its position in court.

With Judge Chattin presiding, the opposing attorneys took more than a day to select a jury. Both Branstetter and A. F. Sloan, the district attorney general, asked probing questions of each prospective juror to discern his or her views on segregation; some heated exchanges took place, and several jurors were seated over Branstetter's objection. Then, before testimony commenced, the judge limited the jury's consideration to two issues—illegal commercial sales and Horton's personal gain. The race issue, like the charges of communism and immorality, would not be argued in court.

(A deposition of Edwin H. Friend of Atlanta was permitted in the court record, however. Friend had attended Highlander's twenty-fifth anniversary celebration in 1957 as an undercover agent for Georgia governor Marvin Griffin. While there, he had photographed the Reverend Martin Luther King, Jr., and others with Abner Berry, a columnist for the Communist *Daily Worker* who also had concealed his true identity from Highlander officials. The photograph was later given wide circulation as "proof" that King had attended "a Communist training school." In his deposition, Friend said his assignment as a Georgia undercover agent was "to go to Monteagle, Tennessee, to the Highlander Folk School and find out whether that malignancy of the NAACP and Communism was leaking out over Georgia.")

The state's case included testimony from beer distributors that they had delivered cases of beer to the school and testimony from others—including Myles Horton—that the school's executive committee had conveyed title to Horton's house and sixty acres of land to him. The property transfer would prove to be the straw the state would seize.

Highlander was shown to have assets of about $175,000, including two hundred acres of land, a dozen buildings, and a library containing several thousand volumes. The school's income of about seventy thousand dollars a year came almost entirely from foundations and was spent on modest salaries for its small staff and on the operation of its workshops and educational programs. From 1932 to 1954 Horton had received only subsistence funds and necessary expenses—no salary. He and his wife and two children lived on the premises, as did his mother and father.

"The executive committee of Highlander transferred the title of my house to me in about 1956," Horton now recalls. "My wife, Zilphia, had died, and the committee wanted to make the transfer so my kids would have a home if something happened to me. We had built the house with our own money on land sold to us by Highlander, and my parents had done the same thing. We paid the school for the land and built on it some years earlier, but we had left it in the name of Highlander, and that's what the executive committee changed. They said I had put twenty-four years of equity into the place, I had earned it, and it should be mine. They also put me on a salary in about 1954—$1,200 a year, as I recall—and by 1959 my salary was something over $5,000 a year.

"Sloan was very clever. He hammered away at that, made it look like the school was being operated for my personal gain and benefit. He told the jury, 'It's not what he's getting, but what he's going to get. He's got it set up so that someday, he can cut the melon—when he gets ready, he can take everything.' The jury was led to believe I would do that—and they convicted me on that."

When testimony ended, there was little doubt of the outcome. Branstetter's passionate assertion that the state hadn't proved its case appeared not to have moved the jury. In their final arguments, Sloan and Kelley bored in on the property transfer. "He got it for nothing," Sloan said derisively. "Deeded it to himself."

In his charge to the jury, Judge Chattin said, "There will be only one issue for you to determine, and that is this: Has Highlander Folk School been operated for the personal gain of Myles Horton?" He made no distinction between legitimate and illegitimate compensation, leaving the concept of "personal gain" to be interpreted in a wholly negative way. Branstetter protested, and after two conferences with counsel at the bench, the judge reluctantly made a clarifying remark to the jury: The payment of salary or conveyance of land in lieu of salary does not constitute personal gain.

But the damage had been done. Highlander's assets were valued at tens of thousands of dollars, and the school received money from out of state, grants from New York foundations, gifts from the likes of Eleanor Roosevelt—and Horton was in charge, he parceled out the funds, and now he held title to a house, to land.

At ten minutes past two o'clock on the afternoon of November 6, the jury filed out. Forty-five minutes later, they were back. The verdict: Yes, Horton had profited; he was guilty.

Four of the jury members who still live in Grundy County vividly recall the Highlander trial. Noah White, Paul G. Cook, Douglas Partin, and the only woman on the panel, Colleen Meeks, remember the issues and the outcome, and they are as convinced now as they were then that their decision was the right one.

"They were selling beer and whiskey without a license," Partin says. "The prosecutors had pictures of it, they had proof."

White goes further. "Horton admitted he took grant money for himself," he says. "He profited, and didn't pay tax on it. All I can say is, justice was done. If that place was down there now like it was then, somebody would blow it away. It wasn't the race thing—that didn't influence me, and wouldn't now."

And Paul Cook: "I didn't want to sit on that jury, but I was sworn to tell the truth. A decision under oath is a very sacred thing. I decided without a doubt in my mind that Myles had profited, and they had sold beer without a license. They weren't paying taxes, either, or having classes, or using textbooks. That integration business, that didn't have anything to do with it. Lots of folks around here resent the colored, and we still don't have any in this county—but they'd have been in trouble without the niggers, and you'd get the same decision now, if the trial was held today."

And finally, Colleen Meeks. She is the postmaster at Coalmont now. "Everybody thought I was just a little housewife out there, with her mind at home," she says. "I had no preconceived idea, knew nothing of it, and I didn't want to be called. I was scared. This was big doings. But I wouldn't be intimidated—I'm not like that. If Branstetter had convinced me, I'd have voted for his side, and I'd have stuck by my guns. It was a simple question: Did Horton profit, or did he not? I decided from the evidence that he did, and my conscience is clear about it. I had no bitterness toward those people. They were good people, some of them. Horton conducted himself admirably. He was a gentleman, an educated man—but he profited from the school.

"And the race thing? Well, this county won't tolerate blacks—never would, and it's still that way—but I honestly don't think that influenced us. I know it didn't influence me."

The final decision was in the hands of Judge Chattin. Three months after the trial, on February 17, 1960, he issued his ruling in the case of the *State of Tennessee* v. *Highlander Folk School*. On the charge of Horton's personal gain, he agreed with the jury's verdict. On the two issues he had reserved to himself, he also ruled against the school: It had sold beer and other commodities without a license, and it had allowed whites and blacks to attend school together, in violation of Tennessee law. He ordered Highlander's charter to be revoked and appointed a receiver to liquidate its holdings. Court costs would be paid from the school's assets. His instructions to Myles Horton were a blunt order to "wind up your affairs."

Cecil Branstetter remembers. He had fought a hard fight. The jurors remember him as "the smartest lawyer I ever saw" and "the man I'd want to represent me if I ever got in trouble." Immediately after the trial, he had filed an affidavit swearing that a deputy sheriff had told him that he, the deputy, had told members of the jury during the trial that Highlander "should be run out of the county." (The state quickly responded with sworn statements from all twelve jurors that no one had tried to influence them.)

Branstetter had sought a new trial, citing thirty-two errors in the proceedings, and when that had failed, he had appealed to the state supreme court. A year later, in April 1961, the five judges of that court had unanimously upheld Judge Chattin's ruling on Horton's gain and the school's sale of beer, but they found it "unnecessary for us to pass upon the constitutional question as to the mixing of white and colored, male and female, in the same school."

Branstetter had then taken an appeal to the U.S. Supreme Court, which on October 9, 1961, denied Highlander a hearing. Burke Marshall, who headed the civil rights division of the Department of Justice under Attorney General Robert F. Kennedy at that time, had written Branstetter a letter of regret, saying the government could not file an *amicus curae* brief on behalf of Highlander because of the lack of "any federal question at all" in the case.

"What was clear from the first," Cecil Branstetter now recalls, "was that the state wanted to get rid of Highlander. The raid was a farce, a publicity thing, the kickoff of the campaign. Once the jury had ruled with respect to Horton's personal gain, it wasn't necessary for the state supreme court to pass judgment on the segregation issue, and they left it out for fear of a reversal—and that's what deprived the U.S. Supreme Court of a constitutional question to consider.

"We could find no precedent for the state's revocation of the charter, and there has been none since, but the law is clear: The charter of a nonprofit corporation can be revoked for cause, and since there are no stockholders, no owners, the property escheats to the state. That's what happened. Everything Highlander had was turned over to a receiver and sold at auction."

Scott Bates also remembers. A French professor at the University of the South at Sewanee, five miles from Monteagle, he had testified at the trial in defense of Highlander, and later he was to serve as president of its board of directors. He remembers May Justus as being "valiant, courageous" in her lonely stand in the community, remembers others around Monteagle who supported the school but were afraid to say so publicly, remembers Horton as "a generous man who never profited from the school, far from it."

And Bates remembers with special clarity the morning of Saturday, December 16, 1961, when all the belongings of Highlander were sold at auction: "It was a grim affair. We had hoped to salvage the library collection, but we had no money. The auctioneers told us they wouldn't sell it unless they got a bid of at least three thousand dollars, but they let it go for five hundred to a second-hand book dealer from

Chattanooga. It was like a picnic, a circus. Hundreds of people came, eager to take away mementos of the school. It was like the dissection of a corpse. Later, some lawyers involved in the prosecution of Highlander bought some of the land."

(The chief prosecutors—A. F. Sloan, A. A. Kelley, Sam Polk Raulston—are all dead. Only C. P. Swafford of Dayton, an assistant attorney general who sat at the prosecution table but took a minor part in the case, is still living. He says he knows nothing about who bought the land. About Highlander, Swafford says: "As I remember, the community just wouldn't put up with it; it was not a good atmosphere, especially for the young people. I really don't remember much about the facts. I had a very small part in the trial.")

Both the house belonging to Horton and the house of his parents were considered assets of the school, though they had built and paid for them with their own money. The houses were included in the auction, along with everything else except the individuals' personal effects. The sale of buildings and land netted $53,700 for the state's treasury. In his book on Highlander, Frank Adams says that "lawyers from the Grundy area bought Highlander's library and turned the building into a private club."

But Highlander, though critically wounded, was not dead, and the controversy surrounding it had not run its course. Even as appeals of Judge Chattin's ruling were being pursued, Myles Horton was addressing an application for a new charter to the Tennessee secretary of state. His request listed new incorporators, a new location (in Knoxville), and a new name—the Highlander Research and Education Center—but the objective was clear: to set up a successor organization dedicated to carrying on the mission of the Highlander Folk School. The state balked, saying such a charter would be illegal, but Horton threatened to sue, and Branstetter, knowing the state had no authority to refuse the application ("it was an administrative function—they couldn't judge it before the fact"), adroitly pressed his advantage. Finally the charter was issued.

Several years later, when Buford Ellington was again Tennessee's governor, the legislature tried once more to investigate the "reborn" Highlander for alleged subversive activities.

"It was in the mid-sixties," Horton recalls. "When I heard what the legislature was up to, I sent Governor Ellington a personal message.

I told him we had cooperated once, but we wouldn't do it again—we wouldn't turn over any information. He would just have to send me to jail, and live with the consequences. I was told later that Ellington tried to get the investigation bill defeated, but he couldn't do it. The legislature had inadvertently failed to pass an appropriations bill to pay for the investigation, though, and Ellington wouldn't let them have the money. Then Chuck Morgan, representing the American Civil Liberties Union, put an end to it all by going into federal court in Nashville and getting an injunction to block the investigation. I think it was the only time an injunction was ever granted to block a state legislative investigation."

Morgan's recollection of the case is also vivid. "They overreached," he says. "Used the word *subversive* without basis. We got it voided for vagueness, got an injunction—and the state didn't appeal."

There were other ironies, early and late—and often unreported. One such incident occurred in 1935, when a coalition of Southern liberals and radicals tried to stage the "All-Southern Conference for Civil and Trade Union Rights" in Chattanooga. The local American Legion got up in arms, and some of its members chased the conference delegates out of town. Most of them, including a small group of students and teachers from Commonwealth College in Arkansas, ended up at Highlander, where they heard speeches and passed resolutions against lynching and other violations of human rights. One of the Commonwealth delegates to the conference was a young radical from the Ozarks by the name of Orval Faubus. The later-to-be governor of Arkansas is best remembered now for his attempt to prevent desegregation of Little Rock's Central High School in 1957; he also sent an undercover agent to look for Communist influences at Highlander in 1959. Faubus has never publicly acknowledged his presence as a radical student at Highlander, but he has been heard to admit it privately.

Another behind-the-scenes incident of note happened in 1965, after the Tennessee State Library and Archives had acquired some of Highlander's private files. While the collection was being cataloged, some unsigned "poison pen" letters were circulated in the state administration, charging that the library director, Sam B. Smith, was "in complete agreement and sympathy with Myles Horton and all that his Communist-backed school stood for." The material was impounded for several months while Smith's job hung in the balance. In the end, he was given a vote of confidence by the commission overseeing the library and archives, and the Highlander papers were finally made available for public use.

One further irony seems worth mentioning, for it still exists. It can be found in the Tennessee statutes. Chapter 37 of the Tennessee Code Annotated, entitled "Segregation of the Races," still contains the 1901 act prohibiting interracial schools. In brackets, the act is designated "Unconstitutional," but it has never been repealed by the legislature.

In the aftermath of the Highlander trial, several of the key figures in the case were advanced to higher positions. Judge Chester Chattin was appointed to the state court of appeals in 1962, and District Attorney General A. F. Sloan, who had been Chattin's close associate since 1947, was named to replace him as judge of the circuit court serving Grundy and adjacent counties. Sam Polk Raulston, another of the prosecution attorneys, also was made a circuit judge. Judge Chattin was further elevated in 1965 to the state supreme court, where he served for nine years.

It is Myles Horton's belief that those promotions were, in effect, rewards. He says: "I think both Sloan and Chattin were told—by Ellington, I suppose—that if they got rid of Highlander, they'd be promoted. And they were—quick."

Cecil Branstetter doubts that things were done that directly. "I have no evidence or knowledge of a deal regarding Judge Chattin or Ab Sloan," he says. "I doubt if there was any agreement, any clear understanding that they would be moved up. That wasn't necessary. What they did simply came out the way the state wanted it to come out—and in the predictable sequence of events, it just naturally follows that their careers would be enhanced."

Branstetter is probably correct. In any case, his assessment is more or less confirmed by Judge Chester Chattin himself—who, like all the others, also remembers the Highlander case.

He lives in retirement in Winchester now, just twenty miles or so from the old Highlander property. He recalls that "the American Legion up there had been pushing against Highlander for years. No disturbance or anything—they just wanted to get rid of it legally. The school didn't teach anybody anything, I don't reckon—they just had a good time, and then Horton turned it into that mess. The main point, as far as I was concerned, was that the trustees had deeded part of the property to him, and that violated the charter. The state brought in all that other business, but the main thing was the property, and I was upheld on that. I also ruled against them on the race issue. I made a mistake on that. The supreme court should have reversed me on that. But Horton was after all the property. He wanted it in his name. Without a doubt, he violated the charter."

And what about Judge Chattin's subsequent years on the bench? Does he consider his advancement in any way an expression of gubernatorial appreciation for his handling of the Highlander case?

"A favor? No, there's nothing to that. I went on to the court of appeals two years after I ruled in that case. Nobody up there tried to help me, because I didn't ask for any help. One of the judges had died, and I called Governor Ellington at the mansion and told him I would be interested in the job if it was open. He said he had already promised it to somebody else, but if the man didn't take it, he'd call me back—and he did. It was Governor Frank Clement who first appointed me to the circuit court back in 1958—and later, in 1965, it was Clement who appointed me to the supreme court. I had managed his first campaign in this district. No, nobody gave me any special help or did me any favors. I was just lucky, being in the right place at the right time."

The old Highlander Folk School near Monteagle is a subdivision now, featuring modern two- and three-bedroom homes on a half-acre or more of picturesque Cumberland Plateau land. There is a cemetery close by, bordered on three sides by dense woods and fronted by a gravel road; among its permanent occupants are the wife and father of Myles Horton. Horton's one-time residence, a handsome log structure, is surrounded by a chain-link fence. A sign on the gate reads DORIS' BEAUTY SHOP.

Across the mountains in Jefferson County, the new Highlander carries on the forty-five-year-old mission of its predecessor. Myles

Horton is still around, but he doesn't play much of an active role in Highlander's adult education programs any more; that responsibility rests mainly with Mike Clark, the current director, and other younger men and women like him. The focus of the education programs has also shifted with the times—from labor organizing to racial equality to the interests of mountain people—but the *idea* of Highlander, the basic purpose of it, apparently hasn't changed at all.

"They called us Communists," Horton remembers, smiling softly, "but they misunderstood. We've always been pursuing something much more radical than communism. What we've been after from the very beginning is democracy."

Myles Horton died of cancer at his Highlander home on January 19, 1990. He was eighty-four years old. At a memorial service in tribute to him later that year, more than a thousand of his friends and associates gathered to celebrate his life. In so doing, they added their individual concerns and strengths to the ongoing life of the Highlander Research and Education Center, still a voice for Southern progress almost six decades after its founding.

∾ THE KING COAL GOOD
TIMES BLUES

The mining of coal is a classic example of an economic enterprise that reaps the highest profit at the heaviest cost to people and the environment. In southern Appalachia, and particularly in the Kentucky, West Virginia, Tennessee, and Virginia portions of that region, coal mining has brought a twentieth-century deliverance of blessings and curses. Martin County, Kentucky, is typical of the unfortunate jurisdictions that rise and fall in response to the extractive machinery. Two pieces I wrote about Martin County—one published in the February 6, 1979, issue of New Times *and the other in the October 18, 1981, issue of the* New York Times Magazine, *are combined here.*

Tom Fletcher had about him a look of awe and astonishment, as if he were in the company of the president of the United States—which in fact he was. There on the mountaineer's own front porch, hunkered down beside him, was Lyndon Baines Johnson, looking attentive and serious as the photographers and cameramen recorded the scene.

It was late April 1964. Spring was nudging to the surface in the mouse-brown mountains of Martin County, Kentucky, a remote Appalachian outpost dubiously distinguished as one of the poorest political jurisdictions in the nation. President Johnson had gone there by helicopter on a whirlwind tour of "poverty pockets," seeking to call attention to his escalating War on Poverty. He had been driven through the little county-seat town of Inez to Tom Fletcher's three-room shack, perched on a hillside close to the road in a narrow mountain valley.

Fletcher was thirty-eight years old, out of work, dead broke. He had a wife and eight children, the two oldest of whom had quit school after the fourth grade (the others were either preschoolers or still enrolled). He had earned four hundred dollars the previous year. The Fletchers were said to be typical of the mass of Martin County's ten thousand people. Official unemployment there was reported to be 37 percent; unofficially, it was estimated that only twenty of every one hundred adults had jobs.

The president chatted with members of the family for a few minutes and then rose to leave. As he crossed the yard, he called back to Fletcher. "Take care of yourself," he shouted. "And don't you forget, now—I want you to keep those kids in school."

Hard times had abided in Martin County for decades before LBJ made his flying visit there. Both the population and the economy had been in steady decline since the 1930s, and the ruggedness of the terrain had always placed severe limits on growth. Rich deposits of nonmetallurgical coal were known to lie underground, but there were neither highways nor railroads to make it accessible.

From the time the area was first visited by white pioneers in the late 1700s to 1870, the year of its formation as one of Kentucky's last counties—and, indeed, for decades thereafter—Martin County was a remote region of dense forests, jagged mountains, and knife-blade-thin hollows where little changed except the seasons. A few small coal camp settlements and company towns existed from the 1870s on. There, men went to work in deep mines with picks and shovels for a few dollars a day; others cut timber or scratched out subsistence crops on the little bit of flat land they could find beside the creeks.

Martin County was a small and insignificant district of 231 square miles and a few thousand people located just across the Tug River from West Virginia. Inez, founded in 1876 and named for a postmaster's daughter, was the modest center of government and commerce, such as they were. Shoehorned into a winding valley between two mountain ridges, the muddy little village was as far removed from the concentrations of wealth and power in central Kentucky as it possibly could have been.

Later came other settlements: Himmlerville, a community of industrious Hungarian immigrant miners; Nigger Hollow, where a few black families lived; Coal Camp, called Tightwad by the miners as an expression of the low esteem in which they held its owners. (Himmlerville and Tightwad now have more euphonious and ironic names—Beauty and Lovely—but Nigger Hollow remains, even though all the blacks have long since departed.)

The first paved road in the county was extended west to east from Paintsville through Inez to the Tug River in 1920, and private investors built a one-lane toll bridge across the Tug. More people left by the road than entered, however, and in spite of intermittent periods of activity in the mines, the chronic pattern of stagnation continued.

By the time Presidents Kennedy and Johnson prodded the nation to an awareness of Appalachian poverty in the 1960s, Martin County was an economic disaster area. Its great store of natural resources—coal, gas, crude oil, and hardwood timber—was thought to be all but inaccessible to large-scale recovery. What little work and political activity there was in the county could be found in just three places: the school board office, the only local bank, and the Republican-controlled courthouse. There was one doctor in the county, one practicing attorney, no newspaper, no hospital, no drugstore. No town, not even Inez, was incorporated. A sheriff and two unpaid deputies were all the local law enforcement there was.

In the early 1960s the level of coal mining in the county was barely enough to keep fifty miners working in the underground caverns for wages of less than twenty dollars a day. Only a tiny fraction of families could depend on annual incomes of as much as five thousand dollars. Welfare, unemployment, disability payments, and retirement benefits from the state and federal governments were being paid to a substantial majority of the county's families. The two local high schools graduated between fifty and seventy-five students a year, and almost all of them quickly fled—some to college or military service and most others to the cities of the North, there to enter the swelling enclaves of mountain migrants who had preceded them.

Then the federal government came to the rescue. The campaign to end poverty brought hundreds of millions of dollars into Appalachia. Through it and other government initiatives, some dating back to the 1930s, a bewildering succession of public assistance programs was assembled—VISTA workers, Appalachian Volunteers, the Appalachian Regional Commission, Aid to Families with Dependent Children, Social Security, Supplemental Security Income, Medicare, Medicaid, food stamps, revenue sharing, unemployment insurance, workmen's compensation, job training, veterans benefits, highway funds, mental health programs, legal services, housing benefits, aid to education, day-care centers, nutrition assistance, occupational safety programs, black lung benefits, flood disaster relief, pension funds. Not all of the programs directly benefited Martin County, of course; nevertheless, the total of expenditures for all federal programs and services there between 1964 and 1980 came to well over $100 million.

The War on Poverty was meant to bring swift and dramatic help to such places as Martin County, but the hot light of public attention focused there by Lyndon Johnson turned out to be as short-lived and ineffectual as a dime-store candle. By 1980, when Ronald Reagan defeated Jimmy Carter and returned the White House to the Republicans, the Democratic tradition of government-induced economic and social change had kept places like Martin County from total collapse but had not transformed them into self-reliant and self-supporting communities.

Power struggles and political controversies often accompanied the new government assistance programs. Bureaucracy grew ever larger but seldom more efficient. By the time money filtered through political hands in Washington and Frankfort (the state capital) and Inez, it sometimes turned out that little was left for the intended recipients. Graft and corruption made a mockery of well-intended programs— as, for example, when Martin County's leading public official, County Judge Willie Kirk, was tried and convicted of embezzling federal flood relief funds. (He was sentenced to twenty years in prison but served only five months before being granted a full pardon by then-president Richard M. Nixon. Kirk subsequently ran for and won the top county office again.)

Though expenditures for social programs increased year by year, there was not much improvement for the poorest of the poor. The aged, the infirm, the disabled, the idle—the Tom Fletchers to whom Lyndon Johnson had pledged a better life—were as impoverished as ever. Whereas fierce pride and independence had marked the lives of their ancestors, many citizens of the region eventually displayed an attitude of resignation bred of habit and hopelessness. Even the most determined among them were hard-pressed to escape the smothering embrace of government on one side and tight-fisted control by the local ruling clique on the other.

Martin County's 1970 population had fallen to 9,377, yet the public assistance rolls were bigger than ever. Most of the recoverable natural gas in the county was piped out during that decade, and much of the prime timber was saw-logged and trucked away. Only the coal remained in abundance, and while the mining of it had increased somewhat, a long period of declining national demand had kept prices so low that there was no incentive to recover the bulk of it.

It is doubtful that the forces of government alone ever would have overcome the widespread poverty of Martin County's citizens or the general inadequacy of local institutions, programs, and services. But in the minds of many people, there was always a glimmer of hope that ways would be found to tap the huge reservoir of mineral wealth that lay buried all about them—and finally, in the early 1970s, the Norfolk & Western Railway turned that hope to bright promise. At a cost of nearly a million dollars a mile, the railroad built a twenty-four-mile branch line from its main route in West Virginia to the heart of the Martin County coalfields, and the boom that began with the coming of the trains has continued with hardly a pause ever since.

When economic recovery finally began to take hold in Martin County in the early 1970s, the symbol of hoped-for prosperity was not Uncle Sam but King Coal. The Arab oil embargo, the energy crisis, and the movement to protect the environment combined to stimulate renewed interest in the nation's huge reserves of low-sulfur coal, which can be burned with minimal pollution in the making of electricity. Doubled production of the once-shunned mineral became a national objective, prices soared from about five dollars to more than twenty-five dollars a ton, and from Pennsylvania to Wyoming, the coal rush was on. Nowhere has the effect of the boom been more pronounced than in Martin County, where geologists have estimated that approximately 1.4 billion tons of coal are buried in thick seams beneath the mountains.

Two coincidental developments—the coal boom and the election of President Reagan—make Martin County an ideal locus for a classic case study of diametrically opposed styles of public policy. The activist philosophy of government initiated by Franklin D. Roosevelt and continued with varying degrees of enthusiasm by four Democratic and three Republican presidents for forty-four years has been given a 180-degree turn by Mr. Reagan, whose expressed determination is to "get the government off the backs of the people" and return the nation's economic destiny to the forces of free private enterprise that controlled it prior to the Great Depression.

Just as it was once a symbol of the government's plan to eradicate poverty, Martin County is now something of a demonstration model of Reaganomics, a small-scale example of supply-side economics in action. Since the early 1970s four giant multinational energy corporations leasing mineral holdings from the Pocahontas Land Company, a subsidiary of the Norfolk & Western Railway, have been extracting coal from surface and underground mines in Martin County at a steadily accelerating pace, and the process is likely to continue for many years to come. This enormous undertaking has brought a measure of economic prosperity to thousands of people and sent the county's average industrial wages skyrocketing from the bottom to the top of Kentucky's hourly pay rankings.

The unfamiliar terminology of the newly ascendant Republican economists and public philosophers still puzzles many people, but there are some in Martin County who seem to understand it quite well. Echoing President Reagan (whose local margin over Jimmy Carter in 1980 was nearly two to one), they argue that too much federal funding of social programs and too much regulation of industrial enterprises such as coal mining have stifled private initiative and kept inflation too high. What is called for, they assert, is a combination of diminished government and expanded private enterprise: reductions in taxes, public spending, and regulation, accompanied by private-sector increases in employment, wages, efficiency, productivity, personal savings, and investment capital.

In Martin County today, virtually all of those characteristics are either in place or in prospect. The economic recovery that liberal government social programs sought in vain to achieve now awaits deliverance by the conservative forces of free private enterprise. It would be hard to imagine a more interesting place to observe this shift of philosophy and power than Martin County, where public and private promises have come and gone, but old-fashioned, rock-ribbed Republicanism has endured forever.

The Norfolk & Western Railway had been planning to tap the Martin County mother lode for years. Through its property management arm, the Pocahontas Land Company, the N&W had acquired four large tracts of property there in the two decades prior to 1960. Those titles, in various combinations of surface land and subterranean mineral rights, totaled more than 100,000 acres, giving the railroad effective control of nearly two-thirds of the county's total land area and almost all of its recoverable coal.

In 1973, just as the new rail spur was going into use, the Arab oil crisis escalated coal prices to unheard-of levels—sixty-five dollars a ton and more—and with what seemed like perfect timing, the N&W began harvesting its virtually inexhaustible reserve of black gold. The four mining corporations leasing its lands—Occidental Petroleum, St. Joe Minerals, Ashland Oil, and MAPCO—extracted the coal, and the railroad got the freight business and a royalty on each ton mined. Though prices have since moderated to an average of about thirty-two dollars a ton, the profits still are enormous. In 1980 the official yield of coal from Martin County was 13.4 million tons—second-highest among all the coal-producing counties of Kentucky. That total works out to more coal mined per day than was mined per year two decades ago.

Before-and-after statistics show the dramatic consequences of the Martin County coal boom. Official unemployment has plummeted from almost 40 percent in the early 1960s to about 3 percent now; per capita annual income has increased seven-fold in twenty years; coal miners' earnings now typically exceed thirty thousand dollars a year. The county's population has increased from just over nine thousand to almost fourteen thousand in the past ten years, and more than five thousand people are now employed by local coal companies. The Inez Deposit Bank has doubled its assets in the past decade, and its savings deposits have nearly tripled in just five years. A weekly newspaper and a radio station now operate in what previously was a complete vacuum of local communication. Nearly a dozen lawyers and as many doctors have taken up practice there. Nobody knows how many millionaires live in Martin County now, but the best guess seems to be about twenty, or roughly one in every seven hundred residents—a ratio that would compare favorably with, say, Saudi Arabia or Kuwait.

The coal companies and the railroad have invested more than $225 million in new technology and equipment to harvest the coal with maximum efficiency. Day and night around the clock, around the calendar (with only a temporary pause in the late 1970s for a national strike of union miners) the corporate giants are gouging Martin County coal from deep mines and strip mines, loading it onto one-hundred-ton railroad cars or highway trucks that hold twenty to fifty tons, and transporting it to electric utility companies in such states as Michigan, New York, and North Carolina, or to ships in Norfolk for delivery overseas.

Some mining officials say that even if the rate of extraction were doubled, the Martin County coal boom still could last sixty to eighty years. With federal and state reductions in taxes and spending now taking place, and with federal regulation of strip mining about to be relaxed, there is every reason to believe that the gross income of more than $400 million a year now pouring into mining company and railroad coffers from Martin County could soon be double or even triple that amount.

Robert M. Duncan, chief executive officer of the bank in Inez, is one of many local leaders who look to the future with optimism and confidence. A thirty-year-old lawyer, Duncan was a Reagan delegate at the 1976 Republican National Convention and an alternate delegate in 1980. He firmly supports the president's program to reduce taxes and government spending and to give the private sector more latitude to solve the nation's economic problems. "It wasn't LBJ who made this boom happen," he says. "It was the railroad and the coal companies."

But for all its rags-to-riches appeal, the story of Martin County's recent transformation also has a negative side. The lion's share of the newly generated wealth, like the coal itself, is whisked out of the community to the corporate headquarters of the land and coal and mining companies in Virginia, West Virginia, Oklahoma, and beyond. Martin Countians have more money in their pockets than they've ever had before, but it is peanuts compared with what accrues to far-flung corporate officials and stockholders, for it is they who own most of Martin County.

The local tax base traditionally has been far too small to support even the most modest public needs, and with the rapid rise in population it has been overwhelmed. Coal mining and hauling are directly responsible for new signs of water pollution, soil erosion, flooding, and serious damage to the already inadequate road system.

In the midst of rapid, irreversible change—for better, and for worse—images of startling contrast are everywhere to be seen: Coal trucks and other vehicles create urban-style traffic jams along the narrow roads and at the Tug River bridge. Sprawling brick homes, some of them with back-yard swimming pools, rise within view of sagging hovels that have no indoor plumbing. Spanking-new Cadillacs and Continentals are parked in the muddy driveways of house trailers. Bustling commerce flourishes in the outmoded business houses of Inez, while the town itself, for all its new money, still wears a woebegone look of drabness. And in the high country away from the valley towns, entire mountain peaks are being sheared off and pushed into the hollows, creating vast stretches of barren land where the only signs of life are a few scattered cattle grazing on incongruous patches of winter grass.

No observant person could look closely at the impact of the coal boom in Martin County without wondering what the future consequences of it will be. The possibilities range from hopeful and encouraging to catastrophic, and it is easy to imagine that both the best and worst of times are coming—first the one, then the other. Many people in the county seem to be thinking in those terms now.

In Inez, much skepticism surrounds the notion that expanding corporate enterprises will be willing or able to pursue the social and economic goals that were the aim of the War on Poverty. Even banker Robert Duncan stops short of saying that the private sector can or should assume those responsibilities.

"We can't make it on our own," he says. "A strong economy will have its trickle-down effects, but government will still have a major role to play." As one example, he cites the federal government's "safety net" social programs, which "will remain essential." And, he declares, Martin County should get a much larger share of Kentucky's coal severance tax, which heretofore has been funneled into the state's general fund with only a tiny fraction returning to the coal-producing counties.

Duncan's ambition is to see all of the parties interested in Martin County's future work together on a long-range plan to assure its survival and improvement. The corporations, he says, should lead the way: "They've had a grace period to recover their capital investments, but that may be over now, and it's time for some decisions. Most of Martin County's mineral wealth is owned by big companies headquartered elsewhere—there is even one large tract that belongs to Harvard University. The profits that are made don't come back here to support education or the arts or programs of that kind, though some parties do put back more than others. It's not hard to tell that the railroad's land company or the subsidiaries of MAPCO or St. Joe Minerals are a lot more involved in the life of this community than, say, Island Creek Coal Company, which belongs to Occidental Petroleum. Island Creek doesn't do much but pay their workers and take the coal.

"If we could get the top executives to come in here and see the whole picture, I think they'd realize what's being taken and what's being put back, and they'd be more charitable. We need to get them all in here—corporate executives, federal and state government officials, local leaders, maybe even the president of Harvard. Working together, we can assure a bright future for Martin County, and I have faith that it will happen. If it doesn't, this place could become a wasteland."

Attorney William McCoy has been practicing law in Inez for forty years. There were seven members of the local bar when he came, but by the 1960s, he was the only one left. He knows from personal recollection the painful dislocations of boom and bust.

"From an economic standpoint, what's happening now is all for the good," he says. "The nation is going to have to use coal in place of oil, so what we have here is very valuable. We can't afford to leave it down there under the ground. I agree that the mountains are pretty, but it wouldn't make sense to leave them untouched if people all over were freezing and everybody here was out of work. Our young people stay here now after they finish school, and many who left years ago are coming back. Everybody who wants to work is making good money. For the young generation coming along, things are better here than they ever were."

But McCoy, remembering the past, worries about the future: "The boom will play out, and if we don't prepare for it, in forty years or less we'll be hurt. We could have ghost towns again. As a son of these hills, that's of more than passing concern to me. I'd like to see at least a portion of this culture survive. I'd hate to see the whole county mined out and people have to leave, with nothing to turn back to."

Martin Countians disagree vigorously on a number of subjects—politics, religion, and the unionization of miners, to name a few—but on the coal boom and its future consequences, they seem almost of one mind. It is hard to find anyone who opposes extraction of the coal by whatever means necessary, within the bounds of safety—and yet, almost as unanimously, they express a fatalistic belief that when the coal is gone, Martin County will be unrecognizable, perhaps even uninhabitable.

Eighty-six-year-old Rufus M. Reed, a local historian, has written admiringly of the rugged old-timers—"conquerers of the dark hills," he calls them—who opened up Martin County for people like him. Now, witnessing the violent conversion of forested slopes into barren high plains, he wonders whether the short-term wealth derived will eventually give way to long-term conditions far worse than those faced by the pioneers. "When the coal is all gone," says Reed, "when the topsoil has washed away and the streams are clogged with silt, what will the people do then? Where will they live? The companies claim there will be plenty of flat land for farms and houses and industries up there on the mountaintops where they're strip-mining now. It sounds good, and I hope it's true—but I really can't see it, myself. When they get done conquering the dark hills this time, I'm afraid there won't be anything left."

Monroe Cassady, a self-described "old man" at forty, left school after the ninth grade and left his Martin County home for Michigan at the age of twenty-one when he couldn't find enough work to support his young family. Nine years later, he gave up a good job as a steelworker to come back to the mines. Now he earns more than thirty-five thousand dollars a year, and he plans to stay as long as he and the coal last. "Things are a lot better here than they used to be," he says. "It won't be as pretty when the coal is gone, and Martin County will be poor again—but there wasn't nothing here before they started mining, and there won't be nothing left after they leave."

Ronnie Maynard, another miner in unaccustomed prosperity, still broods about the long-term cost. "When the boom is over," he says flatly, "Martin County will be finished. That's all there is to it. People just want to get their barrel full and get out. There'll be some level land up there, all right, and it might be good for factories, for farming—but I don't see nobody planning for it. In forty years, my son won't have nothing to do around here. We'll all be left high and dry."

Former county judge Ray Fields sees the problems too. But the coal is there to be taken, he concludes, "and I say dig it. It's a good deal. Everybody's working. I look for it to last twenty or thirty years. Stripping will cause some damage, some flooding, but I'm in favor of mining the coal. What other choice do we have?"

These random voices speak from a community in transition, a place suspended between an unsatisfying past and an uncertain future.

The United Mine Workers of America have never had a strong base in Martin County, and intermittent attempts to organize the mines since the coal boom began have all ended in failure. Only about 20 percent of the miners in the county belong to the UMW (all of them at Island Creek Coal Company). Disputes over the pros and cons of unionization have been particularly intense when organizing campaigns were in progress and when the national union was on strike; during those times, forces in and out of the union have traded accusations of intimidation and violence. What seems to keep the trouble from boiling over each time is the basic consensus within the county that the mines must stay open. "I don't know anybody who doesn't want this coal to be dug," explains one miner. "We've got our differences—but all of us, in and out of the union, want to keep on working."

Lorraine Slone is the wife of a disabled UMW miner, and she is a harsh critic of "big shots," wherever she finds them—in the county power structure, in the coal companies, even in the union. Her husband was injured in a strip mine accident, and she says the union "gave us the run-around" about his disability benefits. Mrs. Slone is not an opponent of the union or of strip mining; she knows that Martin County's coal is going to be mined, and she approves of its taking and wishes all of its mines were unionized and in full production. But she senses a pervasive mood of exploitation without regard for the consequences.

"What I object to," she says, "is greed and corruption. There's an unelected power bloc here—in business, in coal, in banking, in the schools, even in the churches. They have built a majority force by controlling the jobs and the money and the land. Republicans, Democrats, it makes no difference. It's the same old people getting the money, over and over—and if you can't be bought, sold, or traded, you don't get nothing. They'll do whatever is necessary to get the coal out of here. And when they're through, you know what'll be left? Nothing but a flat rock a crow wouldn't light on. They don't expect anybody to live in this county. It'll be a no-man's land, an energy reservation. They're gonna rip it from one end to the other, because in this nation's eyes, the coalfields are worth more than the people who live in them."

At the headquarters of the Pocahontas Land Company in Bluefield, West Virginia, general manager Bob Raines strongly disagrees with that notion. "This is a very conservation-minded company," he says. "We require good reclamation of the companies we lease our lands to, and we're getting it. We have no plans to abandon the land once the coal is gone. Of the forty-eight thousand surface acres we own in Martin County, our objective is to develop 10 to 15 percent—about five thousand acres—over the next fifteen years or so. We're very encouraged by the mountaintop removal method of strip mining. You'll see all kinds of developments up there—orchards, farms, livestock ranges. We want to leave a legacy of towns, manufacturing plants, jobs. Anything on such a big scale is a risk and a gamble, but we've been looking ahead right from the start, and I think we'll end up with something to be proud of."

Raines estimates that the entire process of mining, reclamation, and development in Martin County may take as long as eighty years. "And when we're finished," he says, "it'll be better property, even more valuable than it is now."

For all its vast holdings in the county, Pocahontas has kept a discreet distance from local politics and has generally maintained a low profile around Inez; its office there is in a modest upstairs apartment at the rear of a house on Main Street. No one has suggested—not publicly, at least—that Martin is a "company county," a kept community like the company towns that so many mine and mill owners used to maintain. As long as the only interest of the land company is in extracting coal from mainly empty and unused land—and generating a heavy flow of dollars in the process—charges of paternalism and undue control aren't likely to be heard. Later, when ownership of the land necessitates community development, land-use planning, and cooperative investment rather than extraction, Pocahontas may then find political involvement unavoidable. "We want to look at the overall picture," Raines says. "We want to have a plan, a goal. But we're not that far along yet."

As the parent company of Pocahontas, the Norfolk & Western Railway could be said to have a controlling interest in Martin County. Headquartered in Roanoke, Virginia, the N&W is in a position to determine, quite literally, the future of the county—its life or death. John Fishwick, the company's president, has never been to Martin County, but he speaks with pride of N&W's operations there.

"I look at this [the coal boom] as one of the greatest things that could happen to such a place," he says. "We've turned a wilderness into a habitable place. The coal companies have control now, because we have in effect sold the asset to them, and it's up to them to maximize the coal yield and observe the laws with respect to land restoration. When they turn the land back to us, it'll be more attractive than before. We may try to develop it ourselves or sell it for a profit. It wouldn't be realistic for me to project what the N&W will do when that time comes, because that's a long time off, and I won't be president of the company then. I will say, though, that the future of Martin County is not up to us—it's up to the people who live there. We care about social responsibility, but we won't be taking over the functions of local communities or government or anyone else."

No one seems quite ready to get specific about ways and means and timetables, and no overall vision of Martin County's future has yet come into focus. Only fragments are visible, pieces of the whole. Homer Marcum, a young newspaper publisher in Inez, sees those pieces, the good and the bad—and like so many others, he is ambivalent. "I'd like to think this boom is our golden opportunity to have a better life," he says. "I still hope. But I have to say I honestly doubt it."

In 1977, after the worst flood on record swept through the Tug River valley, an alliance of people and organizations concerned with Appalachian social and economic issues was formed. Concentrating on a wide range of problems, from flooding and strip mining to taxation, housing, and highways, the coalition reached the conclusion that the region's most serious difficulties are either caused by or made worse by absentee property owners who pay a pittance in taxes and put back almost nothing of value for the wealth they haul away.

The Appalachian Land Ownership Task Force was then formed, and with support from the Appalachian Regional Commission the group spent two years poring over deed books and tax rolls in eighty Appalachian counties in six states. Their voluminous study, the most comprehensive land canvass ever attempted in the region, was published in 1981. Among its documented findings was the fact that the Norfolk & Western Railway controls about forty-eight thousand surface acres and eighty-one thousand acres of mineral rights in Martin County—yet its 1978 property tax payment there was "hardly enough to buy a bus for the county school system."

Harvard University was identified in the study as the second largest mineral-rights owner in Martin County, with 9,720 acres of oil and gas rights. Records in the Harvard treasurer's office indicate that the university has held an interest in the property since 1962, when it was received as a gift from descendants of Louis Agassiz, a famed Swiss-born Harvard scientist of the nineteenth century, and his wife, Elizabeth Cabot Cary Agassiz, first president of Radcliffe College. Indus-

91

trialist Alexander Agassiz, a son of Louis and his first wife, was a partner in a large land acquisition in Martin County near the turn of the century. That partnership, known as the Rockcastle Trust, eventually sold its holdings to the N&W—except for the oil and gas rights, which ended up in Harvard's portfolio. The university never has sought to convert the rights to liquid assets, but it does receive an annual income of several thousand dollars from one leased well. It does not, however, pay any tax to Martin County.

The N&W acquired most of its Martin County holdings in the 1940s and 1950s, paying slightly over $2.6 million for 98,600 acres of surface and mineral rights. The company's combined cumulative state and local property taxes since that first purchase amount to less than $400,000. Thus, for an investment of about three million dollars in property (including taxes) and twenty-two million dollars in its railroad spur to the coalfields, the N&W controls an asset that in 1980 alone returned at least fifteen million dollars in tonnage royalties and more than that in freight charges. In other words, the railroad's gross *annual* return is greater than its total investment—and the return will keep coming for at least another half-century.

The N&W's Martin County properties are valued for tax purposes at seventeen million dollars, but the true worth, whether they should be sold now or exploited over the next several decades, can be conservatively estimated at about half a billion dollars. Although recent property transactions in the county's coalfields have shown land to be selling for an average of two thousand dollars an acre, a 1980 move by the local tax assessor to raise the appraisal on the N&W's holdings from fifty to two hundred dollars an acre has been tied up in court by the company's lawyers. The reappraisal would increase the company's state and local property tax bill from its 1979 total of $25,455 to about $67,000—but under the terms of its lease agreements with the coal companies, the tax is routinely passed on to them, so in any case, the N&W pays nothing.

Meanwhile, the Martin County school system, one of the poorest in Kentucky, manages to raise only 7.5 percent of its four-million-dollar annual budget from local taxes. The rest comes from the state and federal governments, both of which are now reducing their appropriations to local schools. And even if higher taxes can be extracted from corporations in the county, a state law limiting growth in local government would lead to a redistribution of the tax burden rather than a budget increase.

Betty Muncy, the tax assessor, says the N&W is "putting practically nothing into this county for the tremendous amount it's taking out. Our resources are being depleted daily, and there is no way we can wait without roads or sewers or adequate schools for industry to come in—they'll never come, unless the ones that are here now pay their fair share of the cost of local government."

Joey Childers, a native of eastern Kentucky, was a law student at the University of Kentucky when he coauthored the Martin County case study in the Appalachian Land Ownership Task Force report. "The extreme contrast of wealth and poverty there," he wrote, "is a classic example of what generally happens when control of an entire community's livelihood is concentrated in the hands of a few."

The coexistence of poverty and wealth is no longer a new phenomenon in Appalachia; it is a common sight. The wealth is evident in profits and wages, in bank deposits, in new homes and automobiles, in the rising number of lawyers and doctors. The poverty is even more pervasive—and more permanent.

When the War on Poverty was declared, between a third and half of Martin County's nine thousand–plus citizens were dependent upon public assistance for their livelihood. The percentage has since declined as the population has increased, but the absolute number of poor people has remained about the same. Betty Endicott, an administrator of public assistance programs, says people in the county are "lots better off overall than they used to be, but the same core group of poor people is still here."

The entire range of programs and services in health, education, and welfare is now being scaled back by governments at every level, and there is no indication that either major corporations or private charities will take up the slack. "At the very best," says Dan Branham, the Martin County school superintendent, "we're facing rising enrollment with a stand-pat budget." Similar reports are being heard across the board: caseload reductions of 15 to 20 percent in food stamps, Medicaid, and Aid to Families with Dependent Children; cuts in job-training programs, highway funds, and legal services; lesser roles for such helping agencies as the Appalachian Regional Commission.

Wages and employment remain high, but much of the "new money" in circulation is being absorbed by inflation, by higher prices and higher interest rates. Gasoline at the pump costs eight cents a gallon more in Inez than in Paintsville, twenty-five miles away—and fifteen cents a gallon more than in Lexington, the nearest large city. Comparable inequities can be found in the supermarkets and drug-stores. Housing—even trailers—is scarce and overpriced, and the same is true of consumer goods such as appliances and television sets.

It has been the poverty of places like Martin County, not the wealth, that has fixed itself in the public mind. Extractive industries have owned the wealth and systematically carted it away for so long that it almost seems by some natural law to belong elsewhere. Only the poverty belongs in the mountains—the mud and dust, the mal-nutrition, the bad food and worse housing, the hardscrabble poverty. The people of Appalachia are commonly thought of as a dependent community, as wards of government, even as parasites.

Such is the common public perception. In light of it, one more statistic from Martin County deserves mention. In 1980 government agencies at the local, state, and federal levels spent close to twenty million dollars in the county; in the same year, all individuals and corporations there paid into the government coffers a sum of taxes and fees totaling approximately forty million dollars.

"Private enterprise is not the only extractive industry at work here," says Homer Marcum, publisher of the weekly *Martin Countian*. "Contrary to the general belief, government also takes out more than it puts back."

For good and ill, coal is the one hope of Martin County; whether or not it assures a bright future, the opinion is widely held locally that there is no future—not even much of a present—without it. Not even the harshest critics of the coal companies are advocates of a cessation of mining.

Peak production of about fifteen million tons a year, two-thirds of it from surface mines, has almost been reached, and estimates of how long uninterrupted mining will continue at that pace fall within a range of twenty to sixty years. Periodic strikes by the United Mine Workers union seem not to have much effect on production. For the foreseeable future there will be plenty of steady, high-paying jobs, so many that hundreds of workers will continue to commute daily from distances of fifty miles or more, and Martin County will not be able to catch up with the demand for housing—or even for empty lots on level ground.

Level land has always been hard to come by in Appalachia—but now, ironically, Martin County is gaining thousands of acres of it on the flattened mountaintops where strip mining is taking place. Can this land be made accessible, stable, fertile? Will the watersheds survive? Can mud and dust, flooding and erosion be controlled? Can new communities take root on the high plains? Can old communities withstand the traumas of transition? The questions are continually asked but never answered; there are opinions, but there are no assurances. The only functional response may be something akin to the mixture of resignation and determined hope expressed by Niles Cumbo, manager of the local water system: "It's too late to yip and yell—it's already started, and we can't turn back. I hate to see the mountains torn up, but the land can be reclaimed. There are ways. It'll take a lot of effort, but it can be done."

The reclaimers—the coal companies—are officially and formally committed to the task. "Times have changed," says Ray Bradbury, president of Martin County Coal, a subsidiary of the A. T. Massey Company, which in turn is owned by St. Joe Minerals Corporation of New York. "The coal industry has been made aware of the social and environmental consequences of large-scale mining, and I believe the companies will meet their responsibilities." Bradbury, an eastern Kentuckian and a one-time union miner himself, says his company is "deeply involved in reclamation and in a variety of experimental land-use projects. We'll do our part to turn usable land back to Pocahontas—and I'm confident they'll bend every effort to develop it."

MAPCO, Incorporated, of Tulsa, Oklahoma, has the largest mining operation in Martin County, with five thousand acres of its own land and thirty-two thousand more leased from Pocahontas. The company's Martiki operation is one of the largest surface mines in the nation. Mike Vallez is MAPCO's vice president in charge of eastern Kentucky operations. "I'm a little sensitive to the charge that absentee ownership is a detriment to development," he says. "Who in Martin County could have invested $100 million in one mine? Who could stabilize and restore so much land to better condition than it was in before? We're going to be here for thirty years. Sometime next year, we'll be ready to sell some restored land—or develop it ourselves— and later we'll be releasing land back to Pocahontas. Long before we pack up and leave, people will be able to judge us by how good a job we've done. We want to do a good job, and we will—that's what our lessor and the law require."

Another of the major mining firms in Martin County is Island Creek Coal Company, a subsidiary of Occidental Petroleum. The chairman of Island Creek is former U.S. senator Albert Gore, Sr., who during thirty-two years as a member of Congress from Tennessee was an unabashed liberal, a champion of "the little man," and a frequent critic of corporate interests. Among other things, Gore fought for passage of a federal law to regulate strip mining, but he was long since gone from the Senate when the law was finally enacted in 1977. Island Creek is now extensively engaged in strip mining in Martin County and elsewhere, and Gore, who says he is "the same bright-eyed optimist and progressive" he was during his years of public service, is not apologetic about it.

"Doomsday is not approaching in Martin County," he declares. "I can't predict what it will be like there in twenty years, but I certainly can't see doom. I'm confident that corporations and government, working together, can bring material progress to places like Martin County. Reaganomics won't last long—corporations won't take over the government's role, and government won't desert the people. The pendulum will swing back. There's a rhythm in politics and economics, the same as there is in nature. Getting government off the backs of the corporations could make matters worse. Island Creek is doing a good job, maybe the best job in Martin County. We're not without imperfections, but we take the law seriously, and we follow it to the letter."

Even so, public records in the Office of Surface Mining in Washington indicate that during 1979 alone, inspectors from the agency issued twelve citations to Island Creek, charging twenty-five violations of various provisions of the strip mine act in the Martin County area.

Attorneys for the company contested each of the alleged violations, and after extensive appeals, proposed penalties totaling $14,300 were reduced to $1,100.

At Morehead State University in eastern Kentucky, former state economic development director Bob Cornett is now working with the coal companies in Martin County to plan for the future. Cornett heads the Appalachian Development Center at Morehead. He believes Martin County will have a strong coal economy for another forty years—but far less time than that to convince its people that life around the mines is getting better, not worse.

"It's a psychological thing," he says. "If people believe there won't be anything left after the coal is gone, it'll be impossible to build a strong community. We've got about ten years to convince them there's a good future there—otherwise, there'll be a mass exodus. The way I see it, the future *is* bright. There will eventually be about twenty-five thousand acres of rolling land up on top of the strip mines— more than enough for a thriving economy. The engineers and the environmentalists assure me it can be done. The biggest problem will be water, and that can be solved. The first phase of this undertaking will start within a year. The corporations are prepared to do a lot, but they can't do it all alone. Other developers and the local people and government at every level will also have to be involved. We've got to work together to make a livable future. If we don't, we may not have much of a future in places like Martin County."

Officials in the federal Office of Surface Mining say the big four mining companies have done a reasonably good job of reclamation in Martin County. The largest strip mine operations, they say, generally have better equipment and management than smaller ones and are also easier for inspectors to monitor, so the big-firm dominance is a point in Martin County's favor.

In the 1982 federal budget, funds for the Office of Surface Mining have been slashed; in eastern Kentucky alone, the agency's staff of inspectors will be reduced from thirty-eight to no more than ten. OSM, like the Appalachian Regional Commission, is on the Reagan administration's "hit list," and Secretary of the Interior James Watt has made no secret of his desire to take the federal government completely out of the mine-inspection business—a move that many in

97

eastern Kentucky, including Morehead's Bob Cornett, say would lead to serious environmental problems.

Staff members at OSM are reluctant to speculate on the long-term consequences of large-scale strip mining in the mountains, with or without close inspection. But from a variety of sources in the federal and state governments, in environmental groups, in mountain communities, and even in the coal industry itself, there emerges a point of view that contrasts sharply with the one expressed by advocates of massive stripping. It is a less-hopeful view, and it can be summarized as follows:

The leveled tops of restored strip mines may offer a limited prospect for some forms of agriculture—tree farms, livestock grazing, grain crops—but the forecast for industries, communities, and other full-scale developments is not favorable. The settling of tons of relocated earth will take years, and until that happens, problems with building foundations, roads, bridges, dams, sewers, and utilities will be severe. Even in agriculture, the poor quality of the soil will require expensive and continual supplementation. Most serious of all will be water problems—the availability of it, the quality, the control. There is no question that strip mining contributes significantly to stream siltation, erosion, flooding; serious damage is also being done to aquifers, groundwater, and entire watersheds. If everything the law requires is done, there may be a few scattered sites where enterprises of some dimension can thrive—but overall, the engineering and environmental problems and the cost will be too great to make development feasible.

Mountain lawyer Harry M. Caudill, author of *Night Comes to the Cumberlands* and now a history professor at the University of Kentucky, has often been critical of corporations and government agencies alike for exploiting the human and natural resources of his native Appalachia. This time, he says, their efforts could turn the region into an uninhabitable land of desolation:

"Mountaintop removal and other massive strip mining operations are a threat to life in places like Martin County. If we had a rain now like the one that caused the 1927 flood, it would devastate the entire region. Those bare flat tops would simply slide away and bury the people in the valleys. It would be like the biblical flood. The Reagan administration isn't going to watch the coal companies, and neither is the state. And even if the rains don't come and the land somehow survives, what good will it be after the coal is gone? With the greatest expense and effort, they can show a little greenery here and there, but the idea of extensive development is just a pipe dream. Historically, neither the corporations nor the government has had much to be proud of in Appalachia. They've treated the region like a colony. When they finish taking what they want from it, they'll just let it go to hell."

Vernal and Gladys Maynard live close to the Tug River in a house built in the1920s as part of a mining company town. Maynard was once a coal miner, and then a shipyard worker in Norfolk. He and his wife, both natives of Martin County, returned there to live in the early 1960s after he became disabled.

"I remember the hard times here," Maynard says, "and they were plenty hard. There was no work to be had. It's all better now. There's still lots of problems, but anytime you've got people working instead of drawing government checks, you have to say things are better."

The coal boom, says Gladys Maynard, has opened up the political process in Martin County as never before: "For thirty or forty years, the board of education controlled most of the jobs, the bank controlled the money, and together they controlled the politicians. A handful of them owned the toll bridge and the coal mines. To learn where the power was, all you had to know was who's in coal, who's in toll, and who's in school. If you got after one, you were against them all, because it was just one big flock. Now, I think those days are gone. All the incumbents were turned out in the last election. The old system has been exposed, opened up. I don't know if the new ones will be any better, but at least they'll be different—and it never would have happened if people weren't earning enough to be independent and if lots of folks hadn't come back here from the North to work."

Gladys Maynard and her friend Lorraine Slone, two middle-aged women long accustomed to fighting for the rights of "little people" against the public and private powers that be, have now organized a

99

local pressure group, Concerned Citizens of Martin County, to keep an eye on "bureaucrats, strip miners, bankers, and the courthouse gang."

"We're bad to say what we think," says Mrs. Maynard. "The sheriff told somebody he dreaded us more than five hundred armed men. They haven't attacked us, though. They're afraid to strike at people who've got facts."

The women also have strong opinions, such as this: "In every federal program there's been in this county, administrators have got all the gravy and poor people have got the scraps. If the government comes in here and makes cuts in these public assistance programs, they'll come off the bottom, not out of the air-conditioned offices of the administrators—and if that happens, it'll be a declaration of war. They might as well drop an atom bomb in here. It's not the programs that's failed—it's the leaders."

The enthusiasm of the Maynards for Martin County's new political prospects is tempered by their concern about the consequences of strip mining. "We had twenty-three inches of water in this house in 1977," Vernal Maynard says, "and four or five inches of it was mud and coal settlings. The river kept cresting, coming in gushes. I've lived around here most of my life, and I never saw it behave that way. Strip mining has to be a major cause. All the stripping and clear-cutting of timber has left the hillsides bare, and with nothing up there to hold the water, it just comes right on down."

Maynard is not opposed to the mining of Martin County's coal, not even necessarily opposed to the strip mining of it. As a one-time union miner himself, he says he would like to see a strengthened UMW and reformed coal companies working together for the prosperity of all. But he doesn't expect that to happen. He has, he says, seen enough political corruption, enough greed, enough coal dust and mud, enough broken roads and broken men—and through it all, enough undiminished and unyielding poverty—to fear for the future of Martin County and most of Appalachia:

"This region was once the survival kit of the country. Everything you needed was here—fruit, nuts, berries, herbs, water, timber, oil, gas, coal. It was like that a long time ago—and not so long ago too, in my lifetime. The people were self-sufficient—they raised their own corn, dug their own coal. You can't even buy coal here now—it's all shipped out. I grew up on a one-hundred-acre farm up there where they're stripping, and I've drunk out of streams you couldn't even bathe in now. By hook or by crook, the big-money boys got it all—the mountains, the streams, everything. They took the timber, the gas and oil, and they're going to get the coal. There wouldn't be any way to prevent it, even if anybody wanted to. It's going to look like the moon up there."

Too much is at stake to stop the coal boom: the nation's energy needs, the investments of the railroad and the coal companies, the livelihood of thousands of miners, the continued recovery of Martin County itself. The mines will reach full production, the trains and trucks will keep rolling, coal tonnage and per capita income will set new records—and numerous other statistics will continue to rise with them: auto sales, property values, crime, divorce, mental health cases.

Of the forty-eight students in the 1957 graduating class at Inez High School, all but three had left the county within a year; now half of them are back, working mainly in the coal industry. More students stay in school to graduate now, but fewer of them go on to college, choosing instead to become coal miners. The school system and the bank are having trouble keeping male employees, because the pay is three or four times greater in the mines. A few women have joined the ranks of the miners, and the average age of mine workers is now down to about thirty.

Martin County remains isolated. The nearest hospital is twenty miles away, the nearest television station, sixty (across the line in West Virginia), the nearest interstate highway and commercial airport, also sixty. There is no public library, no sewer system, no garbage collection, no four-lane highway, no stoplights, no movie theater, no recreation center. Only about 700 of the county's 4,400 housing units are classified as "sound," and only about 20 percent of them have septic tanks; the rest have outhouses or dump raw sewage directly into the streams. What there is in abundance in Martin County is what there has always been: poverty, politics, undying hope, and coal.

"The poor we shall always have with us," says one Bible-quoting citizen. "They've been exploited, used, but never really helped. As far as I can tell, nothing ever touched them."

The politics may be changing, but skeptics prefer to wait and see. Charges of vote-buying, influence-peddling, and misuse of public money are often heard, no matter who is in office.

The undying hope takes many forms, but two expressions of it are heard repeatedly. The first is that money—from government, from industry—will eventually be used to improve the lives of all the people. The second is that when the minerals are all gone, it will still be possible for life to continue.

And finally, first and last, there is the coal:

In the gray gloom of winter, the earth looks wounded, violated. Great, gaping slashes across the faces of mountains expose their bones of stone. Trees are strewn about like broken matchsticks, boulders like discarded building blocks. Strip mine excavations have opened winding caverns of rock and coal in exposed seams, and the barren cliffs stretch endlessly in all directions, too vast to be encompassed in the eye or the mind. The transformed terrain looks more like the wastelands of the West than the mountains of Kentucky.

From the air, there is a different perspective. The hollows are filling up with discarded overburden from the mountaintops, and the decapitated peaks are becoming high plains, tablelands, mountain mesas. Muddy silt ponds and pale green clumps of new grass—part of the reclamation effort—are spotted about like random patches on a quilt.

At one mining site, a monstrous drag line with a bucket scoop big enough to hold a four-room house lifts mouthfuls of matter like some prehistoric beast at pasture. Trains loaded with processed coal wind for miles through the hollows, crawling toward the main line across the Tug River, glistening in the hazy sunlight like giant black snakes. Whenever they pass within hearing distance, the trains and their mournful whistles echo a constant reminder: Martin County is oozing, bleeding, hemorrhaging coal.

The three-room house has been expanded to four. The front porch lists precariously on its concrete-block props. Black smoke from a coal fire curls lazily out of the chimney atop the tin roof.

The front door is standing open. On the wall opposite, a haloed Jesus looks down benignly upon a soap-opera drama being played out in color on the TV set in the corner. There is a beige telephone on one wall. Across the room, a small, frail woman is asleep on the sofa, a blanket clutched closely at her chin. The knock at the door doesn't awaken her, but presently a man comes slowly from the back of the house to the front.

He is about fifty-five but looks much older. His thin, wrinkled face frames deep-set, distracted eyes. His jaw sprouts a stubble of gray whiskers.

All of his eight children are gone, most of them to cities in Ohio. None of them got past the eighth grade in school. The man's wife has been sick, and he himself has been ill and unable to work for several years.

When the War on Poverty began, he was its symbol of destitution and hope; when it ended, he remained a victim, a casualty. The coal boom likewise has failed to touch him. It eventually will, though, for he, like all the other people of Martin County, is living on top of a coal seam. He owns the little plot of ground on which his shack sits, but Pocahontas and the N&W own the coal beneath, and one day they will come for it.

The old man does not want to talk about Lyndon Johnson, or the War on Poverty, or coal mining, or the future. He doesn't really want to talk at all, but he is polite and patient, waiting for his caller's next question.

But there is no next question. All the questions have been asked and answered too many times. There is nothing left to say. In the awkward silence, the stranger finally mumbles thanks, and goodbye.

And the door closes between him and Tom Fletcher.

More than a decade after the Martin County coal boom and the Reagan administration arrived simultaneously to great fanfare in eastern Kentucky, the corporate giants of coal mining and coal hauling were still operating at peak production—about fifteen million tons a year—in the mountains around Inez. But the price of the mineral, having soared to sixty-five dollars a ton in the early 1970s and leveled off at about thirty-two dollars a ton in the early 1980s, had fallen to only half that much by 1990. Worse yet, advancing technology makes it possible for the companies to maintain the level of extraction with only half the work force, and with no substantial union presence to give the miners job security, Martin County is back in its accustomed position of low ranking on Kentucky's economic ladder.

The contrast between the haves and have-nots is greater than ever: high production, a reduced work force, and continued low taxes still result in huge profits for the Norfolk & Western (now Norfolk Southern) Railway and the three or four major energy conglomerates with operations in the county; massive unemployment, a dysfunctional infrastructure, overwhelmed public services, and pervasive poverty still translate into devastating social losses for the county and a majority of its citizens. (The population, having risen by more than 50 percent in the 1970s, fell by more than 10 percent in the 1980s.) As surely as the federal government failed in its War on Poverty to rescue the besieged citizens of Martin County with a welter of uplifting social programs, so did Reaganomics fail to save them with trickle-down doses of spendable earned income after the profits were distributed.

In the higher altitudes where strip mining and mountaintop removal have turned precipitous slopes into flat plains, there is some experimental farming and even an airport for corporate jets, but the grand plans for subdivisions and shopping centers have not come to fruition. The vast majority of Martin County's people still live in the narrow hollows. Gladys Maynard and Lorraine Slone and their Concerned Citizens of Martin County have inspired the creation of a statewide network of grassroots organizations called Kentuckians for the Commonwealth. Tom Fletcher, now nearing sixty-five years of age, still lives in the same battered shack. In the perpetual cycle of boom and bust, bust and boom, Martin County struggles to endure.

A GENTLEMEN'S FIGHT IN PRINCE EDWARD COUNTY, VIRGINIA

The cases that the U.S. Supreme Court consolidated in its historic Brown v. *Board of Education decision outlawing racial segregation in the public schools originated in five widely scattered communities, one of which was Prince Edward County, Virginia. A quarter of a century after* Brown, *it was still hard to tell who won in Prince Edward County. This report from Farmville, the county seat, was researched in 1978 and published in the August–September 1979 issue of* American Heritage.

The Reverend L. Francis Griffin sat in a metal folding chair in the basement assembly hall of the First Baptist Church in Farmville, Virginia. His modified Afro hairstyle, bushy eyebrows, and Vandyke were flecked with gray. Behind horn-rimmed glasses, his brown eyes seemed to suggest a mixture of attentiveness and fatigue, of serenity and sadness.

He had been the pastor of First Baptist for nearly half of his sixty-one years. In the assembly hall where he sat, he had conducted countless hundreds of meetings: with members of his congregation, church committees, Sunday school children—and with striking high school students, civil rights groups, attorneys, the press. Two decades ago, the Reverend Mr. Griffin was the central figure in a long-running effort to achieve desegregation and racial equality for the black citizens of Farmville and Prince Edward County. Now, in the quiet repose of a weekday morning, he pondered a visitor's question for a moment before responding in a baritone voice rich with the accent and cadence of Southside Virginia:

"Who won? It depends on how you look at it. If you're talking about integration in a local sense, then it could be said that the whites won, because there's still a lot of segregation and inequality around here. But if you're looking at it on a national scale, I'd say we won a victory. I believe you could say the black people of Prince Edward County saved the public schools of the South, particularly in Virginia. Had we given in, I think perhaps massive resistance might have become the order of the day throughout the South. So in that sense, we won a tremendous victory."

In his office at the Farmville *Herald,* barely two blocks from Griffin's church on Main Street, publisher J. Barrye Wall, Sr., recalled Prince Edward County's crucible of the 1950s with considerable reluctance. Too much had been said and written about it, he asserted firmly: "Accounts in the national press were all so one-sided. It was a long time ago, and I don't have the time or the interest to look back. I don't want to go into it any further."

Barrye Wall is eighty years old, a short, portly man with white hair and friendly blue eyes. He is a Southern gentleman in the classic mold—formal, courtly, unfailingly polite. Being reminded of an earlier time of discord did not please him, and he searched his mind for proper words to dismiss the inquiry. "My position was right," he said finally. "I stand by everything I wrote about it. It's up to others to make judgments now. I'm through." And having said that, he added what amounted to a personal conclusion, a judgment of his own: "I have never treated a Negro with discourtesy—or been treated that way by one of them. I respect them all. But I was and am for separate education for white and black. We were defending states' rights, state sovereignty. The principles for which Lee and the South fought weren't settled at Appomattox—and still aren't. The South lost—we lost—but it's not settled."

❧

Twenty-eight years after the beginning of a school desegregation controversy in Prince Edward County that attracted national attention and resulted in one of the most significant U.S. Supreme Court decisions of all time, it is still unclear exactly who won what. L. Francis

Griffin and J. Barrye Wall were principal figures in that conflict—personal symbols of diametrically opposed philosophies. For all their differences (and they are many, and vast), the two men brought some common characteristics—pride, confidence, determination, stubbornness—to what has been aptly labeled "a gentlemen's fight." They inspired and influenced large followings—Griffin with the power of his voice, Wall with the power of his press. Now, in retrospect, they speak with ambivalence about the winners and losers, choosing instead such terms as *stalemate* and *cold war* and *peaceful coexistence*. And they are not alone.

Melancholy echoes of the Civil War linger in the recesses of private thought about the past quarter of a century of life in Prince Edward County. Farmville, the county seat, was on Robert E. Lee's route of retreat in 1865, and Appomattox is just twenty-five miles away to the west. Now as then, blacks ponder the meaning of a "victory" that has borne meager fruit, and whites reflect upon a "defeat" that has left attitudes unaltered, lessons unlearned, life largely unchanged. Not all of the residents make such pessimistic assessments, of course, and it would certainly be incorrect to say that nothing is different. Segregation laws have been overturned, and in some sectors of the political, educational, and economic systems, whites and blacks can be found working together as equals.

Nevertheless, few apparently would quarrel with this view expressed by one lifelong resident of the county: "There has been a surface change in race relations here, but no real transformation. The relative circumstances of most whites and most blacks are unaffected, and the basic feelings of whites toward blacks and blacks toward whites are essentially the same as before. If you want to talk of it in terms of winning and losing, I think you'd have to say that nobody won. In the long run, all of us have lost."

Of all the battlegrounds in the struggle for civil rights and racial equality in the South during the 1950s and 1960s, none seemed more unlikely—or in the end more inexplicable—than Prince Edward County. It was a conservative rural jurisdiction populated mainly by small-acreage farmers (slightly more of them white than black), and its Old South traditions of white paternalism and black deference seemed to have survived intact from the nineteenth century. Lacking a history of either radicalism or violence (those being considered forms of extreme behavior unbecoming well-mannered people such as they), the county's citizens seemed incapable of producing a wellspring of black demands for equality or a massive white counterforce of reaction and resistance.

But consider what actually happened in Prince Edward County, in startling contradiction of its past:

• In 1951, almost a decade before organized student protests became a weapon in the civil rights movement, a group of juniors and seniors in the county's black high school in Farmville led a walkout in protest against educational inequities. Virtually the entire student body joined in the strike, keeping the school closed for two weeks.

• Shortly thereafter, black students and adults in the county accepted the aid of the National Association for the Advancement of Colored People in a lawsuit challenging segregation in the public schools. Three years later, when the case reached the U.S. Supreme Court on appeal, it was incorporated with similar ones from Kansas and elsewhere and made the basis for the court's pathfinding *Brown v. Board of Education* decision declaring school segregation laws unconstitutional.

• In 1959, after the state of Virginia had tried and failed to counter the Supreme Court ruling with "massive resistance"—a strategy bordering on open defiance of the federal government—the white elected officials of Prince Edward County shut down their public schools and kept them closed for five years, rather than permit white and black children to attend classes together. A makeshift private school network was set up to accommodate white students and teachers; all blacks were locked out.

Now, twenty years after it closed its schools and fifteen years after it was compelled by a Supreme Court order to reopen them, Prince Edward County clings stubbornly to school segregation. Most of its white pupils attend the all-white private academy, which has become a permanent fixture in the community, and all of its black students are in the public schools with a minority (25 percent) of whites. Thus, even as desegregation has become more the rule than the exception in the schools of the South—and more widely established there than in the rest of the country—most Prince Edward whites have continued on their charted course of racial separation. Only in that—and in a general avoidance of violence—has the county behaved consistently with its past.

∽

By the time it was chartered in 1754 and named for a grandson of the reigning king of England, Prince Edward County had already formed the basic patterns of a way of life that would continue in recognizable form through colonialism, nationhood, civil war, reconstruction, and twentieth-century modernism. It had a tobacco-based agricultural economy, sharp social-class divisions among whites, black subservience, and a general lack of enthusiasm for the notion of formal education for the masses. Before and after the Civil War, it gave its upper-class whites classical education in home-based private schools but provided little for white children of lesser means and nothing at all for blacks until 1870, when some segregated primary schools were opened for both races. The first public high school for whites wasn't built until the turn of the century, and it was nearly forty years after that before black students could complete twelve years of schooling in the county.

The Robert R. Moton High School, named for a Prince Edward County native who had succeeded Booker T. Washington as president of Tuskegee Institute, was opened to 167 students in 1939. Built with forty thousand dollars in state and federal funds, the Farmville school was intended to accommodate 180 pupils, but within eight years it enrolled nearly 400, and three frame-and-tarpaper outbuildings heated by wood stoves were added to handle the overflow.

The principle of "separate but equal" facilities and opportunities for whites and blacks had been set down by the U.S. Supreme Court in 1896, but in the states of the South equality had never really been considered, much less achieved. Moton High School was in no way equal to the high school facilities provided for white students, and the tarpaper outbuildings only served to accentuate the inequity. From time to time there was talk of a new high school for blacks, and the Moton Parent-Teacher Association regularly petitioned the county school board for improvements, but by the beginning of 1951 the board had taken no action on the requests.

That's when a sixteen-year-old member of the Moton junior class,

Barbara Rose Johns, brought together a small group of her class-mates and planned the strike that set in motion thirteen years of con-flict and changed the pattern of white/black relations in Prince Ed-ward County.

On the morning of April 23, 1951, the 450-member student body was called to the auditorium, there to be met by Barbara Johns and her companions. The two dozen members of the faculty were asked to return to their classrooms, and reluctantly they did so; the school principal was away from the building, responding to an anonymous telephone message that two of his students were in trouble at the Farmville bus station.

Quickly, the case for a protest strike was put before the student body: their school was grossly inadequate and unequal, their educa-tion was being severely shortchanged as a result, and they should walk out together and stay out úntil county officials promised them a new school. Protest signs were stored and waiting (WE WANT A NEW SCHOOL OR NONE AT ALL and DOWN WITH THE TAR PAPER SHACKS). The mass of students rose cheering, took up the signs, and marched out. The strike was on.

The student leaders made two telephone calls that afternoon. One was to the Reverend L. Francis Griffin at his church in Farmville; the other was to the Richmond law office of Spottswood Robinson and Oliver Hill, attorneys for the NAACP. Two days later, in the assembly hall of First Baptist Church, the lawyers and Griffin met with a dele-gation of students, and the following night, an estimated one thou-sand students and parents crammed into the Moton High auditorium to hear and approve, with only a few dissenting voices, a plan for legal action—not simply to obtain equal educational facilities but to end segregation in the Prince Edward County schools.

White reaction to these developments was by stages disbelieving, confused, alarmed, and resentful. There were meetings with student leaders, letters to parents, promises of an all-out effort to secure funds for a new school, accusations that the principal of Moton and others (including Griffin) had masterminded the strike. A formal pe-tition was presented to the school board by the NAACP attorneys calling for desegregation of the educational system, and when it was rejected, the lawyers promptly took the case into federal court. The black students then returned to school to await the results.

It proved to be a long wait. M. Boyd Jones, the Moton principal, was fired at the end of the year by the school board. The family of Barbara Johns, concerned for her safety, sent her for her senior year to Montgomery, Alabama, where she lived with her uncle, the Reverend Vernon Johns, an expatriate Prince Edward Countian (and predecessor of Martin Luther King, Jr., in the pastorate of Montgomery's Dexter Avenue Baptist Church). Pressure to abandon the lawsuit was brought to bear upon many blacks in Prince Edward County, including some in Francis Griffin's church, causing him to put his job on the line by calling for a vote of confidence (and getting it, almost unanimously). Local and state officials, hoping to blunt the desegregation suit by making "separate but equal" a reality, came up with $800,000 and went quickly to work building a new Moton High School. The months became years. The NAACP lost its case and appealed. Finally, three years after Barbara Johns and her young allies had raised the issue of discrimination and inequality, the U.S. Supreme Court sought to settle it.

In *Brown* v. *Board of Education,* a consolidation of the Prince Edward case and four others dealing with the same issue, the court concluded "that in the field of public education the doctrine of 'separate but equal' has no place." Unanimously, the nine justices declared on May 17, 1954, that "separate educational facilities are inherently unequal."

But school desegregation—in Prince Edward County, the South, and the nation—was still a long way from reality.

During the fall of 1954 J. Barrye Wall of the Farmville *Herald* and a local businessman named Robert B. Crawford became principal figures in the creation of a legal–political action organization called Defenders of State Sovereignty and Individual Liberties. With strong backing from Virginia's senior U.S. senator, Harry F. Byrd, and other leading politicians, the group soon built up a membership of several thousand persons across the state. The Defenders also gained quick control of the political machinery of Prince Edward County, and in the spring of 1955 they persuaded the county board of supervisors and leaders of the white parent-teacher organization to make plans

111

for a shutdown of the public school system and the creation of a segregated private school network for white children.

In truth, little persuasion was necessary. White public sentiment had swung fiercely against the Supreme Court decision. The board of supervisors was prepared to fund public education on a month-by-month basis as long as it remained completely segregated—and to cut off all funds and padlock the doors as soon as any court ordered white and black children to attend the same school. As for the PTA, it led the way to formation of a foundation to operate private schools and raised funds to pay the salaries of all white teachers in the event the public schools were closed.

In Congress, Senator Byrd and Virginia congressman Howard W. Smith introduced the Southern Manifesto in 1956 and used that document of defiance against the Supreme Court's *Brown* decision to erect an almost-solid wall of resistance across the South. And in the state capitol at Richmond, the Byrd machine—with ideas and encouragement from Richmond *News Leader* editor James Jackson Kilpatrick—developed a plan of "massive resistance" against the authority of the federal government.

As court orders implementing the *Brown* decision were handed down across the state in 1958, Governor J. Lindsay Almond followed the massive resistance plan and ordered the closing of some schools in Charlottesville, Norfolk, and Front Royal, but the courts quickly struck down the state laws upon which the strategy of defiance was based. Against the angry objection of Byrd, Governor Almond capitulated rather than risk being jailed for contempt of court, and massive resistance died a quick death.

Meanwhile, Prince Edward County officials, still determined to close their schools rather than desegregate them, continued to wait for the dreaded implementation order they knew was inevitable. Complex legal maneuvers had kept their case tied up in the lower federal courts since the *Brown* ruling. Finally, in the late summer of 1959, all appeals on the particulars of implementation were exhausted, and desegregation was ordered to begin. The Prince Edward supervisors, true to their word, promptly cut off all funds to the school system and shut it down. Even as Virginia's strategy of recalcitrance was being shattered and token desegregation was beginning to take place in a few schools scattered across the state, little Prince Edward County prepared to go its chosen way alone, without regard for the consequences.

When September 1959 arrived, almost all of the fifteen hundred white pupils in the county were enrolled in Prince Edward Academy, the new entity that was holding classes in sixteen temporary locations. They had the same white teachers and administrators as before, the staff of about seventy having moved virtually en masse from the public payroll to the private one. For the seventeen hundred black students and approximately twenty-five teachers, there were no classes, no jobs, no schools.

For all practical purposes, the Prince Edward County government, the private academy, and the local Defenders of State Sovereignty and Individual Liberties were all dominated by the same people. Throughout the more than eight years of turmoil that enveloped the community, the whites never broke ranks. Not even moderate expressions of dissent or suggestions of compromise were tolerated. Two who voiced mild objections to the closing of the schools—a high school principal named James Bash and a Presbyterian minister named James R. Kennedy—were gone from the community within a year. Another, a history professor at Longwood College in Farmville named Gordon Moss, grew increasingly critical of white intransigence as the crisis dragged on, and while he remained in the community, his was an isolated and lonely voice.

Among blacks, public support of desegregation was also muted. Only the Reverend Mr. Griffin, whose livelihood was beyond the reach of the white establishment, was consistently outspoken. The NAACP, of which Griffin was both a local and a state leader, continued its efforts in the federal courts to win desegregation and equal educational opportunity for Prince Edward County blacks, but the legal proceedings were agonizingly slow. The beginning of the private school program for whites seemed a signal to one and all that a long stalemate was beginning, and as that realization sank in, the various parties became more determined and uncompromising than ever.

In the fall of 1959 a group of white segregationists offered to set up a private school program for blacks, ostensibly in response to the plight of idle students and teachers. Most blacks were suspicious of the idea, however, seeing it as a cynical ploy to legitimize segregation, and in the end only one application from a black child was received by the sponsors.

Since the state legislature had set up tuition grants for students attending private schools, the Prince Edward segregationists may have wanted a private school for blacks in order to demonstrate that the tuition grants were available to both races and thus nondiscriminatory. Furthermore, the whites badly needed school buildings for their academy, and there was some speculation that if both whites and blacks had private schools, the padlocked facilities of the public system might somehow be reopened to accommodate them. A dispute over that issue in 1960 led to the only serious split between whites in the community during the entire school crisis. In the opinion of Lester E. Andrews, Sr., chairman of the public school board, it was imperative that the public schools be reopened as quickly as possible. Two former chairmen and close friends of Andrews', B. Calvin Bass and Maurice Large, shared that view. But in the leadership of the private academy there appeared to be a consensus that public schools in the county had been abandoned for good. Neither group favored integration, of course—but the Andrews faction believed that it would be economically disastrous for the county to try to function permanently without a public school system, while the academy backers were willing, even eager, to go that route.

The split between the two factions became deep and serious. Andrews and four others on the six-member school board resigned rather than vote to sell Farmville High School to the academy. In the summer of 1960 Andrews, Bass, Large, and others held a series of private meetings, some with blacks in attendance, to talk about compromise moves that might break the deadlock between whites and blacks and settle the long legal dispute.

But social ostracism and pressure against the compromisers—derisively dubbed the Bush League—grew quickly in the white community. In short order, the effort was abandoned, and the only sign of serious dissent to arise during the school crisis faded and died as quickly as it had arisen. Four more years of closed public schools and dreary stalemate lay ahead for Prince Edward County.

Over the years, a number of national groups and organizations tried with varying degrees of success to assist the black children who were locked out of the Prince Edward schools. The NAACP, the National Conference of Negro Women, the American Friends Service Committee, Kittrell College in North Carolina, and numerous others offered assistance. Some students were sent away to schools in other communities and states; some got a little help in makeshift centers set up to operate part-time in the county; some were aided by summer school programs organized by groups of teachers and others from outside the community.

But most of the black children—by one estimate, at least eleven hundred—received virtually no schooling during most of the five-year shutdown. Carlton Terry, one of the fortunate few to be educated elsewhere under the sponsorship of the American Friends Service Committee, called the Prince Edward blacks of the 1959–1964 period "the crippled generation . . . [a] generation left lame."

With assistance from officials in the administration of President John F. Kennedy, private funds were raised to set up a "free school" for black students in the county in 1963. Colgate W. Darden, Jr., a former governor of Virginia and former president of the University of Virginia, was named chairman of the private body's board of trustees, and Neil V. Sullivan, a nationally prominent public school educator, was brought in as director. Prior to the opening of the program in four formerly all-black public school buildings, a hot summer of demonstrations and discord in Farmville had raised for the first time the threat of widespread violence in the county. Prince Edward was by then a beleaguered county, and a wounded one; its troubles had been told to the nation by television and the press, and in the growing struggle for civil rights that was then enveloping the South, it seemed near to becoming a battleground of major importance. One way or another, the stalemate there appeared certain to be broken.

But somehow in that barren soil, a few fragile seeds of hope took root. The summer demonstrations ended without disastrous results, the protesters who had come in from other places departed, and a measure of calm was restored. The free school program received some cooperation from state and local officials during its first term in 1963–1964, and the effort yielded some positive results. Prince Edward Academy was firmly entrenched in a new school plant it had built, but its enrollment slipped to about twelve hundred, and some people ventured the opinion that reopening the public schools would result in gradual desegregation and a further decline in the academy's hegemony. At the very least, the prospect of some interracial contact in education no longer was unthinkable to all whites in the county.

And at long last, in the summer of 1964, the U.S. Supreme Court concluded once and for all that, in the interest of equal protection of the laws guaranteed by the Constitution, Prince Edward County had to maintain a public school system and that the county's elected officials could be forced, if necessary, to appropriate funds to that end. At a cost beyond measure, the county and the state of Virginia had fought in the courts to prevent that conclusion for thirteen years; in the end, they submitted quietly, and the schools were finally reopened in September 1964.

The free schools went out of business after just one year of operation. Fewer than a dozen white students and approximately seventeen hundred blacks enrolled in the "new" Prince Edward County public schools. The number of blacks in school was about the same as in 1959, before the schools were closed—but they were not, of course, all the same children, and it would prove impossible to determine exactly how many had been deprived of schooling permanently (the total almost certainly ran into the hundreds). As for the white children, the commonly expressed belief that they had not been affected adversely by the school closings appeared not to be borne out by the facts: In the eight years prior to 1959, white enrollment in the county had grown by 18 percent; by 1964, the total (that is, the enrollment in Prince Edward Academy) had fallen about 20 percent below the 1959 number. No accounting for the loss has ever been made.

When it was all over, the people of Farmville and Prince Edward County could look about them and wonder what their "gentlemen's disagreement" had wrought. Desegregation had begun, but in a way and to an extent unsatisfactory to virtually everyone; segregation still reigned, but at a cost burdensome to all. No other political jurisdiction in the United States had taken the extreme measure of closing its entire public school system to avoid desegregation. It was a reactionary step taken with deliberation by mild-mannered whites against mild-mannered blacks, and it was ultimately fruitless and destructive.

A Norfolk newspaperman named Bob Smith wrote a meticulously detailed and balanced account of Prince Edward County's years of trouble in a 1965 book called *They Closed Their Schools*. From his perspective, soon after the schools reopened, he concluded that victory had eluded all sides. "Everybody lost something," he wrote, and "what was won is pitifully inadequate payment for what was lost." If they could agree on nothing else, the whites and blacks who lived in Prince Edward County in 1965 could almost certainly agree on that.

"People feared the worst," said James M. Anderson, the Prince Edward County superintendent of schools, recalling the long crisis, "but things were never as bad as they were thought to be. There's great potential here, and we're making real progress."

In 1978, fourteen years after the schools were reopened, Anderson counted nearly six hundred whites and a stable total of seventeen hundred blacks in the public school enrollment. "When I came here in 1972," he said, "I was told we would never reach 20 percent white. We're about 25 percent now."

Anderson is white himself, and a native of Prince Edward County; he was teaching in the school system of a neighboring county during the years of turmoil. "It was like living next door to a couple who were having a fight," he recalled. "You kept your distance—and even now, you don't bring up the old fight. That's fine with me. I happen not to be a person who likes to dwell in the past."

Even so, he is not ignorant of it. "The closing of the schools was a great trauma," he said, "and there were serious long-term consequences. Now, we're seeing steady improvement, especially in the lower grades."

The new Moton High School, erected after the strike in the early 1950s, is now called Prince Edward County High School. A modern vocational-technical school has been opened across the road from it. Slightly more than half of the school system's 125 faculty members and 3 of the 8 school board members are black. Consolidation has reduced the number of school buildings in use in the county to five. Teacher salaries average about ten thousand dollars a year. Half of the 120 or so annual high school graduates regularly go on to some type of postsecondary education. There has been growth, change, improvement; public schools are back to stay, and the future, in Anderson's view, is full of promise.

But memories linger, and divisions remain. "There is no adversarial relationship between our schools and Prince Edward Academy," the superintendent said. "We go our way, and they go theirs." Given that atmosphere of peaceful coexistence, of proximity without contact, he would not speculate about future increases in white enrollment in the public schools. "Our goal is to try to educate all the students who come to us," he said. "I think our enrollment will take care of itself."

The headmaster at Prince Edward Academy is Robert T. Redd. He has been an administrator and teacher at the school for all of its twenty years. His office is in a building adjoining the academy's sixty-classroom facility, built in 1961.

"The papers tried to crucify us," he said. "They called us a fly-by-night operation, said we wouldn't last a year. But we've proved them wrong. We've shown that we can deliver excellence in education under a controlled environment. Eighty percent of our graduates go on to college or some kind of post–high school education—and they're going to high-quality institutions like the University of Virginia and Virginia Tech, and doing well there."

Admission to the academy is not selective, Redd said, "except that we avoid known discipline problems." The school has enrolled nonwhite students, he added—"Koreans, Chinese, American Indians, Spanish"—but no blacks: "None have ever applied. We have no written policy on that. If they came, I suppose we would handle them the same as we do all the others."

According to Redd, Prince Edward Academy's enrollment was stabilized at about twelve hundred for a number of years, before tapering off over the past five years to the present level of about one thousand. Tuition has increased gradually but steadily, from a low of $240 in 1960 (the first year was free) to the present charge of $850 for high school students and $800 for students in the lower grades. Teacher salaries have also risen, from less than four thousand dollars a year in the beginning to an average of about eight thousand now.

"Our pay scale isn't as high as the public schools," the headmaster said, "but we don't have any trouble getting teachers. All of our class-room teachers are certified, one-third of them have master's de-grees—and this year, we had about a hundred applications for two vacancies. The best teachers want to come here because we don't have any discipline problems. We run a tight ship."

In spite of rising costs, Redd said the academy is not in danger of becoming too expensive for most Prince Edward County whites. "I doubt if we'll be forced to admit only the affluent," he said. "Tuition will continue to rise, but we're trying to stay within the capacity of people to pay. We provide partial scholarships for about 120 students now. We want to serve all, not just the wealthy few."

The academy operates a fleet of seventeen buses, some of which cross over into four neighboring counties to pick up students, and that service has been a help in maintaining a large enrollment. An-other help has been the school's extensive program of interscholastic athletics. It competes—and wins consistently—in a thirteen-member league of Virginia private academies and plays against a few schools outside the state as well. None of its opponents enroll black students. "We used to play some of the public schools," Redd recalled, "but as they became integrated, we stopped playing them. Birds of a feather flock together."

The relationship between Prince Edward Academy and the public schools of Prince Edward County is not unfriendly, both sides agree—not close, but not hostile either—and while it might be stretching a point to say they wish each other well, it is certainly safe to assume that they watch each other closely, and with keen interest.

And, no doubt, both of them also watch a third educational enter-prise in Farmville: the Campus School, a kindergarten-through-sev-enth-grade program operated since 1970 by Longwood College. The school has about two hundred students, including a small number of blacks.

Longwood, formerly a state teachers' college for women, is now a general liberal arts institution that includes a few hundred males and a hundred or so blacks in its student body of about twenty-five hun-dred. Some veteran members of its faculty recall that in the early 1960s the college raised the salaries of its employees whose children attended Prince Edward Academy. ("It was a fringe benefit," said one of them, "a cost-of-living increment to help offset the private school tuition.") The Campus School ostensibly was created as a laboratory school, a training center for future teachers, but education majors from the college are not assigned to do their practice teaching there.

One Longwood professor indicated that the school was started "in part to prove that integrated education can work around here." Another said it resulted from "a general dissatisfaction with both the public schools and the private academy." A third suggested that its beginning was "purely coincidental" and unrelated to the chronic education problems in the county. Whatever the case, the Campus School is there, providing free education for a limited number of elementary school children, most of whose parents work at the college. Children of Longwood employees have first priority for inclusion in the school's enrollment. The vast majority of Longwood's employees—and all of its faculty—are white.

All the heat of the 1950s and early 1960s in Prince Edward County has long since burned out. The people have adjusted, adapted— some with relief, others with resignation—to the new arrangement. Many are pleased with the outcome, satisfied that no great harm has been done and no cataclysmic changes have resulted from a little desegregation. Many more are saddened, convinced that no fundamental adjustments have been made, no lessons learned—and now life goes on as before, in the spirit of pretending that nothing ever happened.

And some, like J. Barrye Wall, Sr., feel that too much has changed beyond any hope of restoration. In 1960 the managing editor of Wall's newspaper, John C. Steck, wrote an account of the Prince Edward story that the paper published in booklet form and circulated widely as a "factual account of what has happened." In the booklet, Steck wrote that "the mixing of the races at the insistence of voices we cannot sanction, by means we deem illegal, is not something to be lived with; not a pill to be swallowed. It simply cannot be tolerated. . . . Time has demonstrated that [the white people of Prince Edward County] have not tolerated it."

Four years later the pill had to be swallowed and tolerated—and most managed to do it. Barrye Wall never could. In 1978, as firmly as in 1948, he could speak kindly of blacks—even of an adversary like L. Francis Griffin—and in the same breath reaffirm his undying conviction that anything short of total and absolute segregation of the races is immoral, unconstitutional, and probably fatal for the American nation.

"I believe in public education," he declared. "I always have, and I've said so many times. I never was for the abolition of the public schools, then or now. But I am for segregated education, with equal expenditures."

There are men in Prince Edward County—pillars of the white community—who agree wholeheartedly with Wall's unreconstructed view of the past. And there are others, equally as influential, who speak privately of "the diehards, the rigid and inflexible men who never fully accepted public education in the first place, and never have accepted the fact that segregation is dead and gone forever."

The disagreement between these two groups became bitter and pronounced in 1960, when the schism developed on the question of selling public school property to the private school. In some respects, they still hold different views. For example, the "diehards" will not acknowledge, as the "compromisers" do, that Prince Edward Academy is "costing more than people can afford" or that there is "a distinct put-down of whites who don't go to the academy."

But by and large, those who temporarily parted company in the heat of the moment almost two decades ago have long since made their peace, and their differences now are subtle and indistinct. "The wounds have healed," said B. Calvin Bass, a former chairman and long-time member of the public school board. "After we refused to sell the high school, people shunned me; today, we sit down and enjoy meals together. Not just whites, either—blacks, too—and the adamant diehards are right there, sitting with the Negroes, and enjoying themselves. There's been a mellowing, and there's no more bitterness."

Apparently, virtually all of the whites who lived through the years of discord in Prince Edward County believe that desegregation has greatly diminished the quality of education in the public schools and that Prince Edward Academy has been a "safety valve" and a "saving grace" for the community. Few will say—as one man did, off the record—that they have changed their minds about segregation, that they now believe integration is in the long-term best interest of the county, or that they expect someday to see black students enrolled at Prince Edward Academy.

Lester E. Andrews, Sr., a one-time chairman of the county school board, now serves on an electoral commission that appoints new members to the board; he also serves as a member of Prince Edward Academy's governing body. When he resigned the school board chairmanship in 1960 rather than vote to sell school property, Andrews lost some friends. Recalling that, he said: "People didn't understand what we were trying to do. We were trying to keep the black schools open. I have no regrets about my role in it—or about the outcome. The blacks lost five years of school, and they were hurt immensely by that—but now, they're probably getting a better education. The academy was hard-pressed to begin with, but whites have also ended up getting a better education than before. In a way, you could say we've got pretty much what we had before, only better."

Looking to the future, Andrews said, "I think the academy will stay about the same as it is now—and hopefully, will remain all white. The public schools will stay about the same too. The blacks had a real serious beef—what they had wasn't right. Things are a lot better now. Black/white relations are different—closer, stronger. We never had a really bad situation, no violence—these are level-headed folks—but there were problems, and now I think they've been resolved."

If such men as Lester Andrews and Calvin Bass could find themselves alienated from white society in Prince Edward County for the positions they took twenty years ago, it is hard to imagine the isolation of someone like Gordon Moss. A native of nearby Lynchburg, he had first gone to Farmville in 1926, and by 1960 he had taught off and on at Longwood College for two decades. He was popular among the students and was not known as a boat-rocker on the race issue. But when he finally came to the conclusion that segregation was a wrong he had to speak out against, he was instantly branded as an outsider, an alien, and made a pariah by his fellow whites.

Moss dug in and held his ground. He sent his son out of the county when the public schools were closed and brought him back when the free schools were opened in 1963. In interviews and speeches, the professor bluntly criticized the closing of the schools. At one point, he was under heavy pressure to be silent or lose his job, but somehow he managed to hold on. In 1968 he retired from teaching but stayed in Farmville; he lives there still, a seventy-eight-year-old scholar with a Sandburgian shock of white hair and a still-active mind.

"Most people seem to have finally accepted me," he said, sitting in his book-lined study. "Back then, less than half a dozen did—publicly, anyway. I never thought of leaving, though. I didn't enjoy the un-pleasantness of it, but I saw it as a chance to do something about an injustice, to right a wrong. I couldn't have lived with myself if I had failed to speak when confronted."

His assessment of the outcome of the Prince Edward County school closings is quietly, matter-of-factly negative: "Most of the blacks got no education at all and have grown up uneducated. Some went away to school and profited greatly from the experience, but the vast majority were simply lost. I'd say the white segregationists won. They have to obey the letter of the law now, but not the spirit—and they don't. There is no longer total segregation, but the whites still get what they want. As long as they can raise enough money to keep their academy going strong, they've won. Not many lessons have been learned. I'm afraid we accomplished very little."

Of all the people who figured prominently in the Prince Edward County conflict, L. Francis Griffin could be said to have been the central character. Many whites—and not a few blacks—saw him as a radical disrupter of the peace and perhaps the instigator of the student strike and the NAACP lawsuit. Young blacks active in the pursuit of change looked to him for advice and leadership. The NAACP lawyers and all those who tried in one way or another to bring pressure to bear from outside the community found it necessary to reckon with him.

In terms of his personal health and that of his wife, the welfare of their six children, and the general well-being of those he chose to represent, the Reverend Mr. Griffin paid a heavy price for his dissent. Sitting in the two-story brick church his father pastored before him—a structure that had served as a hospital for Union soldiers during the Civil War and as the sanctuary of a white congregation before that—he reflected on the Prince Edward ordeal and its consequences:

"I thought of leaving several times, but I always concluded that it would be wrong for me to do so. I saw it as a matter of human rights—trying to help and defend the oppressed, those who were being taken advantage of, including some of the whites. I had to debate with myself whether I had the moral authority to take people through such wrath, knowing that many of them couldn't see where it was leading. Whether I had the moral right to involve my family and others in such a movement was always a question I had to struggle with. I decided that I did, but that decision didn't come easy. I do feel now, though, that I did the right thing, and I have no regrets—though there are some things I might do differently if I had it to do over."

One of those things, Griffin said, would be "to keep the outside help away, and let it be strictly a local fight with no holds barred." He acknowledged that the NAACP attorneys were indispensable and that such organizations as the American Friends Service Committee gave vital aid to children barred from school. But most of the others who came and went, he said—marchers, demonstrators, even some educators and members of the press—did more harm than good:

"There were too many frustrated, poorly adjusted, uncommitted people mixed in with the good ones. They competed among themselves for recognition and credit. Some of them were dangerous. One woman from New York tried to create an incident for news purposes—tried to get some youngsters to commit violent acts against older people. And the free school was a problem, too. A good school system was operated for one year, there's no question about that—but Neil Sullivan, the man in charge, was too much of a self-serving opportunist. He presented himself to the nation as a man who had risked physical danger to rescue these black children from ignorance, when in fact he was not in danger and he didn't perform any miracles. The issues were clear enough, and the fight was on a high moral level; there was no need of exaggerating. Sullivan, and many of the others, were more interested in promoting themselves than in help-ing the oppressed people of this county."

Concerning the "high moral level" of the struggle, Griffin offered this insight: "I could respect the local whites for the honesty of their position. Their feelings were firm and out in the open. They were not deceitful. I think it's fair to say they respected me, too. I was frank—I would tell them what I was going to do, and I'd do it. It was sort of a gentlemen's fight. There was no overt violence, such as was common in Mississippi and elsewhere. What little violence there was was iso-lated and unorganized. There were reprisals, yes, but they were more tactful and sophisticated. It was a more insidious form of viciousness. Though we disagreed completely, I think we understood one another. Both sides could be very firm in their positions, without becoming bitter. I almost reached bitterness a couple of times in the process, but I never did, and that helped me to remain here and keep my sanity."

The youngest of the Griffin children is a student at Prince Edward County High School now, and Mrs. Griffin is a teacher there. The older children are all grown and gone; one of them graduated from Harvard and is presently engaged in doctoral study there. "They missed four years of school, the same as most of the others," Griffin said. "As long as any black child was without education, I couldn't in good conscience let mine go off to school somewhere else. After the schools reopened, I did send two of them away. It's hard to say how much damage was done to children here by the closing of the schools, but many had tremendous gaps in their learning after they returned, and many others never continued school at all."

The quality of the schools now, in the Reverend Mr. Griffin's opin-ion, "is comparable with that of schools elsewhere in Southside Vir-ginia—and I don't know if that's saying a lot. I think they're working up to standard, and I hope they'll continue to improve. But it's still a question of money and politics. All American schools seem to be in trouble, and these are no different." The Prince Edward Academy, he added, "is pretty much like it has always been, and I don't see any-thing other than economics changing that. It would have to fall of its own weight. Many people thought that would happen soon after it opened, but I didn't believe it. Rising costs, though, could eventually make it impossible to sustain."

The changes he has seen in Prince Edward County since he returned there to live almost thirty years ago have left Francis Griffin with mixed emotions. He has seen land ownership by blacks decline sharply as small-acreage family farming has become virtually an impossible means of livelihood; at the same time, he has seen some industry come into the community, with the result that many blacks—and whites—have steadier employment and higher incomes than they have ever had before. Some blacks now serve on the county board of supervisors, on the school board, in other offices of government, and in law enforcement—but there are fewer black craftsmen and small-business owners than in previous years.

Race relations, too, are both changed and unchanged, he says: "Among young adults, I think things are better—there's more contact, more pragmatic cooperation. My hope is with those young adults—and of course, there's always hope for the little ones, even though the continuation of segregated education establishes attitudes that are difficult to overcome. With the older generation, things are the same as always—most of them haven't been affected by any of this, not really, and since that's where the power still is, it's hard to see much real improvement in race relations. The whites see that what little they've given up didn't cost them much, so they let a black in here and there, and the crisis has passed, and they feel no pressure. On the black side, something similar has happened: There's a sense of having arrived, having accomplished something. People have let down, relaxed. We're squatting and resting on our laurels, white and black."

Of the county's white power elite, the men who were his adversaries, the Reverend Mr. Griffin said, "I see some of them now and then. We talk. Some of them have told me they feel what happened was for the best. They may not tell you that, but they've told me. A few of them have told me they now see and appreciate what I was trying to do—but I doubt if you could find any who would say, even in private, that they think integration is right. Even now, they would be afraid to be identified with that position."

And what of the future? "Unless something drastic, such as a major economic crisis, forces further change," he said, "I don't see things being much different in another twenty or twenty-five years than they are now. In essence, there's a new status quo here. This is still a battle-ground, the lines of separation still exist—but the pressures are not such that there will be skirmishes, or all-out fighting. It's a cold war now, and I look for it to go on."

He pondered that conclusion for a moment, and then the Reverend L. Francis Griffin shook his head slowly. "It's a very peculiar thing," he mused. "I've wondered about it a great deal. I've wondered why this ever happened at all. Why did they close the schools? Why here, of all places? Vernon Johns, who was Barbara Johns's uncle and one of my mentors, a remarkable man, once said it happened here for no reason at all—it was simply an accident, a freak of nature, like a fixed star leaving its orbit. He may have been right, but I keep thinking there must be some explanation. I'd surely like to know what it is. It's a great mystery to me and has been throughout all these years."

Barbara Rose Johns never returned to Farmville to live; she has spent most of the intervening years of her life in Philadelphia and is there now. Most of the other members of the Moton High School "strike class" of 1951 also left the community. One of them, James Samuel Williams, returned to Farmville in 1977 from Buffalo, where as a Baptist minister he directed a ghetto education and social action program for nine years.

Williams said the school strike and subsequent developments "didn't end racism and exploitation in Prince Edward County, but they raised people's consciousness permanently, raised black expectations, gave them a sense of personal worth, and taught them the meaning of justice and equality. Reverend Griffin is responsible for that."

The basic problems of the county are essentially the same as before, Williams said: "Racism and economic stratification are dominant here, as they are everywhere else in the country. But I do see some change for the better since I left. We've got a better chance to make it than many places—better than Buffalo—and I'm glad to be back."

Other young adults have begun to manifest a more independent and progressive outlook in the county's businesses and professions, and in government and politics. The local Democratic party organization, long dominated by conservatives, is now in the hands of a committee carefully balanced with whites and blacks, progressives and conservatives, young and old, men and women. (Women, virtually invisible in the upper echelons of any social or political organizations in the past, are finally beginning to be seen and heard around Farmville.)

Donald Stuart, a young English professor at Longwood College and the current chairman of the Democratic party, has made clear his position on race. "The rigid segregationist is a dying breed," he said. "The world is changing. Younger people are coming into this community who don't have any hang-ups about race. I wouldn't call them liberal—they're just color-blind. They want everybody to participate—not necessarily for social reasons, but simply because it's good for business."

Marshall Ellett, a thirty-one-year-old attorney and a native of Southside Virginia, is another activist in Prince Edward's political "youth movement." A self-described "pragmatist," he helped to fashion the "exotic coalition" that now bids to become the new voice of political power in the county. He acknowledges that racial inequities still exist. "We're still paying for the troubles of the past," he said. "That's a cross we bear. But we're trying to pick up the pieces, and though it may take fifteen or twenty years, I think we can solve our racial and economic and educational problems."

Some whites in the community are still not confident enough to speak with openness of the racial problems the county had and has. They will say privately, as one of them did, that "twenty white families, in order to keep from having to mix with blacks, made all the other whites pay the heavy price of private schools." Or they will say that "the white power structure drew the line, fought tooth and nail, lost—and learned nothing, still feels just the same, still clings to white supremacy." And they debate among themselves the pros and cons of segregated private schools and integrated public ones.

There is much more diversity of thought and opinion among the new generation of young people than existed previously. Some aspire to nothing more than a seat in the inner circle of directors who control the banks, the businesses, the academy (all of the thirty-nine directors of the county's three banks are affluent-to-wealthy white males, and most of them are over fifty). Others yearn to break up that tight circle, to integrate it with blacks and women and working-class people. Whatever their motives, the younger adults who are moving now to the fringes of power in Prince Edward County seem willing to proceed according to a new rule: that power, in order to be effective, must be dispersed, inclusive, and accessible to all.

And finally, there is James Edward Ghee, Jr. He was born and raised in Prince Edward County. When the schools were closed in 1959, he was about to enter the ninth grade at Moton High School. He was out of school for two years, a member of the "lost generation." But James Ghee was not lost. He was one of sixty-seven children sent to schools in other parts of the country by the American Friends Service Committee. Ghee attended high school for four years in Iowa City, Iowa, and went on to graduate from the University of Iowa in 1969. Returning to his home state, he was admitted to the University of Virginia Law School. After earning his degree there and gaining three years of experience elsewhere, he returned to Farmville in 1975. He is the only black attorney between Lynchburg and Richmond and the first ever to practice in Prince Edward County.

"I think I always knew I was coming back," he said. "I knew there was a need—not just for a lawyer, but for someone who could help as I have been helped. The best way to make a difference with my life, I felt, was to go back home—and it's a real good feeling to be back."

James Ghee is a principal figure in the group of young adults seeking to reform the county Democratic party. He has a thriving law practice on Farmville's Main Street, representing white as well as black clients. He is near his parents (his father is a laborer, his mother a maid) and near friends, old and new.

"I'm really satisfied here," he said. "There is a sense of great possibility, a reason to be optimistic. There has been some change—and there's more coming. The old traditions and customs are falling. Over time, the younger generation will change things here. Yes, it feels really good to be right in the middle of that."

The Reverend L. Francis Griffin died in January 1980, and many of his contemporaries, including J. Barrye Wall, Sr., of the Farmville Herald *and Gordon Moss of Longwood College, have also passed away. The public schools of Prince Edward*

County enrolled almost twenty-five hundred students (including about nine hundred whites) in the fall of 1990, and Prince Edward Academy's enrollment of fewer than seven hundred included a token few black students. Blacks have won election to the Farmville town council, the county school board, and the county board of supervisors, and the Prince Edward County Democratic party has a black chairman. Barbara Johns, the heroine of Moton High School in the 1950s, is now a librarian in Philadelphia. Attorney James Ghee observed the fifteenth anniversary of his Farmville law practice in 1990. In 1989 Prince Edward County gave a majority of its votes to L. Douglas Wilder, the first black candidate in U.S. history to be elected governor of a state.

≈ HERITAGE OF A HEAVYWEIGHT: THE ANCESTRY OF MUHAMMAD ALI

In that characteristic way in which small-town Southerners know who among them is kin to whom, attorney Granville Clark of Russellville, Kentucky, knew that some of Muhammad Ali's forebears came from the tobacco-growing countryside around Russellville. It was Clark who put me on the trail of this fascinating story, which was published in the September 28, 1980, issue of the New York Times Magazine.

At his Deer Lake training camp in the Blue Mountains of Pennsylvania, Muhammad Ali was summoning the discipline to prepare himself for the ordeal of all-out combat. The thirty-eight-year-old fighter was only weeks away from what might finally be the last boxing match of his long and legendary career, a world heavyweight title fight with Larry Holmes, the current champion.

Against the advice of numerous ring-wise counselors, Ali had come out of retirement to seek the heavyweight crown for the fourth time. (He is already the only fighter ever to hold it three times.) The Holmes fight looms as his most challenging in a quarter-century of ring battles, for Ali is the underdog contender this time, the old man bucking the odds (currently two to one). And the stakes are enormous: When he steps onto a Las Vegas canvas with Holmes next Thursday night, he will be going for the fifty-seventh victory of his sixty-fight career—and for a guaranteed purse of eight million dollars, an amount that will raise the former champion's lifetime ring earnings to about sixty million dollars.

In his private quarters at Deer Lake, Ali was trying to relax after a heavy workout. He was bone-weary and craving rest, but to all outward appearances, he seemed unscarred by a lifetime of formal violence. He had lost thirty pounds since the start of his training. His smoothly handsome face and his powerful, polished-walnut physique could have belonged to a weight lifter—or a dancer. He didn't look like a man who had made himself world-famous by conquering all comers with his fists.

His voice, too, was a surprise. The strident, stinging lash of fury and near-hysteria that had come to characterize his prefight public rhetoric was muted. For a moment, he was not on public display, and his thoughts were not on his fights but on his family. He spoke softly, just above a whisper: "I never knew much about my ancestors until now. It makes me proud to learn something about them, about people like Tom Morehead—honest, hard-working people, strong people. When I'm gone, I want my grandchildren and great-grandchildren to give me credit for what I did—and in the same way, I'm happy to know about my ancestors so I can give them credit."

Ali studied a faded photograph of Tom and Lizzie Morehead, two of his great-grandparents. He listened intently to stories of slaves and free blacks who returned to Africa, or fought for the Union in the Civil War, or struggled against racial discrimination after the war. He heard the facts and the circumstantial evidence that linked blacks and whites as victims and aggressors, as friends and enemies, as literal and figurative brothers and sisters.

These long-forgotten ancestors penetrated his consciousness. Their lives were a revelation to him. He was fascinated by them, drawn to them. They, too, had fought on against heavy odds, and some of them had prevailed, if only in modest ways. He sensed a kinship, a connection that bridged the generations.

"I've heard about Henry Clay and Cassius Clay, about the slave owners and all," Muhammad Ali said at last, "but this is the first time I've heard much about my black ancestors. I'm proud and honored for them to be recognized. Someday I'd like to dig up everything that can be found about all the people I'm descended from."

After two tumultuous decades of national and international exposure, Muhammad Ali is certainly one of the best-known personalities in the world—and, in the eyes of millions, he is probably also the most respected. Most rankings of the best boxers in history confirm what Ali himself has long claimed: that he is "The Greatest." Outside the ring, he has been an irrepressible and often controversial figure. He has overcome the wrath of Christians and patriots, asserting his right to embrace Islam and to reject his country's call to military service. He has often returned the scorn of whites with scorn and has lived to hear their praise echoing the praise of nonwhites the world over. He has seen the bottom and the top, not once but several times, and with great effort he has secured a place for himself at the top. More than a fighter, he is now an international celebrity, a global black hero, a worldwide symbol of black pride and strength. Such is his fame that he seems almost to have transcended the traditional boundaries of politics and religion, race and class, nationalism and ideology.

And yet, for all that has been said and written about Ali, little is known of his ancestry. Sports writers and biographers have told of the brash and cocky black kid who rose from the segregated streets of Louisville, Kentucky, to seize attention in the ring. They have noted that he was born in Louisville on January 18, 1942, the first son of Cassius Marcellus Clay, Sr., a sign painter, and Odessa Grady Clay, and that he was given the name of his father. Some writers, pointing to the fact that one of the most notorious white men in nineteenth-century Kentucky was a firebrand abolitionist and gentleman-warrior named Cassius Marcellus Clay, have suggested that the Louisville boxer was a worthy successor to the name—and perhaps a blood relation of the historical figure as well. One biographer, John Cottrell, also wrote that there was a "family claim" that the young fighter "was the great-great-grandson of Henry Clay," the famous Kentucky senator and presidential candidate of the mid-1800s who tried in vain to lead the nation away from civil war. But those assertions were made without attribution or proof. The gap between the white Clay family of the nineteenth century and Muhammad Ali's father—a gap of at least two generations—has never been bridged.

When his career was in its early stages, young Clay liked his name, even though he had learned that the Clays had been slave owners. "Don't you think it's a beautiful name?" he used to say to interviewers. "Say it out loud: Cassius Marcellus Clay." Then in 1964 he joined the Nation of Islam and became Muhammad Ali, renouncing "Cassius

Marcellus Clay" as a "slave name." His distressed father's initial reaction was that his son was "trying to rub that name out, and I'm trying to make it strong."

The seriousness of Ali's commitment to his Muslim faith has been frequently tested but never found lacking. Even so, he has retained a sense of humor and irony about his former name. In 1974, during a visit to the Capitol in Washington, he stood before a statue of Henry Clay and joked, "So that's what the great-great-grandfather looked like."

But in his autobiography, *The Greatest: My Own Story*, written with Richard Durham in 1975, Ali said there was "very little knowledge, if any, of 'white blood' from any source" in his family, and he added, "If slaveholder Clay's blood came into our veins along with the name, it came by rape and defilement." As for the abolitionist Cassius Marcellus Clay, he may have gotten rid of his slaves, Ali wrote, "but [he] held on to white supremacy." Ali concluded: "Why should I keep my white slave master's name visible and my black ancestors invisible, unknown, unhonored?"

(In truth, Cassius Clay's attachment to slavery went even farther than Ali imagined. In spite of his abolitionist fervor, Clay apparently owned more slaves in 1865, when the Thirteenth Amendment to the U.S. Constitution finally forbade the practice, than he had inherited from his father thirty-seven years earlier.)

Ali wrote with special fondness in his autobiography of two of his paternal aunts, Coretta and Eva Clay. Coretta is dead now, but her sister Eva Clay Waddell still lives in Louisville.

"My father was Herman Clay," she said, "and my mother was Edith Greathouse Clay. They were Muhammad Ali's grandparents, and they were still living when he was growing up. I can recall back in the 1930s when four generations on my mother's side of the family lived on the same street, Twelfth Street, here in Louisville. Besides my mother and me, there were my mother's parents, Montgomery and Betsy Jane Greathouse, and my mother's grandmother, Patsy Alexander, who lived to be 115 years old. But I never even knew the names of my father's parents. They both died before I was born. All I ever heard about them was that my grandmother was a woman from Madagascar, and that she and my grandfather [Muhammad Ali's great-grandparents] were married in Louisville, and that their children were born here. My father was one of them, of course, and I believe he had an older brother named Cassius."

(According to census records and other public records in Louisville for the years 1865–1900, a black laborer named John Henry Clay and his wife had nine children, among whom were sons Cassius, Henry, Daniel Webster, Claudius, and Herman. Herman's age was the same as that of Mrs. Waddell's father, who she said was seventy-seven when he died in about 1955.)

"He used to tell us he was a grandson of Senator Henry Clay," Mrs. Waddell recalled. "Said he got teased about it a lot when he was young, and got into plenty of fights because of it."

Ali's aunt spoke with warmth and pride of the Clay and Great-house relatives she had known. "No doubt some of their ancestors were white," she said, "but that doesn't concern me one way or the other. It's nothing to hide. Those things happened back then."

Cassius and Odessa Clay, Muhammad Ali's parents, are now separated, but both of them still live in Louisville. They are sought out frequently by strangers inquiring about their son, and as a consequence they have become reluctant to enter into conversation about him, or about family matters in general.

Odessa Lee Grady was born in Hopkins County, in western Kentucky. Her parents, John Grady and Birdie Morehead Grady, were divorced about fifty years ago, after which Mrs. Grady moved to Louisville with her children. There, Odessa eventually met and married Cassius Marcellus Clay, Sr.

Little is known about the Grady side of the family, except that a cousin of Muhammad Ali's recalls hearing that John Grady's father was born to a black woman and a "white Irishman" named Grady, or perhaps O'Grady. But the Moreheads—the parents of Birdie Morehead Grady, the grandparents of Odessa Grady Clay, the great-grandparents of Muhammad Ali—are another story. The Moreheads were special.

∾

Gillie Bell Morehead Plunkett is not certain of her age. She could be eighty—or ninety. She has lived in Louisville for almost a half-century, but she was born a Morehead in rural Logan County, Kentucky, 140 miles southwest of Louisville, and she is the unofficial keeper of her family's history.

"I'm the oldest living grandchild of Tom Morehead," she said. "He had lots of children—seven by his first wife, six by his second. My father was Virgil Morehead. He belonged to the first set, to Tom Morehead and Georgia Ann Lyons. Birdie Morehead, who was Muhammad Ali's grandmother, belonged to Tom and his second wife, Lizzie Bibb. I remember my grandfather well—I was a young girl when he died in 1913."

Mrs. Plunkett recalled the land of her childhood: "Green Ridge, Gordonsville, Bibbtown—they were all little communities close together, running along the Highland Lick Road a few miles out of Russellville, the county seat of Logan County. It was rich land, good soil, and my grandfather owned over two hundred acres of it. Part of what he owned was inheritance land, passed to him from his father's holdings.

"My grandfather was half-white. I never knew what his father's first name was, but he was a Morehead, a white man, and he had Tom by a slave woman named Dinah. I was always told that. At about the same time, that Morehead man and his white wife had a son named James. Jim and Tom were half-brothers—they grew up together, played together, worked together. They were real close. After Tom married, he named his first son Jim—that was my uncle, my father's brother."

Mrs. Plunkett searched through a large box full of photographs and family memorabilia, looking for a picture of her grandfather. "Tom Morehead went away and served in the Union Army in the Civil War," she continued, "and I heard him tell of fighting until blood ran like water in the trenches. He wasn't afraid of nothing. He was some nice-looking man, too, the best-looking man I ever saw: tall and straight, light-skinned, had long black curly hair and dimples in each cheek. He carried himself with pride, didn't bow to no man."

She found the photograph she was looking for, a tan and tattered picture of two neatly dressed adults and four small barefooted children gathered around a lace-draped chair in which infant twins were propped. "That's Tom Morehead and Lizzie Bibb and their six children," she explained. "See that little girl standing close to her father?

That's Birdie—that's Muhammad Ali's grandmother. This picture must have been made soon after 1900, because Birdie looks to be eight or nine, and I think she was born in 1893."

Mrs. Plunkett studied the picture for a moment. "My grandfather was right prosperous," she said. "His land was supposed to stay in the family, and it did for a while after he died, but then it got away somehow—white people got it. One of my uncles' wives let a white man buy it from her. There's not any Moreheads left around there now, black or white. They've all died, or moved away."

The photograph of Tom Morehead and his wife held Mrs. Plunkett's attention. "I used to know some white people that claimed kinship to my grandfather," she said after a pause, "and they were proud of it. When he died, there was as many whites as blacks at his funeral. He was buried in a cemetery between Gordonsville and Green Ridge, I believe, and he had a big tall tombstone. Both his wives were buried there too, and so was his mother. All his life, Tom Morehead stood high. He was *somebody*."

On the wall of her sitting room, just above a large television set, Mrs. Plunkett has a framed picture of her young cousin, Cassius Marcellus Clay. He is poised in a crouch before a punching bag, and he is wearing a U.S. Olympic team jacket. She looked up at the picture and smiled.

"There's something about Cassius people don't understand, isn't there?" she said. "How did he come to be so famous? When he was little, we never dreamed he'd be famous. But I can remember when he was just a little boy, he'd go around saying, 'I'm gonna be a boxer, and I'm gonna whip everybody.' I told him to hush up, to go on to Sunday school and church and stay out of trouble." She shook her head and laughed. "Maybe he knew what he was talking about all along."

Russellville and Logan County are located near the midpoint of a fertile farm belt that stretches for about a hundred miles along Kentucky's border with Tennessee. Land-seeking white men from Virginia and the Carolinas explored and occupied the region two hundred years ago, and for generations, people of the area have taken great pride in their community's substantial contributions to Kentucky history.

Residents of Russellville in particular pay reverent attention to the past. In the years between 1800 and 1860, their town evolved from a rugged frontier village in an outlaw society to a place of some refinement and productivity, and now its shady streets are graced by numerous fine old houses. Local histories note that the town and county have produced four Kentucky governors, five governors of other states, five U.S. senators, and six congressmen. (Also claimed are James Bowie, the famous knife-fighter who died at the Alamo, and Robert James, who went with the generous aid of two local bankers to study for the ministry. The latter would hardly be worth mentioning were it not for the fact that two of the minister's sons came back years later to rob the same benevolent bankers—and thus began the outlaw career of the notorious James brothers, Jesse and Frank.)

But of all the names of prominent local people in Logan County's nineteenth-century "golden age," none were more notable than the Moreheads and Bibbs. Three Morehead brothers—Charles, Armstead, and Presley—migrated to the area from Virginia in about 1800, and their family name stayed in the public eye for the better part of a century. One of the contemporaries of the Morehead brothers was Major Richard Bibb, a Revolutionary War officer turned Methodist minister who acquired large holdings in land and slaves in his new Kentucky home.

One particular story about Major Bibb has survived to the present day: Apparently feeling some conflict between the teachings of his religion and the practice of human bondage, he reportedly called his slaves together on the front lawn of his Russellville home (this in the 1820s, when Bibb was about seventy) and offered them a choice: immediate repatriation to Africa or freedom in Kentucky upon his death. About thirty of the slaves chose the former and were transported to Liberia in 1829, never to be heard from again; more than fifty others chose the latter, and in 1849 they were emancipated and given fifteen hundred acres of Logan County farmland, in accordance with the deceased major's will. The ones who stayed in Kentucky took the Bibb surname along with their freedom—and in the 1850 census, virtually all of the free blacks in Logan County were named Bibb.

Sons of Richard Bibb, meanwhile, went in different ways to make their own history, one becoming a Whig member of the U.S. Senate from Kentucky in the 1830s, and another—John Bibb of Frankfort, Kentucky—hybridizing a popular leafy vegetable now known far and wide as bibb lettuce.

The Moreheads and Bibbs have long since faded from prominence in Logan County—the names appear only a few times in the county telephone directory, and elsewhere hardly at all—but some local citizens remember the families quite well, and a few also know that Muhammad Ali's Morehead and Bibb ancestors were born there.

Two Russellville sisters, John Ella Dickerson and Willie Belle Dickerson Bibb, recall that their father, Walter Dickerson, was a nephew of Tom Morehead's. "We're cousins of Odessa Grady Clay," said Miss Dickerson, a retired schoolteacher, "and also cousins of Gillie Bell Plunkett. Cousin Gillie is right—Tom Morehead's father was a white man, a Morehead, but we don't know what his first name was. I doubt if anybody around here knows that story. Tom Morehead has been dead nearly seventy years. He's buried out around Green Ridge, but I don't even know where the cemetery is. I do remember hearing, though, that he was a soldier in the Union Army, and that he owned a lot of land after the war—some of it inherited from his father's family."

Attorney Granville Clark's roots in Russellville go back a long way, and his fascination with history has paralleled his interest in civil liberties and the law. His office near the courthouse is in a historic old home where a delegation of Kentuckians met in 1861 in a futile attempt to take the state out of the Union and into the Confederacy.

"I've known for years that Muhammad Ali is descended from Bibbs and Moreheads who once lived in this county," he said, "but I never knew just what the connection was. For some reason, I've always thought of it as having something to do with that story about old Major Bibb freeing his slaves. That's a great story—it would make a fine novel. Just think: One of the blacks who went to Liberia might be an ancestor of some national leader of modern Africa—and one of those who stayed here might be an ancestor of Muhammad Ali."

139

In the Logan County courthouse and in the public library in Rus-sellville, some of the information linking Ali to the Moreheads and Bibbs of the past can be found. The record is incomplete, but it does contain some helpful clues. This is the essence of what it shows:

The Morehead brothers who migrated to Logan County at the be-ginning of the nineteenth century took an active part in the public life of the county and state. Charles, the eldest, served in both the house and senate of the Kentucky legislature, and his son, Charles S. Morehead, later held numerous state offices, including that of gov-ernor. Presley, the youngest of the brothers, also served in both houses of the legislature.

Armstead, the middle brother, was the first postmaster of Russell-ville and the first circuit court clerk of Logan County. One of his sons, James T. Morehead, was governor of Kentucky from 1832 to 1834, and in 1841 he joined his fellow Whig Henry Clay in the U.S. Senate.

Another of Armstead's sons was Armstead S. Morehead. Like his father, he stayed in Logan County. While his brother James was pur-suing a career in politics, A. S. Morehead (as he commonly signed his name) was living a more conventional and anonymous life, farming on the family holdings in the Green Ridge section west of Russellville. He was married twice, possibly three times, and his wives had at least four children, one of whom was James W. Morehead, born in 1836. There also were several blacks attached to A. S. Morehead's family— some slaves, others free—and one of them was Thomas Morehead, born in 1837.

A. S. Morehead died in 1865. His son James inherited large tracts of land, including a 150-acre tract of the family farm on Duck Lick Creek. In 1870 James and his wife, Elizabeth, then living in Robert-son County, Tennessee, adjacent to Logan County, sold 161 acres on Duck Lick Creek to Tom and Sam Morehead ("both men of color") for $350 in cash and four promissory notes of $650 each, to be paid annually through 1874. The land was identified in the deed as "a part of the tract on which A. S. Morehead . . . lived, and on which [Tom Morehead] is now living." In 1877, when part of the debt was still outstanding, James and Elizabeth Morehead accepted seven farm an-imals and twenty acres of tobacco as payment in full, and nine years later they sold Tom Morehead eighty more acres in the same vicinity.

The record shows that Tom Morehead married Lizzie Bibb on December 24, 1890, and that the couple subsequently donated land for a Baptist church in the Green Ridge neighborhood. In 1901 they deeded one acre to the county as the site for a school—probably the first school for blacks to be built there.

The public record of the lives of Tom Morehead and Lizzie Bibb, Muhammad Ali's great-grandparents, thus concludes—and like all public records, it leaves many questions unanswered. There is no indication of Tom Morehead's parentage or of his military service, nor is there any record to show when he died, where he was buried, or who his survivors were.

For American blacks in general, as for the Moreheads and Bibbs in particular, documentary evidence of this nature is sparse, if it exists at all. It may be assumed that the black forebears of Tom Morehead and Lizzie Bibb were the property of white Moreheads and Bibbs whose family roots can be traced far back into colonial Virginia (in the case of the Moreheads, all the way back to 1630), but no record exists to prove that assumption. Census data customarily listed the slaves of each master only by age and sex, not by name. Marriages, births, and deaths of slaves were seldom recorded, and even more rarely recorded was the evidence of black children fathered by white men.

In light of the fact that the importation of slaves to Virginia from Africa ended at about the time of the Revolutionary War—and some sixty years before Tom Morehead's birth—it is probable that the blacks from whom Muhammad Ali is descended, no less than the whites, had lived on American soil for generations before their migration to Kentucky. Their link to the land of their origin was no doubt lost beyond recovery long before they saw Logan County—and even there, a generation passed and disappeared without a trace before Tom Morehead was born.

The Highland Lick Road wound past summer-green fields of tobacco and corn and soybeans. Random inquiries at a half-dozen houses yielded no clues to the location of a country cemetery in the

Green Ridge–Gordonsville area. Finally, a farmer seemed to recall having seen the long-abandoned site. "If they was Moreheads," he said, "they was colored. They used to own a lot of this land around here, including my place."

Another false turn, another request for directions, and finally, the farm of J. W. Stratton—and nearby, in a tangled thicket of undergrowth and trees, the cemetery.

Stratton had often wondered about the graves, most of which were unmarked and all of which were carpeted with a dense mat of moss and creeping vines. He quickly found one stone, lying almost hidden under the leaves. It belonged to Lizzie Morehead, and it showed that she was born in 1870 and died in 1919.

"There's another stone here somewhere," Stratton said. "I've seen it many a time." He walked slowly, his eyes fixed upon the ground. Then, abruptly, he stopped: "Here's the gentleman, right here."

The stone was three feet high—or would have been, had it been standing. It lay half-buried in the soft brown earth, its inscription facing skyward through a coat of dried leaves. When the leaves were brushed away, the words stood out as a revelation and a puzzle:

> Thos. Morehead
> Co. E.
> 129 U.S.C.I.

At the National Archives in Washington, military service records indicate that Thomas Morehead of Logan County, Kentucky, served a little more than one year in the Union army, rising from private to sergeant in that time. Years later, when his health was failing and he was unable to work, he sought the aid of a Russellville lawyer to help him obtain a pension for his military service.

There was some confusion about the number of Tom Morehead's military unit; he remembered it as the 122d U.S. Colored Infantry, but it might have been another—the 129th, perhaps. There was also some question about his exact age, and about the nature of his disability. Then his lawyer died, and the application papers were lost, and the bureaucracy in Washington moved very slowly.

Tom Morehead spent twenty-five years trying to gain the pension to which he was entitled. Finally, in 1902 he was awarded a monthly payment of eight dollars. Within a short time he began an appeal for reconsideration and a higher award.

In 1908, when he was seventy-one years old and still mired in disagreement with pension officials, Tom Morehead reached back to the years of his childhood to summon help. Thus it was that twice in that year, the commissioner of pensions in Washington received letters from James W. Morehead of Springfield, Robertson County, Tennessee. One letter read in part:

> I, James W. Morehead, do hereby certify that Thomas Morehead and my self is about the same age. I was born Dec. 14th 1836 and am drawing a pension on that age. I am drawing 15 dollars per month. There is but little difference in my age and Thomas Morehead. Thomas Morehead belonged to my father A. S. Morehead and we bouth lived with him till the last civil war and I joined the 8th Ky. Cavelry, U. S. and Thomas Morehead a infantry Regiment U. S. I dont know the No. of his Regiment and I did not see him any more until after the war. I am confident there is not as much as 12 or 15 month different in our age. My Mother died when I was about 16 months old and I have often heard Thomas Morehead's Mother say that there was not much difference in our ages.

Thomas Morehead followed each of the letters from James Morehead to the commissioner with letters of his own. "I have give you my age by one who we was boys together," he wrote, referring to James. "We worked together untill the war . . . and we was bouth in the millertery severic." When no increase in his pension was forthcoming, he persisted with a patience that barely hid a tone of exasperation. On September 14, 1908, Morehead wrote once again: "I have give you true reports to my age. You ask me for Bibb evidents but I could not give that, but I give you J. W. Morehead evidents and my mother raise us bouth and that is the best evidents I can give you."

The government's records on Tom Morehead are in some respects quite detailed and descriptive. They indicate that he was a farmer and a carpenter, and that he was five feet eight inches tall, with brown eyes, black hair, and a "yellow" or "light brown" complexion. They even detail his physical problems—afflictions of the liver, heart, bowels, and lower back.

But the pension commissioner apparently could not ascertain to his satisfaction the old soldier's eligibility for higher benefits. It was not until a year before he died at the age of seventy-five in 1913 that the pension office finally accepted his word and the word of James W. Morehead that Thomas was the age he claimed to be. Accordingly, the weary veteran of the 129th U.S. Colored Infantry had his pension raised to the lofty sum of twenty dollars per month.

During his two years of retirement from boxing, Muhammad Ali turned his hand to more pacific endeavors, among them acting and diplomacy. In "Freedom Road," a television movie adaptation of the Howard Fast novel by that name, he played the part of Gideon Jackson, a black veteran of the Union army who struggled on against racial discrimination in the South after the war. More recently, Ali went on a brief but highly publicized goodwill mission to Africa on behalf of the Carter administration. During neither experience was he aware that one of his own ancestors had been a soldier for the Union, or that others, farther back, may have been among a small group of free blacks who journeyed to Africa from a small town in Kentucky.

Now the restless fighter is preparing for battle once more. Having refused to quit a loser after his defeat by Leon Spinks in 1978 and having retired as the only three-time heavyweight champion after conquering Spinks in a rematch, his return to action now is puzzling. He is inching toward forty, an ancient age for a boxer, but the principal source of his wealth and fame and the focus of his greatest glory still beckons him irresistibly: an elevated canvas ring, twenty feet square, rope-bordered, surrounded by a screaming throng—and inside the ropes with him, one last man to overcome, one more opponent standing between him and safety. The seductive whisper lingers in his ear: one more fight, one more victory, one more unmatched and unmatchable achievement. It is almost as if he cannot quit a winner.

"I'm shooting for immortality," Ali has said repeatedly. "I want to be the only four-time world champion."

"Aren't you already immortal?" a reporter asked him recently.

"Yeah," Ali replied, "but not immortal enough."

So he is fighting on against heavy odds, risking security for a dream—and in that show of determination and stubbornness and courage, perhaps there is a spark of Tom Morehead, of the Clays and Greathouses and Bibbs and Gradys and all the others from whom he came.

"You can't know about yourself, or what makes you the way you are," Muhammad Ali said. "I'm a part of my ancestors, and they're a part of me. Maybe some of what I am, what I do, goes back to those people. Maybe it's them, coming out in me."

Muhammad Ali lost his October 2, 1980, title fight with heavyweight champion Larry Holmes by a technical knockout in the tenth round, and thus ended the sparkling twenty-year career of the most dominant figure in boxing history. Now, more than a decade later, as he nears his fiftieth birthday (in 1992), Ali is still an exceedingly popular public personality in American life. The man with the "most recognized name and face in the world" still lays claim to a charmingly immodest and distinctive title: The Greatest.

**CLAUDE PEPPER'S
LAST CRUSADE**

*Longevity and liberalism combined to give Claude
Pepper a singular role in Southern politics for fully
half of the twentieth century. His last crusade was a
spirited fight for the rights of the elderly. This profile
of the Florida congressman appeared in the November 29, 1981, issue of the* New York Times Magazine.

If ever a constituency could be ex-
pected to belong to a public official, the twenty-five million Americans
aged sixty-five and over should belong to Ronald Reagan. At seventy,
he is one of them, the oldest person ever to be elected to the White
House. Millions of older Americans share the general tenets of his
conservative Republican political philosophy. He is an attractive and
glamorous man, a personification of usefulness and productivity in
later life, an inspiration to old and young alike.

But Mr. Reagan has serious competition for the loyalty of the elderly—and, indirectly, for their votes. It comes from a short, homely
looking, outspoken, and indefatigable congressman from Florida,
eighty-one-year-old Claude Pepper of Miami. A New Deal Democrat
and an unwavering liberal from the day he first gained a seat in the
U.S. Senate in 1936, he is now the oldest member of either house of
Congress. He is also chairman of the House Select Committee on Aging and is widely regarded as the leading congressional authority
on—and advocate of—federal assistance to the elderly.

When the third decennial White House Conference on Aging begins its four-day meeting in Washington tomorrow, the twenty-two
hundred voting delegates will be primed for a clash between the Reagan and Pepper philosophies, if not a confrontation between the two
men themselves. Pepper will not only be a featured speaker but also

plans to attend every session of the conference. President Reagan has also been invited to address the delegates, as his Republican predecessors Dwight Eisenhower and Richard Nixon did when the first two conferences were held in 1961 and 1971.

The curious fact that Reagan and Pepper have never met only adds more drama to the prospect of their appearance at this forum, and their sharply contrasting reputations precede them like advertisements for a prize fight. At a meeting of Pepper's committee a few weeks ago, some White House Conference delegates charged—as Pepper himself had previously—that the Reagan administration, through the Republican National Committee, was attempting to "sabotage" the conference, as a means of blunting criticism sure to be expressed there against presidential budget cuts affecting the elderly. A highly placed Reagan aide added fuel to the fire by calling Pepper "the perfect embodiment of the Democratic philosophy of big spending that has almost destroyed this nation's economy." Pepper responded in kind by excoriating the president's economic policies as "a blueprint for disaster" that will "bring shame to our nation and misery to millions of older Americans."

In what might best be characterized as the long and colorful autumn of his remarkable career, Claude Pepper has made a special constituency of the nation's older population. In doing so, he has often pictured conservatives in general and the Reagan White House in particular as heartless exploiters of the aged, the infirm, the disabled, the poor. Vexed Republicans have alternately ignored the congressman, dismissed him as a toothless tiger, denounced him as a demagogue—and Mr. Pepper, with consummate oratorical skill and the benefit of a half-century of experience in public life, has responded by stepping up his attacks on the administration's budget cuts, its proposals to reduce Social Security benefits, and its "multibillion-dollar tax transfer to the rich."

The White House Conference on Aging is not the only forum in which the Reagan and Pepper schools of thought will be joined in battle in the months ahead. The congressman has been chosen by Speaker Thomas P. O'Neill to represent House Democrats on the fifteen-member bipartisan Social Security review commission proposed by President Reagan. And if the Democrats retain control of the House in next year's elections, Pepper will be in line to become chairman of the powerful House Rules Committee and thus will control what legislation goes, or doesn't go, to the House floor for a vote.

And so, from opposite ends of the American political spectrum, the president and the gentleman from Florida have come to center stage as perhaps the two most prominent and powerful public figures in the lives of the nation's senior citizens. However direct the confrontation between the two men turns out to be, the symbolic imagery it inspires is exquisite: a political "High Noon" in the streets of Washington, a classic showdown on Pennsylvania Avenue, with two battle-wise and utterly fearless old men striding toward a fight to the finish for the favor of widows and orphans and sundry other defenseless souls.

Mr. Reagan has not yet directly acknowledged his adversary. Mr. Pepper, for his part, is waiting calmly. "I have no ill will against the president," he says, "but his has been the most reactionary voice in public life for the past fifteen years. He is an affable man with foolish, dangerous ideas. When the two positions we represent come into conflict, as they inevitably will, it will be an interesting fight, and I look forward to it. In fact, I'll relish it."

Pepper's long-time colleague from Miami, Congressman Dante Fascell, says he "can't see Claude losing this battle. He's been around for a long time, and he understands the dynamics of politics, the fine points of positioning and timing. Claude doesn't fall into traps—he might spring a few, but he won't get caught in any. If the president insists on a major overhaul of the Social Security system, I think he'll have to back down. If I were a betting man, I'd put my money on Pepper."

Two weeks after President Reagan's inauguration last January, the Select Committee on Aging presented a briefing for members of the House on "the status of the elderly in America." Citing statistics from a variety of government sources, Chairman Pepper asserted that 15.7 percent of the elderly—nearly four million people—have incomes below the poverty line (pegged at $3,941 for single, elderly individuals); 60 percent would be in those circumstances were it not for Social Security; and more than 75 percent of all senior citizens presently have incomes of less than $7,000 a year. Medicare, Pepper told his colleagues, is estimated to pay only about 38 percent of the health bills of the elderly, and only "the poorest of the poor" are eligible for Medicaid.

Yet, said Pepper, "there are many voices sounding the call for re-treat. . . . Social Security, they say, must be slashed—and they would say deeply—in order to balance the budget, in order to make it possible to cut the taxes of many . . . who hardly need tax reduction as much as the elderly need the benefits they are receiving. Social Security is the most successful government program in existence in the world today. . . . Social Security is a sacred trust between the American people and their government."

Far from cutting benefit programs, Pepper advocated "a comprehensive legislative package to improve the state of the elderly in America." Among its features would be increased minimum benefits for people who have worked all their lives under Social Security only to find themselves living below the poverty line; increased private pension coverage to compensate for needs not met by Social Security; and expanded coverage and protection under Medicare.

Although he has not spelled out where the money to provide these benefits would come from, Pepper has suggested that most, if not all, of the long-term financial problems of Social Security would be solved if a large portion of the medical expenses now drawn from Social Security funds were to come instead from general tax revenues. He also believes that substantial additional funds would be available if more people were encouraged to postpone retirement, thus reducing the number of elderly drawing from the system while increasing the number still putting money into it.

When Pepper's committee invited David A. Stockman, director of the Office of Management and Budget, to testify last April on what impact the fiscal year 1982 budget cuts would have on the elderly, Stockman presented figures indicating that total federal tax dollars in support of programs for the elderly would actually rise, from $144 billion in 1980 to $191 billion in 1982. "In my view," the budget director said, "it is adequate, it is a generous level of support." He went on to summarize the administration's proposed "economies": elimination of the minimum monthly benefit under Social Security and a phase-out of certain survivor and death benefits.

In his characteristically courtly manner, Mr. Pepper complimented the "distinguished" and "able" and "honorable" Mr. Stockman: "You are very familiar with these figures, of course, and you present them very well. As a matter of fact, if the elderly people had been listening to you they would think you would be conferring a blessing on them by making these cuts." Then Pepper asked: "Are you able to assure us, Mr. Stockman . . . that [these cuts] comply with the assurance the president gave to the people that his program for budget-cutting would not adversely affect the truly needy of the country?"

"I think in the main I can give you that assurance," Stockman replied.

Pepper was unconvinced. In July his committee issued a report claiming that the administration's proposals would result in Social Security benefit reductions of $10.65 billion in fiscal 1982—and over the long run, estimated expenditures for the program would be cut by 23 percent.

"They want to make a raid on the Social Security trust funds to finance their own programs and balance the federal budget," Pepper said later. "I'm going to fight like the devil to prevent that. Congress may need to make some adjustments in benefits and funding, as it has done fourteen times since the Social Security Act was passed, but the trust funds are not going bankrupt, as the administration claims, and we're not going to cut benefits and take away from the American people the little bit of security they have paid for all their working lives."

When the Social Security Act was first passed by Congress in 1936, payroll workers were taxed twenty dollars a year—1 percent of the first two thousand dollars of their earnings—to finance the system. As the number of recipients has grown and benefits have been expanded, the cost has risen sharply. In 1982 payroll workers will pay 6.7 percent on the first $32,400 of their earnings, for a maximum Social Security tax of $2,170.80, with their employers paying a matching percentage. Self-employed persons will pay 9.35 percent on the first $32,400 of their earnings, for a maximum tax of $3,029.40. Additional increases in the future have already been mandated by Congress.

But in spite of these rising contributions, the three trust funds into which Social Security taxes are paid—the retirement, disability, and health funds—have faced a problem of diminishing reserves in recent years. Opinions differ widely on the causes and possible solutions to the problem. Most experts appear to agree that some relatively simple stop-gap measures, such as borrowing from one of the trust funds to shore up another, will provide temporary relief. But the long-term problem is a demographic one: Whereas 3.2 workers now pay into the system for every beneficiary, in another forty years or so the gradually aging population will have cut that ratio to 2.1, and the trust funds will eventually be exhausted—some say as soon as the year 2025.

There are, at bottom, only two possible solutions to this long-term problem: increased revenue from higher Social Security taxes, or reductions in either the number of recipients or the amount of benefits. Last spring the Reagan administration proposed thirteen different reductions in benefits or recipients, for an estimated saving of more than eighty-eight billion dollars over the next five years. Three of those proposals have now passed into law, but one of them—elimination of the $122-a-month minimum benefit paid to some three million retired persons—has since been partially reinstated after strong public opposition caused Congress and the White House to reconsider.

It has been the position of the Democratic leadership in the House of Representatives that major surgery is not needed to cure the ailing Social Security system—that interfund borrowing and perhaps partial funding of the health trust fund from general revenues will correct the problem. Congressman Pepper has been a stalwart supporter of that position—some would say the originator of it. Some Democrats—notably J. J. Pickle of Texas, chairman of the House subcommittee on Social Security—have proposed raising the retirement age of beneficiaries and lowering the automatic cost-of-living increases they receive annually as compromise measures to correct the long-term deficit prospect. But for the moment, the party leaders and Mr. Pepper are arguing that such compromises are not necessary; indeed, says Pepper, "changes of this magnitude would amount to a capitulation to the administration and a breach of faith with the elderly."

In the White House, Pepper is viewed as a serious impediment to the administration's plan to achieve a balanced budget. "He's got a safe issue—nobody can be against old people," says a high-ranking official there. "And, he's got a committee that's stacked with people who won't face the hard choices this country is up against. Committees of that kind explain why the Democrats lost so heavily last year. They're undisciplined big spenders, and Pepper may be the worst of the lot. Everyone admires him greatly for his courage and vitality, but if his view prevails on the funding of entitlement programs for the elderly, the long-term implications are frightening. There's no way this country can afford such enormous expenditures."

Such comments bring a knowing smile to the congressman's face. "I think we have a defensible position," he says confidently. "I refuse to believe a country as rich and powerful as ours can't afford to guarantee the basic comfort and security of its older citizens. I know we can do it—and I intend to be long and loud about it."

Throughout his fourteen years as a senator and nineteen as a member of the House—sandwiched around a twelve-year law practice—Claude Pepper has always spoken his mind. His Washington career encompasses the administrations of nine presidents. He was a bellwether for Franklin Roosevelt, a headache for Harry Truman, a loyal opponent of Dwight Eisenhower, a nemesis of Richard Nixon, a valuable ally of John Kennedy, Lyndon Johnson, and Jimmy Carter. He has had private audiences with popes and kings and private interviews with such giants of history as Joseph Stalin and Winston Churchill. He has hunted birds with Bernard Baruch and drafted bills with Walter Lippmann. He has been branded a warmonger, a peacenik, a Communist, a nigger-lover. He was a Cold War victim of McCarthyism before the rise of Joe McCarthy—and later a resurrected freshman in the House, a survivor of slander, at an age when most people are winding down toward retirement.

Mr. Pepper is an anomaly: a Southern liberal in an age of conservatism, a surviving Democrat in a sea of Republicans, a vigorous old man among generally much younger colleagues. Now, with most of his contemporaries of the 1930s either in their dotage or gone altogether, he is embarked on a civil rights crusade in behalf of a class of citizens to which he himself belongs. "Ageism is as odious as racism and sexism," he declares, and with the energy of a man half his age, he scurries about like an octogenarian Paul Revere, calling people of advanced years to their own defense and demanding that the rest of the population recognize their rights and their worth.

"All his life Pepper has been a partisan," a *Saturday Evening Post* writer said of him in 1946. He has always been known as a liberal, too—and that in itself is anomalous, considering his background.

He was born Claude Denson Pepper, the oldest of five children in a family of yeoman farmers, near Dudleyville, Alabama, in the first year of this century. Both of his grandfathers fought for the Confederacy. Amid the poverty of their time and place, his parents could be thought of as middle class—they were small-plot landowners, mainline Baptists, loyal Democrats. In 1910 the family moved a few miles west to the Tallapoosa County town of Camp Hill, where Pepper's father was first a merchant and later the police chief, and Claude finished high school there in 1917.

After a brief succession of jobs as a hat blocker, a schoolteacher, and a steelworker, he entered the University of Alabama in 1918 and graduated three years later, having also become a military veteran by virtue of his brief wartime induction into the Student Army Training Corps. He lost his first political contest at the university, too—a bid to be president of the student body. "From the time I was fifteen," he recalls, "I wanted to be in public life." His interest in oratory, debate, and campus politics throughout his school years won him the nickname Senator—a title he later earned and still carries among friends and members of his staff.

Pepper went from the University of Alabama to Harvard Law School, and he never again lived in his native state. After Harvard, he taught for a year in the University of Arkansas Law School (J. William Fulbright, later a fellow senator, was one of his students there), and in 1925 he borrowed three hundred dollars to finance a move to Perry, Florida, and a start in law practice.

Three years later Pepper won a house seat in the Florida legislature and campaigned for Al Smith, the Democratic presidential nominee. During his term in the legislature, he voted against a resolution condemning Mrs. Herbert Hoover for inviting the wife of a black congressman to a White House tea, and his Perry constituents promptly turned him out of office in 1930. The young politician's luck was not all bad, though; the following year he met Mildred Webster of St. Petersburg, "a beautiful girl in a yellow dress," and five years later they were married.

Pepper ran in 1934 against a popular but inactive U.S. senator, Park Trammell, and lost in a primary runoff by just four thousand votes. Two years later, after the other Florida senator, Duncan Fletcher, died suddenly, Pepper was nominated by his party to finish Fletcher's term. He was subsequently elected to full terms in 1938 and 1944.

"If you want to know about Claude Pepper," says Jack Ossofsky, executive director of the National Council on Aging, "go back and read his maiden speech in the Senate in 1937. He could give that speech today and it would be relevant. He is deeply respected now for the consistency of his concern."

In that first speech, the young senator was responding to the assertion of a colleague that economic recovery from the Great Depression had been achieved, and the time had come to cut costly New Deal programs in order to erase the national debt and balance the federal budget. Noting the short life of "the idealistic impulse," Pepper expressed a suspicion that "even here in this body the old sentiments of conservatism . . . are beginning to reassert themselves." And, he went on, "when we talk about more housing, when we talk about more jobs, when we talk about the improvement of public health . . . the timid or the fearful, the recalcitrant or the selfish, get in the way of the program, and they decide suddenly that it is better not to go ahead."

Such convictions quickly caught the attention of President Roosevelt, and he and the young senator soon established a strong bond of mutual admiration. "If I knew anything," Pepper recalls, "I knew the South needed help, and Roosevelt was our only chance to get it. He inspired me, and I wanted to be identified with him." Having arrived in Washington favoring old-age pensions and federal aid to education, it was a natural progression for the senator to become an early advocate of Social Security, minimum wage and hour laws, and national health insurance. Before his easy election victory in 1938, his picture was on the cover of *Time* magazine above a line that read, "A Florida fighting cock will be a White House weather-vane."

Pepper went to Europe in the fall of 1938 and came back advocating support of England and France against Hitler and preparedness for war at home. When he proposed a national military draft in 1940, angry isolationists denounced him as a traitor and hanged him in effigy on the Capitol grounds. A year later he almost single-handedly persuaded the Senate to support lend-lease aid to the European allies (columnist Walter Lippmann secretly helped him with the final draft of the bill). But somehow, his advocacy of social programs and military preparedness, while it provoked controversy among conservatives and isolationists, was not enough to get him into deep trouble at home. (Then as now, says his House colleague Sam Gibbons of Tampa, "Claude was an effective, well-organized servant of his constituents.") His reelection in 1944 was not a landslide, but he did manage to win by a margin of ten thousand votes.

Pepper went back to Europe after the war, meeting with Churchill, Eisenhower, and Stalin. He praised the Soviet leader and, because Moscow had been an ally, advocated a Marshall plan of sorts for war-torn Russia. He later called for the destruction of all atom bombs as the surest way to prevent nuclear war. He was an early backer of Henry Wallace for president in 1948, but when the left-wing former secretary of agriculture went the third-party route, Pepper, who had always done his fighting within the party, quickly left him and pleaded with Eisenhower to seek the Democratic nomination. When that failed, he briefly announced as a candidate himself before finally coming around to support Harry Truman. In those volatile times Pepper seemed to bounce from one controversy to another; he opposed the union-regulating Taft-Hartley bill, supported anti–poll tax measures, and advocated laws to guarantee fair employment practices.

It was all finally too much for the liberal senator's enemies. In 1950, led by the giant DuPont empire's Florida boss, Edward Ball, and with help from such groups and individuals as the American Medical Association, the U.S. Chamber of Commerce, former ambassador Joseph P. Kennedy, Senator Spessard Holland, and possibly President Truman himself, the anti-Pepper forces sought and found a candidate to run against him. Their chosen man was a tall, handsome young congressman and Pepper protégé named George Smathers.

⸎

Claude Pepper ruefully remembers helping George Smathers get his first job out of law school—an assistant district attorney's post in Miami. Later, Pepper and Thomas G. Corcoran, a long-time Roosevelt crony, interceded with the secretary of defense to get Smathers released from the Marine Corps so he could run in 1946 for a Florida congressional seat. "Smathers had been a Pepper man up until then," Corcoran recalls, "but after he was elected to the House a couple of times, he flipped over and ran against Pepper—and Joe Kennedy was one of his chief backers."

Robert Sherrill, in his book *Gothic Politics in the Deep South,* called the Pepper-Smathers race "the most elaborate crusade of political annihilation ever conducted in southern politics." Among its features were a widely circulated photograph of Senator Pepper standing beside singer Paul Robeson, who was black and blunt and publicly accused of being associated with Communist causes. In the closing days of the campaign, a booklet called *The Red Record of Senator Claude Pepper* was distributed all over the state; even Ralph McGill, the liberal Atlanta columnist and editor, chipped in with an article in the *Saturday Evening Post* praising Smathers and painting Pepper in unflattering shades of red. (It was the *Post* that in 1946 had labeled the senator "pink," leading to his inevitable defamatory designation as Red Pepper.) McGill later said he regretted his part in Pepper's demise, but the damage had been done.

Smathers won the bruising primary battle by sixty-seven thousand votes and went on to serve three terms in the Senate. Since 1969 he has been a lawyer and lobbyist in Washington. His remembrance of the 1950 campaign—and of Claude Pepper—has mellowed with time.

"It was a good, tough campaign," says Smathers. "I never said a lot of the stuff about Claude that was attributed to me. Harry Truman asked me to run against Claude and get him out of the Senate, and I finally agreed to try. I thought Claude was way off track. I felt he was soft on Stalin—he was wrong on a lot of things that gave comfort to the Communists. I said it then, and I still say it. But that was a long time ago, and now, happily, fortunately, we're friendly when we see each other. He's a remarkable man. There's nobody who can better speak for the aged than Claude. He can carry the fight on Social Security, and I'd be happy to see him do it. I think he and President Reagan will have a meeting of the minds. Claude just gets better with age, like a good wine—and now he's the right man in the right place at the right time."

Pepper responds to the assertion that President Truman was behind the Smathers campaign against him by saying, "I never had any reason to believe that. If it's true, the president lied to me, because he led me to believe he was working behind the scenes to help me." Tommy Corcoran, who has been a close friend of Pepper's since they were in law school together at Harvard, says he "wouldn't be surprised if Truman put Smathers up to the race" but adds that he has no proof of it. "I do know, though," he says, "that Truman once spoke of Claude and me as 'two SOB's who should be kicked out of the Democratic party.' I think he and Joe Kennedy were both against Pepper. In politics, there's no such thing as personal loyalty."

In spite of the pervasive campaign against him, Pepper believed until the end that he would squeeze past Smathers. "Of all the people close to me," he recalls, "my wife Mildred was the only one who told me I was losing. I found it hard to believe. Now, looking back, I find it hard to believe I came as close as I did. It was a vicious campaign, a smear campaign of innuendo and guilt by association. Richard Nixon started the trend in 1946, the year he and Smathers were elected to the House. Later, that low style of smear tactics personified McCarthyism, but Joe McCarthy didn't invent it—Nixon did, and Smathers refined it."

With a sizable debt and little income, Pepper returned to Florida and resumed the practice of law. He opened an office in Tallahassee, then another in Washington and a third in Miami, where he eventually took up residence. In spite of his left-wing reputation, he attracted well-heeled clients (Westinghouse, Bethlehem Steel, *Time* magazine). He also became a partner in a savings and loan association. In 1958 he tried to unseat Senator Spessard Holland, an archconservative, but failed by more than fifty thousand votes. "I was out of politics," he says, "but I was doing all right otherwise. Our law firm had nine lawyers by 1960, and my income was up to about $150,000 a year."

Through it all Pepper remained a loyal and active Democrat, working for Adlai Stevenson, for Joe Kennedy's son Jack, and later for Lyndon Johnson, Hubert Humphrey, George McGovern, and Jimmy Carter. In the meantime the 1960 census gave Dade County and Miami an additional House seat, and Pepper won it in a crowded field in the 1962 election. The district is a mostly Democratic mélange of retirees, white-collar and blue-collar workers, Hispanics, blacks, and relocated New Yorkers. It includes parts of Miami Beach, the Cuban and Haitian refugee communities, and the troubled black ghetto of Liberty City. In that diverse mixture of humanity, Pepper has felt right at home, winning reelection nine times without serious opposition. Even in 1972, when Richard Nixon reached Republican high tide in Dade County with 60 percent of the vote, the congressman got 63 percent against his own Republican opponent, and in 1980, he beat a Cuban-American Republican by a three-to-one margin.

The story of the rise and fall and rise again of Claude Pepper covers so many years that it has a quality of timelessness, as if his tenure in Congress had no beginning. Few people seem to remember how controversial he once was. Democrats and Republicans alike praise his gracious manner, his wit and wisdom, his political skill, his staying power. "He is the quintessence of a good public servant," says Congressman Pickle of Texas. "He'll always be Lord Chesterfield to us."

Representative Millicent Fenwick of New Jersey, a member of Pepper's committee on aging, lauds him as "a dear, kindly, gallant gentleman whose concern for the elderly is absolutely genuine. Some feel he goes too far in his zeal, but none doubt his sincerity or his influence. Any debate on the future of Social Security in this country has to include him. Others may be more expert on actuarial tables and taxes, but someone has to speak for the heart. Claude speaks for the heart." In a similar vein, Maggie Kuhn, leader of the Gray Panthers, says Pepper "is not a special pleader for the elderly but an advocate of social justice for the whole society. He sees and serves the larger constituency. He's an amazing person."

Two freshman House members young enough to be Pepper's grandchildren compliment him from opposite sides of the aisle. Republican John LeBoutillier of New York, at age twenty-eight the youngest member of Congress, says the administration "really blew it last spring when they suggested cuts in Social Security. They've never recovered from that. They gave Pepper the ammunition to beat them with, and he has made the most of it. He's a very able politician who has made his age an asset." Democrat Ron Wyden of Oregon, age thirty-two, was working in legal and social programs for the elderly when he first met Pepper. "The opportunity to serve with him was a major reason I decided to run for Congress," he says. "He's a bulldog for the elderly, a passionately committed defender. He's an inspiration."

New York Democrat Mario Biaggi, a House colleague of Pepper's since 1968, praises him as "a Southern gentleman in the best sense of the term. He's a man of integrity and principle. In the earlier years of his career, when anything less than vocal and vigorous defense of white supremacy was political suicide for a Southern politician, he still managed to speak and act in opposition to racism. I think he is greatly appreciated among all minorities now for his humanitarian concerns."

Indiana Democrat Andrew Jacobs served with Pepper in 1967 on a special committee appointed to consider sanctions against New York congressman Adam Clayton Powell for his documented offenses against the rules of the House. Jacobs, who later wrote a book about the episode, remembers Pepper as "taking a harder line for ouster" than the other members of the committee: "He was the only Southerner among the nine members, and it was a time of great emotion on the race issue, and Powell was a black man whose flaunted indiscretions outraged many whites. Pepper, perhaps with an eye on the folks back home, advocated Powell's expulsion, but he finally agreed to a unanimous committee recommendation of fines and censure— and then the House voted to deny Powell his seat anyway. Considering the times, I think it would be unfair to use Claude's performance

159

in that case as a measure of his true feelings on race. Without knowing in detail what positions he took earlier in his career, I can say now
that he is a breathtakingly articulate champion of the elderly poor of
all races, and no one doubts the depth of his commitment."

James Southerland, once a top administrative aide on Pepper's
staff, says the congressman "was persuaded by me and others" to seek
Powell's ouster: "He had voted for all the 1960s civil rights legislation
and somehow kept the favor of his constituents, but we felt it would
be disastrous for him not to take a hard line on Powell. In my opinion,
his doing so enabled him later that year to cast a decisive vote in favor
of open housing legislation in the House Rules Committee."

As he himself recalls, Congressman Pepper was in favor of Adam
Clayton Powell's expulsion "not because he was black but because he
was corrupt. He was an extremely intelligent and able man who
squandered his great talent." As for the other positions he took on
civil rights issues, Pepper remembers one in particular that he regrets: "In 1938 I filibustered for eleven hours against a bill to make
lynching a federal offense. It was the last time I ever opposed a civil
rights measure." Even so, more than twenty years later, in his futile
attempt to unseat the segregationist senator Holland, Pepper
struggled uncomfortably to avoid being branded as an integrationist.
It was not until he returned to Congress in 1962 that he was able to
stake out an unequivocal position on racial issues.

Democrat Harold Ford of Tennessee, a member of the committee
on aging and of the Congressional Black Caucus, has worked closely
with Pepper for seven years. "I have watched him in action," Ford
says, "and we have campaigned for each other, and all I've ever seen
is a genuine man, an articulate, dedicated warrior for the poor and
the elderly. I don't think race enters into it with him. He's solid for all
who are old and poor."

Since his early years in the Senate, Mr. Pepper has practiced a style
of liberalism that skillfully blends pragmatic and idealistic concerns.
He was instrumental in the creation of the National Science Foundation and the government's cancer research programs; he has given
strong support to Cuban refugees and has regularly denounced the
Castro regime in Cuba; he has sought middle ground on the issues
of gun control and abortion; he was not an early critic of the war in

Vietnam; he has voted consistently for the military budgets proposed by the House Armed Services Committee, in the firm belief that the nation can afford both guns and butter. In general, he is a proponent of government activism as the surest and fairest way to peace and prosperity, much as Lyndon Johnson and Franklin Roosevelt were.

Now, as an octogenarian, his activism has found sharp focus in the concerns of the nation's older citizens. In recent years he has introduced legislation to abolish mandatory retirement, to fight crime in housing projects for the elderly, to cut Amtrak fares for senior citizens, to make nutritious meals available to the elderly. His committee on aging, though it lacks the power to draft legislation, had kept up a steady schedule of hearings on subjects of wide-ranging interest to older people. His staff-written newspaper column, "Questions and Answers on Aging: Ask Congressman Pepper," is now syndicated in more than seven hundred papers all over the country.

"We all look to him," says William Hutton, executive director of the National Council of Senior Citizens. "He's the focal point of the older American's interests in Congress. Since his wife died, he has lived completely for his job. He's the nearest thing this country has to a national congressman."

Mildred Pepper's death from cancer in 1979 ended what Congressman Dante Fascell called "a true love match." The couple, who were childless, had been virtually inseparable for forty-two years. At Florida State University in Tallahassee, the Mildred and Claude Pepper Library has been established to house their papers—and hers, the congressman says, "are as important as mine. She was a very active and involved person."

After a period of adjustment to his wife's death, Mr. Pepper resumed his full schedule, staying on in the modest Washington apartment they had occupied for a number of years. He typically works nine-hour days on Capitol Hill, attends numerous evening functions, and returns to Miami almost every weekend to "be available" to his constituents. And increasingly, he is immersed in the last crusade on his agenda: the welfare of the elderly. He expects the job to keep him busy indefinitely. "I hate to think I'll have to quit someday," he says. "My goal is to see this century out—and get the next one off to a good start—before I give any thought to retiring."

Claude Pepper's gray eyes scanned the headlines of his morning paper. Over a light breakfast in his condominium on Biscayne Bay during a recent weekend visit to Miami, he was gearing up for a busy day out among the voters. He tossed down his breakfast napkin and chuckled.

"Mr. Reagan says the economy is in recession," he sneered. "Well, well. I wonder who told him. Mr. Stockman, I guess." The elder statesman's amusement was short-lived: "How in the world he could be seventy years old and have so little feeling for the elderly, I'll never know. He seems to have no compassion. He disdains the poor."

At the White House, aides of the president are equally as puzzled, as one of them put it, that "after fifty years of government profligacy, the Claude Peppers of this world still want more. Their idea of serving is simply to spend more money. That's not a solution to this country's problems—it's the primary cause of them."

The fundamental clash of philosophies approaches once again: private enterprise versus government activism, Reaganomics versus "the Claude Peppers of this world," perhaps even Ronnie versus Claude.

Comedian Bob Hope, who is seventy-eight, may be the one and only close friend of both men. "I admire them both very much," he says—but not even for laughs will he "get into the political side" of the differences between his two friends. Those differences will soon require resolution—and the outcome will determine the nation's response to its older citizens for years to come.

It seems fitting that two public servants of advanced age should have so much to do with the settling of this issue. They are both certainly equal to the challenge, mentally and physically. Mr. Reagan's health has been one of his great strengths. Mr. Pepper, though he is eleven years older than the president, seems equally fit. For exercise, he plays eighteen holes of golf every week or two, pedals a stationary bicycle in his apartment on rainy weekends, and walks farther and faster than any member of his staff.

On the first Saturday in October, doctors at Walter Reed Hospital in Washington inserted a pacemaker under Claude Pepper's skin. It was, he says, "a preventive maintenance measure to keep my heart strong." Two days later he was back on the floor of the House to support a bill extending the life of the Voting Rights Act. Then he was off to Florida for a busy week of speeches and public appearances.

"I asked my doctor how long the battery in this thing would last," he remarked later, patting his chest. "He said it was good for about ten years. I told him I'd just take three of them with me now, and come back for more later if I needed them."

Claude Denson Pepper died of cancer at Walter Reed Army Medical Center in Washington on May 30, 1989. He was eighty-eight years old and had spent almost half of his life representing Florida in the U.S. Congress.

∾ MAURICE MAYS AND THE KNOXVILLE RACE RIOT OF 1919

The crime for which Maurice Mays was charged and eventually convicted set off what the Tennessee history books call the Knoxville race riot of 1919. In truth, it would be more accurate to describe what happened after the murder of Bertie Lindsey as a lynch mob's invasion of a black section of the city. The murder, the white reaction, the trial (a transcript of which was preserved), and the eventual outcome and consequences were full of dramatic surprises and ironic twists. This reconstruction of the events was published in the July–August 1983 issue of Southern Exposure.

T he administration of capital punishment in America has taken many forms since the beginning of European colonization almost four hundred years ago. Convicted criminals have been put to death by beheading, strangling, burning, pressing, sawing, hanging, shooting, gassing, poisoning, asphyxiation, electrocution, and lethal injection. No complete records exist to show how many people have been legally executed, but Watt Espy, a researcher in the University of Alabama Law Library, has found documentation for more than 13,500 official killings dating back into the early colonial period.

These should not be confused with lynchings, or illegal and unofficial executions. Statistics compiled at Tuskegee Institute indicate that an average of 146 lynchings a year took place in the United States in the last two decades of the nineteenth century, and that 1,799 blacks and 196 whites were lynched between 1900 and 1962. The overwhelming majority of lynch victims throughout our history have been black males put to death in the Southern and border states. Nine states, all Southern, accounted for more than two hundred lynchings each between 1882 and 1962; the total number of such killings in those same states during that eighty-year period exceeded thirty-three hundred.

A rough correlation can be seen between the prevalence of lynchings and official executions within a given state. Tennessee, for example, is one of the nine states in which two hundred or more lynchings have occurred (of 204 blacks and 47 whites, to be specific), and it is also a typical Southern state with respect to capital punishment. Espy's research shows that nearly two hundred people, a majority of them black, were legally hanged in the state before 1913. In that year an electric chair was installed at the main penitentiary in Nashville. The Tennessee legislature abolished capital punishment in 1915 but reinstated it four years later. Since then, the state, which is 85 percent white, has electrocuted eighty-six blacks and thirty-eight whites, all of them males from the bottom end of the socioeconomic scale. (Due to legal challenges and other complications surrounding the practice of capital punishment, there has not been an electrocution in Tennessee since 1961.)

Twelve of the 124 Tennessee offenders to die in the electric chair—eight blacks, four whites—were residents of Knox County, which is more than 90 percent white. One of those Knox Countians, the eighteenth man to be put to death in the state's electric chair, was thirty-four-year-old Maurice Mays, a black man from Knoxville; he was pronounced dead at 6:16 A.M. on Wednesday, March 15, 1922.

This is an account, pieced together from the public record and from other sources, of the life and death of Maurice Mays.

The Times

Since the Civil War, Negroes in east Tennessee had been celebrating freedom. We had a history of thinking we lived among the best white people in the South. But when the summer of 1919 came around, we found out it wasn't true.
—Ninety-eight-year-old Y. D. Bryant of Knoxville, in a 1982 interview

August 1919:

Fresh from a resounding victory in the war to make the world "safe for democracy," the United States seemed headed for an era of social progress on the domestic front, and Tennessee was a willing partner in the march. Across the country, public education was reaching the masses; automobiles were replacing buggies, and paved roads were extending in all directions to accommodate them; the Eighteenth Amendment to the U.S. Constitution had been ratified as a national response to alcohol abuse, and the Nineteenth Amendment, giving women the right to vote, had been passed by both houses of Congress. Even the sensitive issue of race relations was receiving some attention, in part because black war veterans who had risked their lives for democracy were determined to share in its fruits.

Tennessee was not laggard. For nearly two decades the state had been rushing to reach all its children with public schools. It had more than seventy-five thousand automobiles—triple the number just three years earlier—and the development of a highway network was deemed second in importance only to the education program. Prohibition had been a statewide legal requirement since 1909. Women were already allowed to vote in state and local elections—and Tennessee in 1920 would become the state whose ratification of the suffrage amendment would make it the law of the land.

White moderates on the race issue in Tennessee (there being no liberals or radicals of note) were encouraged by the fact that lynchings and other atrocities by white mobs had declined from ten a year to two, on the average, since the turn of the century. The Law and Order League had been organized by a group of white citizens in 1918 to "combat the evils of lawlessness"—particularly lynching. And when Chicago was staggered by an outburst of racial violence in July 1919, Tennessee governor Albert H. Roberts welcomed black refugees from that city with these words: "We need the Negro here, and I do not fear that Tennessee will ever be the scene of such troubles as are now existing in Chicago."

Like the rest of the South, Tennessee lived by a rigid set of segregation laws and customs, but the self-image its white majority liked to cultivate was one of patient and kindly paternalism toward the lowly black race. White supremacy was simply taken for granted, as if it were a divine right, and as long as blacks were submissive to the status quo, unprovoked acts of aggression against them were publicly frowned upon as unkind, unwise, and unnecessary.

The state did not legally deny blacks the right to vote; rather, it discouraged them with poll taxes and party primaries that strongly favored whites. Likewise, educational opportunity for blacks was not denied, so long as it was dispensed in isolation from whites. The most benevolent white citizens of Tennessee in the postwar period tended to be outspokenly opposed to lynching and other lawless acts, supportive of black legal rights within the bounds of segregation, and fearful of just two things: the social elevation of nonwhite men and women, individually or collectively, into the exclusive realm of the majority race, and the prospect—even the hint—of sexual attraction between black men and white women. (Sexual contact between white men and black women was a widespread and long-standing occurrence at that time, though the subject was almost never acknowledged publicly.)

If Tennessee thought of itself as different—more segregationist than its Yankee neighbors, but more tolerant and charitable than its Rebel cousins—then Knoxville could claim to be the most different of its cities. It was an urban oasis in the mountains, a busy city of brick streets and electric trolleys and bustling commerce, of telephones and theaters and trains, of people in rich and motley assortment. "Staid old Knoxville," as an out-of-town editorial writer called it, was the principal city in a region of the state that had stood with Lincoln and the Union in the Civil War, a region that remained staunchly Republican. The city's eighty thousand people included fewer than twelve thousand blacks—not even half as many proportionally as Memphis or Nashville or Chattanooga. The state university was also there, and it lent an air of serious and responsible maturity.

The last place anyone—least of all a Knoxvillian—might have looked for signs of impending racial violence was surely in this east Tennessee community where Mayor John E. McMillan, a Democrat, had denounced the Ku Klux Klan and gained a following among blacks as well as whites. The formation of a local branch of the National Association for the Advancement of Colored People—considered a radical and possibly subversive group by many whites, even in the North—may have given Knoxville's white establishment some cause for concern, but the chapter was small and ineffectual, and it included none of the recognized local black leadership.

White Knoxville was quiet and complacent, proud of its supposed tolerance, sure of its basic goodness. Only an outrageous and sensational breach of racial laws and mores could have provoked either blacks or whites into violence—or so it seemed.

But then, in the early hours of Saturday morning, August 30, 1919, a young white woman was shot and killed in the bedroom of her home, and before dawn a black man had been arrested and charged with the crime. Within hours the complacency of Governor Roberts and other white Tennesseans was shattered, and the peace of Knoxville was no more.

The Crime

Bertie Smyth was twenty-three years old when she moved to Knoxville from the mountains of southwest Virginia in 1915. That same year she met Daniel B. Lindsey, a twenty-one-year-old carpenter and a migrant from neighboring Jefferson County. They were married in December 1916, and later they bought a three-room frame house at 1216 Eighth Avenue in north Knoxville.

In late May 1919 Daniel Lindsey left Knoxville for a job in Akron, Ohio. His wife stayed behind, living alone in their home until mid-July, when her twenty-one-year-old first cousin, Ora Smyth, moved in with her from her parents' farm on the Clinton Pike in Knox County.

Several weeks later, as the rainy and humid night of Friday, August 29, edged into the predawn hours of Saturday morning, Bertie Lindsey and Ora Smyth were asleep in a double bed in the front room when someone entered the house. The women were awakened. There was an encounter with the intruder, and then a pistol shot was fired. The bullet struck Bertie Smyth Lindsey in the chest, killing her instantly.

After the intruder had fled, Ora Smyth ran next door to the house of Emmett Dyer, a Knoxville policeman. Her frantic calls roused

Dyer's wife, who let her in. As soon as Ora Smyth had told the couple of the shooting, Dyer called the police station and summoned help. By 2:30 A.M.—less than half an hour after the incident—several officers were on the scene.

One of the policemen responding to the call was thirty-seven-year-old Andy White. He and the others questioned Ora Smyth, who identified the intruder as "a colored man" with a gun in one hand and a flashlight in the other. Patrolman White then got his superior officer's permission to go with three others in search of a man whom White considered a prime suspect. The man's name was Maurice F. Mays.

Maurice Mays, age thirty-one, was a familiar and somewhat controversial figure on the streets of Knoxville. His light complexion, his dapper appearance, and his smooth manner had won him both strong friends and bitter enemies among whites as well as blacks. Handsome and articulate, he was often seen in the company of women of both races. Though he was married, he did not live with his wife—or with his mother and stepfather, Frances and William Mays. He was known to have connections among gamblers and prostitutes, and he was adept at delivering black votes to white politicians. He had a ninth-grade education—above average for blacks in that time and place. He had at one time been a deputy of the Knox County sheriff, with a permit to carry a pistol, and before that, at the age of fifteen, he had been convicted—and subsequently pardoned—for killing another black man.

One white person who especially disliked Maurice Mays was Officer Andy White; on more than one occasion he had been heard to threaten him for associating with white women. One who had a special fondness for him, on the other hand, was Mayor John McMillan; it was rumored about town—and even hinted at in the newspapers—that Maurice Mays was the mayor's illegitimate son.

White and his fellow officers went first to the home of William Mays on Campbell Street, a mile or so from the scene of the crime. There they learned that Maurice Mays had his own house at 313 Humes Street, a few blocks away in the same neighborhood. At 3:30 A.M. the policemen arrived there and found Mays in bed.

He answered their knocking and let them in. White immediately asked to see his pistol, and Mays pointed to a dresser drawer. White opened it and took out the gun, a .38-caliber Smith and Wesson five-shot revolver. It was fully loaded. He sniffed the barrel and then put it back in the dresser. The police asked Mays a few questions, examined his clothing, and then, without telling him the reason for their visit, ordered him to get dressed and come with them.

Mays got into the patrol wagon with White, the other three officers, and William Mays, who had followed them there from his home. They drove to the corner of Eighth Avenue and Gillespie Street, a few houses away from the murder scene. While Mays and his step-father waited there under a streetlight with the other policemen, Andy White went to get Ora Smyth. A few minutes later he led her out of the shadows to within a few feet of Mays and asked her if this was the man she saw kill Bertie Lindsey. She replied that he was. It was the only "lineup" Mays ever got.

Dawn was just breaking as Maurice Mays was taken to the police station and booked for murder. Within hours the one indisputable fact in the case—that a white woman had been shot and killed in her own home—was embellished by an outpouring of rumor and speculation. A "flower of Southern womanhood" had been robbed, possibly raped, and certainly murdered in cold blood—and the man who stood charged with the crime was Maurice Mays, a notorious "bad nigger."

The Riot

By noon milling clusters of agitated white men could be seen and heard reacting to the crime on street corners throughout the central city. Their mood was angry, menacing; trouble was in the wind, as palpable as an impending summer storm. Sheriff W. T. Cate, in consultation with other criminal justice officials, decided to move Mays to a jail in another city for his own safety. The sheriff and some of his deputies then managed to spirit their prisoner away in a heavily guarded automobile to a nearby town, where they caught a train for the one-hundred-mile ride to Chattanooga.

Late in the afternoon the scattered groups of men began to congregate in the downtown market square. Guns were everywhere in evidence. The crowd became a throng, then an angry lynch mob; it swarmed down Market Street in the hot and muggy air, headed for the county jail on Hill Street.

At the jail, leaders of the mob demanded that Mays be released to them. Deputies insisted that he was not there. Three times, delegations of men were allowed to enter and see for themselves that the prisoner had been removed, but the mob was not satisfied. Just before eight o'clock, in the last hour of daylight, fighting broke out in the streets, and shots were fired. Two squads of soldiers from a nearby Tennessee National Guard training camp had been called in to reinforce outnumbered city policemen and sheriff's deputies, but their presence seemed only to fuel the mob's anger. More guardsmen from the same unit—the Fourth Tennessee Infantry—were summoned, but their support was too little and too late. As darkness fell, the mob stormed the jail.

A telephone pole was brought up as a battering ram to smash down the main door to the building, and the mob surged through the hallways. Most of the white prisoners were released, including three under murder charges. The black prisoners were neither freed nor harmed. Law enforcement officials and militiamen defending the facility were quickly overwhelmed. The mob seized from a storeroom a large quantity of confiscated illicit whiskey, as well as all the guns and ammunition available. In the sheriff's adjacent residence and in the jail itself, virtually everything that could not be taken away was vandalized and demolished.

Numerous calls had been made to Governor Roberts in Nashville in the meantime, and he subsequently declared martial law in Knoxville and ordered the entire Fourth Infantry to move in and enforce it. The eleven-hundred-member unit, together with nearly three hundred special policemen and deputies, joined some two hundred Knox County law enforcement officers in the effort, but the mob still outnumbered them.

Responding to rumors that armed blacks were roaming Vine Avenue eight blocks away, the mob turned up Gay Street and headed in that direction. The intersection of Vine and Central avenues was the heart of black Knoxville, the crossroads at which large numbers of blacks commonly gathered in the evenings. While the rampaging whites were smashing windows and taking more guns and ammunition from hardware stores and pawnshops along the way, soldiers rushed to set up machine guns at Vine and Central and at other points in the vicinity.

Accounts vary widely on what happened in the battle that raged there into the night. Officially, the death count was placed at two—a black man, Joe Etter, whose body was found on the street, and a white guardsman, Lieutenant James W. Payne, who was accidentally riddled with machine-gun fire by his own men. Unofficially, the count was much higher; one sheriff's deputy claimed that twenty-five to thirty men were killed.

By dawn, a nervous calm had settled over the empty streets. Throughout the long night and on into the days that followed, the tyranny of the mob was gradually transformed into repression by the military forces, and the effect on the black citizens of Knoxville was devastating. Blacks were placed under a strict curfew, relieved of what civil liberties they had, and subjected to personal abuse by patrolling guardsmen. Homes were entered and searched, sometimes forcibly and always without warrants. All blacks entering the city by train were questioned and searched, and many were mistreated. Hundreds of black residents fled the city, some never to return. Between the violence of the mob and the repression of martial law, black Knoxvillians could hardly make a distinction.

Whites, on the other hand, were generally left alone by the authorities. Thirty-six white leaders of the mob were arrested and charged with felonies, but when they were tried before an all-white jury six weeks later, thirty-one of them were acquitted; the other five were freed after a mistrial was declared in their cases.

The daily newspapers of Knoxville and other Tennessee cities did not bestir themselves to deplore the outburst of white violence. On the contrary, the tone of the news coverage and such editorial comment as there was implied that Maurice Mays was guilty and that the crime was outrageous enough to justify the actions of the mob and the military. One state official, Senator John C. Houk of Knoxville, dismissed the violence as "merely a mob . . . a white mob engaged . . . in disturbing the peace." A month later, when racial violence erupted in the town of Elaine, Arkansas, the Nashville *Tennessean* blamed it on "organizations at work preaching the doctrine of social equality and urging the negroes to stand up for their rights." The *Tennessean* had made no editorial comment at all on Knoxville's tragedy.

But the force of law was much more swift and relentless in the case of Maurice Mays. From the moment of his arrest, he had steadfastly maintained his innocence; the state, with equal steadfastness, moved rapidly to convict and punish him. A grand jury indicted him four days after the crime, declaring that Mays had "unlawfully, feloniously, willfully, deliberately, premeditatedly and maliciously" assaulted and murdered Bertie Smyth Lindsey, "against the peace and dignity of the state." On Wednesday, October 1, 1919, a month after the murder, Case no. 508—*The State* v. *Maurice Mays*—commenced in Knox County criminal court.

The Trial

With Judge T. A. R. Nelson presiding, the names of 520 white men were drawn from the jury pool, and from them twelve were chosen to hear the evidence and decide the guilt or innocence of the defendant. Governor Roberts had appointed former Knoxville mayor S. G. Heiskell as special prosecutor to handle the state's case against Mays. He was assisted by R. A. Mynatt, the district attorney general, and Fred C. Houk, a Knoxville criminal lawyer.

The defense team was headed by Reuben L. Cates, a former district attorney general. His principal assistant, curiously, was Lincoln C. Houk, the father and law partner of prosecutor Fred Houk. (John Houk, the state senator who had dismissed the riot as a mere disturbance of the peace, was Lincoln Houk's brother.) Three others "signed on" as defenders but questioned no witnesses: W. F. Yardley and John W. Huff, two of the three black attorneys then practicing in Knoxville, and James A. Fowler, one of the city's most prominent white citizens. Fowler had run for governor in 1898 and had served as a top official in the U.S. Department of Justice under presidents Roosevelt and Taft from 1908 to 1913.

Clearly, Maurice Mays was not without able counsel. It was widely rumored that the national NAACP was paying for his defense, but the temper of the segregationist times suggests otherwise. Another speculation now seems more plausible: that the white defense attorneys acted out of friendship for—or perhaps with payment from—Mayor John E. McMillan, who was a banker by profession and a man of substantial resources. (The story that Maurice Mays might be McMillan's son was never mentioned at the trial or in press coverage of it, but such allusions had appeared earlier. On the afternoon before the Lindsey murder, Mays and his stepfather had been actively campaigning for the mayor's reelection. A week later, when Maurice was in jail, McMillan was soundly defeated at the polls.)

During the first two days of testimony, fifteen witnesses were called, including the husband of Bertie Lindsey, the doctor who examined her body, and several of the police officers who were involved in the investigation. But by far the most attention was paid to two others: Ora Smyth, the eyewitness, and Andy White, the arresting officer.

Under questioning by Attorney General Mynatt, the young woman said that when she was awakened by her cousin's voice, she saw a Negro man standing beside the bed. He had a gun in one hand and a flashlight in the other. The man threatened her, Ora Smyth said, and told her to lie still, and she never moved. In the reflected light of his flashlight, she said, "I saw him in the face. . . . I could see his face plain." Further, she said, "He laid his hands on me . . . on my private parts." Bertie kept getting up, she testified, and the man kept making her lie down again; then she took a step toward the door, and when she turned to look back, he shot her.

Again, Mynatt asked the witness if she had seen the man's face clearly. She replied that she had, several times, as he changed the flashlight from one hand to the other. And was that man now in the courtroom? Yes, she answered firmly, pointing to Maurice Mays at the defense table. "Could you be mistaken?" Mynatt asked. "I could not," Ora Smyth responded.

After the shot, she said, the man came back and put his hands on her again, and she told him to "spare my life, but take my money." She directed him to the dresser, where he took some loose money and Bertie Lindsey's pocketbook. Then, she said, the intruder left the room and went out the back door. She then ran to the front door, she testified, and there she heard the man fall and get up in the dark yard, and in a moment she saw him run past and cross the street in front of the house.

An hour or so later, when the police brought a man to the corner of Eighth Avenue and Gillespie Street and asked Ora Smyth to come and look at him, she testified that she twice identified Maurice Mays as the killer. "By his form, by his face and by his voice, and his clothing," she said, she was positive of her identification.

In his cross-examination, defense attorney Reuben Cates concentrated on whether or not a flashlight in the hand of the intruder could have given Ora Smyth a clear view of the person's face. He asked no probing questions about the appearance or actions of the intruder or about how he managed to fondle her while holding a flashlight in one hand and a gun in the other, and he asked nothing about her identification of him under the streetlight. The questioning was over in a matter of minutes, and Ora Smyth was never called back to the witness stand.

When Andy White testified, he claimed that his suspicion of Maurice Mays was prompted by his questioning of Smyth and her description of the assailant. He said he had then asked permission of Captain Joseph Wilson to go in search of Mays. In a patrol wagon driven by a black police employee named James Smith, White and two other officers went first to the home of William Mays and then to the Humes Street address of his stepson. It took several minutes of loud knocking and shouted calls, White said, to induce Mays to let them in.

White first asked for his pistol, and Mays said it was in the dresser. "I smelt a faint smoked powder on it," he testified, adding that he kept the fully loaded gun. White also claimed that Mays's shoes had fresh mud on the soles. The officers then told Mays to get dressed so they could take him to "let some people see him." When they arrived at the corner of Eighth and Gillespie, White said, he and another officer walked to the Lindsey house to get Ora Smyth. Then, according to White, the young woman twice stated that Mays was the killer.

During the officer's testimony, several disputes arose between the opposing attorneys—over whether or not White had coached Smyth before she saw Mays, over whether or not Mays had denied her accusation, and finally over Mays's alleged possession of photographs of white women. With the jury out of the courtroom, prosecutor Heiskell told the court he wanted to ask about such pictures. Mays, he said, "is a negro, considered to be such. His association naturally would be with negroes, and if he got to running after white women that would be something unusual, at least in this part of the United States. That would indicate . . . a state of mind in which the defendant was, that he was running after white women." Judge Nelson ruled that such evidence was inadmissable because it would "unduly prejudice the jury against the defendant and it would not throw any light upon the homicide at all."

Attorney Cates, in his cross-examination, drew from White some seemingly important admissions—that he had looked for but failed to find a flashlight in Mays's house; that he had not, in fact, kept Mays's gun but had returned it to the drawer; and that he had accused Mays of having a second pistol, which implied that the first one appeared not to be the murder weapon. Cates also suggested that White had long held "unkind feelings" toward Mays, but White denied it.

Another officer did take Mays's gun to the police station, but it was never positively identified as the murder weapon. The bullet extracted from Bertie Lindsey's body was never matched to that or any other gun, and no spent shell was ever found. No reports on fingerprints or ballistics or an autopsy were presented in evidence. Lindsey's pocketbook was found in her yard, but it was not linked in any way to Mays, and no flashlight ever turned up.

White and other officers testified that Mays's trousers were damp—presumably from running through wet weeds—and that his shoes matched prints found in the mud at the Lindsey home, but the testimony was directly contradicted and shown to be highly circumstantial, even speculative. In the case of the shoe print, the prosecution contended that a badly worn left heel print matched Mays's shoe, but the defense introduced his only pair of shoes in evidence to show that the heels were hardly worn at all.

As the trial entered its third day, Cates called White back to the stand for more cross-examination and attempted to show that he had nursed a long-standing grudge against Mays and was trying to frame him for the Lindsey murder. White had focused his suspicion on Mays even before the investigation, Cates suggested. Anger rose on all sides, and the judge also seemed to be disturbed, but Cates persisted: "Before you ever had a description, didn't you . . . state that

Maurice Mays had committed the crime?" White categorically denied having made such a statement to anyone at any time.

Shortly after that exchange, the state rested its case. It had failed to establish a motive linking Mays to the crime, failed to show that he was ever at the scene, failed to prove that his gun had been fired or even that it was of the same caliber as the murder weapon. There had been much discussion of muddy footprints and damp trousers and the faint smell of powder in his gun barrel, but there was nothing of substance—nothing except the word of Ora Smyth that she saw Mays fire the shot.

The first defense witness was Mays himself. In a soft-spoken but confident manner, he described his activities on the day of the crime—an afternoon of campaigning with his stepfather on behalf of Mayor McMillan, an evening of casual socializing with several friends. Between 12:30 and 1:00 A.M., he said, he went home, undressed, read the paper, and went to sleep. At three o'clock he was awakened by loud voices and knocking. He said he went to the door and found three policemen. They came in, searched his room, looked at his gun, asked him some questions, told him nothing; then, he said, they ordered him to dress and follow them.

His stepfather had arrived in the meantime and was allowed to ride with Mays in the patrol wagon. At a street corner in north Knoxville, Mays said, he waited under the watchful eyes of the other policemen while Andy White went alone to a house up the street. "Someone has been shot by a colored man," one of the policemen finally explained to Mays and his stepfather. When White returned with Ora Smyth, Mays said, she accused him of the crime. Then, he testified, "I told her she was mistaken. I said, 'Mr. White, please bring the lady back and let her look at me better than that,' and I said, 'Certainly I am not the man,' but she didn't come back."

Under questioning by Reuben Cates, Mays testified that he had known Andy White for three or four years and that White had been unkind to him, had cursed him several times, had called him a "little black son of a bitch" and a "little yellow negro." White hadn't spoken to him in four or five months, Mays said, and he quoted Jim Smith, the black driver of the patrol wagon, as saying that White "thinks you would do anything."

It was then S. G. Heiskell's turn to cross-examine Mays. Against repeated objections from the defense, some of which were overruled by Judge Nelson, the prosecutor established that Mays had three indictments pending against him, that one of them was for carrying a pistol, and that the pistol in question had been taken from him by the police. He also got into the record a hint that Mays had once shot and killed a man and an assertion that he sometimes followed white girls.

Heiskell pressed hard with questions about Mays's whereabouts at the time of the crime, the condition of his pants and shoes when he was arrested, and his confrontation with Ora Smyth under the streetlight. He also suggested—and Mays denied—that he once had interfered with White's attempt to arrest some men who were gambling in a café run by Mays.

The prosecution objected to three witnesses called by Cates. Judge Nelson sent the jury out while he heard the three, all white women, say that they had been assaulted in their homes by black intruders after Mays was in jail. One of the women said her assailant threatened to "shoot me like he did Bertie Lindsey." The judge sustained the prosecution's objection and excluded the testimony of all three of the women.

The defense called twenty more witnesses to support Mays's claim of innocence. Among them was a twenty-nine-year-old black lawyer, George McDade, Jr., who said that he knew both Mays and White and that he had heard White call Mays a "little yellow son of a bitch" who was shielding thieves and ought to be put in jail. Another witness was Dave Saunders, a white police officer and former deputy sheriff, who said he examined Mays's pistol at the police station and detected no smoke or powder smell. Saunders also testified that he and his wife had conducted an experiment with a flashlight in a dark room and found that the holder of the light could not be seen. (Earlier, a police witness had claimed a similar experiment produced the opposite result.)

Perhaps the most effective witness in Mays's defense was James Smith, the black driver of the patrol wagon and an employee of the department for twelve years. On the way to the Lindsey house to investigate the crime, he said, Andy White had "guessed Maurice Mays was the man who killed the woman." White hated Mays, Smith testified; he cursed him often, called him a "yellow bastard" and a "dirty nigger," and vowed to "catch him with his pants down and put him in the penitentiary." Under cross-examination by Mynatt, Smith denied that he had a personal dislike for White. He claimed that others had also heard White curse Mays, but he declined to name them.

Some brief and inconsequential rebuttal testimony followed. Then the questioning was over, closing arguments were heard, and finally, late in the afternoon of Saturday, October 4, Judge Nelson gave his charge to the jury. The trial's ending was curiously anticlimactic, devoid of any surprising or dramatic developments. In what seemed almost like an atmosphere of collective resignation, the participants and spectators settled back to wait for a verdict.

It was a short wait. In less than twenty minutes the jury was back. They had found Maurice Mays guilty of murder in the first degree. The judge had already indicated that the penalty for such a finding was death in the electric chair.

The defendant, in the words of one newspaper, "maintained the most perfect appearance of calm." He was quoted as saying to those who had helped him in the trial: "I want to thank you all for what you have done for me, but I don't want you to get it into your head that I am guilty of the crime. . . . I want to proclaim standing here that I did not commit the crime. It is simply a case of prejudice."

Two weeks later the defense moved for a new trial on five grounds: that racial passion and excitement in the community had prevented a fair trial, that defense testimony concerning three similar assaults had not been permitted, that the judge had incorrectly charged the jury, that the sentence had been incorrectly fixed, and that late testimony contradicting Ora Smyth's sworn statements had not been allowed.

In denying the motion, Judge Nelson asserted that Maurice Mays "had an absolutely fair trial. He was ably defended. He was given the benefit of every single doubt. The jury having heard all the evidence returned a verdict of guilty of murder in the first degree, and returned it in only a few minutes. And that verdict meets with the hearty approval of the court. I am convinced beyond a peradventure of a doubt that he is the man who committed the awful atrocious crime." Nelson directed that Mays be taken to the state penitentiary in Nashville and there electrocuted on November 28, 1919.

In separate statements made that same week, Judge Nelson and Attorney General Mynatt had deplored the action of another jury that in the meantime had freed all of the white men charged in the August 30 riot. But in the case of Maurice Mays, both men expressed their satisfaction that justice had been done, swiftly and surely.

The Wait

It had taken the state just thirty-five days after Bertie Lindsey's murder to arrest and convict the only suspect and prescribe his punishment—but two and a half years would elapse before that punishment was administered. Through appeal, reversal, retrial, reconviction, renewed appeal, and final verdict, Maurice Mays remained imprisoned but ever hopeful, even confident, that his innocence would finally be declared. Three times he was taken from the Knox County jail to the penitentiary in Nashville to await execution, only to be returned to Knoxville for more waiting.

The Tennessee supreme court's consideration of the first conviction postponed Mays's November 1919 execution date, and in January 1920 the court reversed the conviction on a technicality concerning the manner in which the death penalty had been fixed. More than a year later, on April 18, 1921, another criminal court jury was chosen to retry the case in the court of Judge Xen Hicks. The same two teams of attorneys returned to battle, and most of the same witnesses were called. Once again, Ora Smyth (the eyewitness, since married to a store clerk named Ray Parsons) firmly asserted that Maurice Mays was the man she saw shoot Bertie Lindsey—and just as stoutly, Mays repeated his declaration of innocence.

And once again the outcome was the same. On April 23 the jury found the defendant guilty of first-degree murder and sentenced him to die in the electric chair. Six months later the Tennessee supreme court affirmed the verdict, finding no trial errors and no technical flaws to warrant another reversal. The execution was scheduled for December 15, 1921.

In the meantime, Tennessee had elected a new governor—Alfred A. ("Uncle Alf") Taylor, a seventy-two-year-old Republican from east Tennessee. A former congressman, he had earlier waged and lost a campaign for governor against his brother, Democrat Robert Love

Taylor. With his election in 1920, Alf Taylor inherited the final responsibility for the fate of Maurice Mays.

As soon as the supreme court upheld Mays's conviction, Taylor was swamped with letters, phone calls, telegrams, and petitions on the highly emotional and controversial case. Some urged him to permit no delay in the execution; others, with equal fervor, pleaded for reconsideration and reprieve. Taylor responded by appointing three prominent Tennesseans as a commission of "disinterested" counselors to study the case and recommend a course of action to him. He also granted a ninety-day postponement of the execution—to March 15, 1922—in order to allow petitioners for Mays to examine purported new evidence in the case.

Sentiment in Knox County was reported to be "about equally divided" between those who were convinced of Mays's guilt and those who believed he was innocent. The three-man commission reported to the governor its considered opinion that Mays had committed the crime but suggested that he may have been insane at the time. Finally, Governor Taylor, saying he had read the entire case record and listened carefully to all sides, announced that he would render a final judgment before the scheduled execution date. He would, he said, be guided "by a sense of justice and conscience."

The weeks slipped by. Mays, ill and on crutches in the late winter of 1922, saw his hopes fading. Finally, on March 14 the governor ended his long silence. He had found no new evidence to indicate that the court had erred, he said; therefore, he would not interfere with the verdict. Maurice Mays would die at sunrise.

The Nashville *Tennessean* reported that the decision caused the governor to be "beseiged with visitors pleading for the life of the man convicted of one of the most brutal crimes in the annals of the state." One such petitioner was James A. Fowler, then a special assistant to the U.S. attorney general in Washington and formerly one of Mays's defense lawyers; others included prominent black Tennesseans who, the newspapers reported, had raised "a fund of $10,000 or more" to provide Mays with "capable counsel in his legal battle."

But it was all to no avail. The governor issued one last statement concluding that "the responsibility for the fate of Maurice Mays rests with the courts and juries of Tennessee, and not upon me." Two criminal court judges, two juries, the state's highest court, an independent commission, and two governors had rendered their collective verdict: Maurice Mays was guilty as charged.

"The only statement I have to make," said former defense attorney James Fowler when all hope was gone, "is that they are electrocuting an innocent negro."

The Execution

William Mays went to the death house inside the state penitentiary to be with his stepson for the last time, and he was a tearful witness to the condemned man's baptism by two black Methodist ministers. With tears in his own eyes, Maurice Mays assured his stepfather once again of his innocence.

As the night wore on, Mays twice asked to be taken on to the chair. He had made his last appeals; he was resigned to the inevitability of his death. "I am to die to satisfy a few Republican politicians," he said. "The governor hasn't man enough in him. You might as well talk to a rock. Some Republicans told him he'd lose twenty thousand votes if he helped me."

In his final statement, Governor Taylor had said that the case "turned upon the testimony of Ora Smyth" and that the defense had been unable to discredit her. "Therefore," he said, "she stands in the case unimpeached and unimpeachable." The defense attorneys had, in fact, missed numerous opportunities to challenge the truthfulness of Ora Smyth in her brief and uncontentious time on the witness stand.

Maurice Mays understood clearly that the young woman's testimony would determine in the end whether he would live or die. He had written an open letter to Ora Smyth Parsons, begging her to admit that she was wrong. "My life," he wrote, "is to be taken from me solely upon your word alone. God knows and I know that I am entirely innocent. . . . After I am dead it will then be too late, but God will teach, and may make your life miserable. He will bury it in your heart as long as you live that I died innocent upon your word alone." No response to the letter ever came.

In the early morning hours of March 15, some of those who waited in the death house with Maurice Mays said they heard him "pray to his Maker to cleanse the sinful hearts of men who have dipped their fingers in my innocent blood." Then, one newspaper reported, "It was almost uncanny, the way Mays fixed a smile on his face, walked to the chair from the death cell, and, upon sitting in the chair exclaimed, 'I am as innocent as the sun that shines.'"

At twelve minutes past six o'clock the first electric shock was sent surging through his body. It continued for four minutes. When the current was turned off, the attending physician quickly determined that Maurice Mays was dead.

William Mays took his stepson's body back to Knoxville for burial. An estimated two thousand of the city's twelve thousand black citizens filed past the open casket at the Wheeler Funeral Home on Vine Avenue.

The Confession

For many months, the people of east Tennessee, white and black alike, found it difficult to rid themselves of the bitter aftertaste of murder and execution. In some quarters, Maurice Mays was remembered with contempt as "an underworld figure" and "a bad nigger." In others, he was praised as "a martyred victim of white racism." There would never be agreement on the question of his guilt or innocence. But on one conclusion there was virtual consensus: The "capital offense" of Maurice Mays was that in a society of unremitting white supremacy, he had dared to assume the liberties of a white man—and for that "crime," he paid with his life.

Assaults similar to the one that cost Bertie Lindsey her life continued in the Knoxville area for more than five years. By the end of 1924 a total of thirty-two such crimes had gone unsolved; eight women had been murdered, and about two dozen others had been raped or robbed. At one point a private detective claimed that a single white man had committed all of the assaults, including the one on Bertie Lindsey. No convictions were ever obtained after the Lindsey case.

The segregationist status quo prevailed in Tennessee and throughout the South. Finally, in the fullness of time, the wounds of William and Frances Mays, of Daniel Lindsey, and of the city of Knoxville scarred over and healed. At length, no one spoke any more of the murder and execution that had stirred such emotions and caused such deep divisions in the community.

Then, in August 1927, five and a half years after the execution, a twenty-eight-year-old white woman walked into the police station in Norton, Virginia, 130 miles northeast of Knoxville, and calmly told the officer in charge that she was the murderer of Bertie Lindsey. In a signed confession, Sadie Mendil said that she had suspected her then-husband, John Roddy, of carrying on an affair with Daniel Lindsey's wife. Seeking revenge, she had dressed in men's clothing, blackened her face, and entered the Lindsey house, where she shot Bertie Lindsey as she lay in bed with another woman. Then, Sadie Mendil said, she had made her escape.

The Norton authorities were impressed with the sincerity of the confession and with Mendil herself, who said she had decided to make the statement because of a "troubled mind and heart." But Knoxville police chief Ed M. Haynes quickly discredited her story, saying that "confessions" were commonly made after sensational crimes. There were, said Haynes, some serious discrepancies in Sadie Mendil's account of the murder. He advised the police chief in Norton to release her.

Four days later a man who identified himself as Mack Mendil appeared in Haynes's office and said that his wife, Sadie, had given a false confession to the Norton police because she "has become temporarily demented from brooding over her baby," a two-year-old son who was being cared for by another family. That explanation completely satisfied the Knoxville authorities; the Lindsey case, they said, had already been solved, and they considered the matter closed forever. The confession of Sadie Mendil was thus ignored, and no one ever questioned her about the crime again.

April 1982:
Sixty-two years after Bertie Lindsey was murdered and fifty-four after Sadie Mendil claimed responsibility for the crime, it was still

possible to find a few uninvestigated leads in the musty pages of the public record in Knoxville and elsewhere in Tennessee.

A chance discovery of the trial record and the subsequent confession had drawn me into a study of the case, but some of the frail clues quickly evaporated as I tried to pursue them. Ora Smyth Parsons and her husband apparently had moved out of Knoxville after Maurice Mays was executed, and I could find no trace of them. Mayor John E. McMillan, for all his visibility at the time, is all but invisible in the city's recorded history now. (I did, however, locate a nephew of his who volunteered the information that Maurice Mays was "my Uncle John's bastard son.") Governor Alfred A. Taylor's public papers include none of the extensive and voluminous materials generated in his office by the Mays case. Attorney James A. Fowler left an extensive memoir, but it contains no mention of his role in defending Mays, nor even an acknowledgment of the murder, the riot, or the execution.

And what of Sadie Mendil? She would have been eighty-three years old in 1982, and her son would have been fifty-seven. Were they still alive?

Before her marriage to Mack Mendil, she had divorced John Roddy in a Tennessee mountain county courthouse. I found the record there, dated June 30, 1926. Along with her single status, Sadie had also taken back her maiden name. Then, in another county soon thereafter, she had married Mack Mendil. Might she have eventually left him too, and again resumed her maiden name, and returned to the county of her childhood and youth? Or might she at least be known there by her family name? I decided to make some discreet inquiries.

The name is a common one in that mountain community. It would seem invasive of the privacy of many people to call Sadie Roddy Mendil by her maiden name here, so I won't use it now; I'll just call her Sadie Brown.

In every courthouse office, I asked if anyone knew a woman in her eighties named Sadie Brown. The question drew blanks at first—but finally, a middle-aged clerk said the name rang a bell. She sent me to the next town down the road, where I met a woman who seemed to recall the recent death of a Sadie Brown in yet another town nearby.

I called at the local funeral home. The records showed no death and burial of anyone by that name. But, said the undertaker, "there's a Reverend Buell Brown around here. He'd probably know. He lives out in the county. You might want to give him a call."

The Reverend Buell Brown (age fifty-seven, I learned later) answered the phone cordially, but when I spoke Sadie Brown's name to him, his voice turned suddenly cool, wary. Who was I, he demanded; why did I want to ask about her? My answers were unsatisfactory to him. "Yes, I know Sadie Brown," he said at last, "but I won't talk to you about her, or tell you where she lives. It's none of your business where my mother lives." Abruptly, he hung up.

I knew I would not have long to do what had to be done next. As quickly as I could, I rushed to the local post office and engaged a friendly clerk in conversation. I was looking for Mrs. Sadie Brown, I explained. Could she tell me where she lived? "Oh, yeah," said the clerk. "She lives in an apartment complex right here in town, just a few blocks from here."

Within minutes I stood at her door, knocking. A short, pleasant-faced, white-haired woman appeared. "Are you Mrs. Sadie Brown?" I asked, trying hard to be friendly and casual.

"Yes, I am," she replied with a smile. I took a deep breath and began to talk, spilling out the story as I had pieced it together, taking every precaution I could to keep from offending or frightening her.

She listened politely. Her pleasant expression did not change. I came at last to the key question: Was she *that* Sadie Brown, the one I had described?

She hesitated a moment and then said, "That was my sister-in-law. She was born Sadie Brown; I got the same name, but by marriage. She confessed that killing, but she didn't do it. She was afraid of her husband, Mendil. He kept her under close watch, and she wanted to get away from him, so she ran to the police and said she was the one that killed that other woman. They locked her up, and then my brother went and got her out, and that's how she got away from Mendil."

I waited for her to continue, but there was no more. "What finally happened to Sadie?" I asked.

"She married again—and then she died about two years ago."

"Where did she die, and what was her name then?"

"She died in Knoxville, but I can't remember what her married name was."

I tried another tack. "The newspaper story said she had a son before she was married to Mack Mendil. Do you know where he is, or what his name is?"

"I think he may be dead too," she replied.

We stood in the shade of Sadie Brown's front porch, looking calmly at each other, showing no outward emotion. I glanced over my shoulder, wondering how soon the Reverend Buell Brown would be there. With a feeling of barely controlled desperation, I searched my mind for the right things to say, the right questions to unlock the mystery. No words came. The silence filled the space between us.

Sadie Brown stepped back inside and stood behind the screen door, still smiling faintly. "Goodbye," I said lamely. "And thank you."

The door closed. Walking back to my car, I thought about the whole story, the long-buried mystery, and I wondered if I had finally found the end of it—or another beginning.

The murder of Bertie Smyth Lindsey is officially recorded as the criminal act of one man, Maurice Mays. The subsequent assault on black citizens by a lawless mob of white men is still referred to as the Knoxville race riot of 1919. Mays's conviction and his execution for the crime in 1922 are generally seen, when they are remembered at all, as proper acts of legal punishment administered by the state. Neither Ora Smyth Parsons, who was Mays's accuser, nor Sadie Brown Mendil, who attempted to exonerate him, has ever again spoken publicly about the crime, and the case remains officially solved and thus closed, presumably forever.

THE ENDURING MYSTERY OF JAMES EARL RAY

Nearly twenty years after Dr. Martin Luther King, Jr., was assassinated in Memphis, I interviewed his convicted killer, James Earl Ray, at the Tennessee State Prison in Nashville. That conversation and others I had with about three dozen people directly affected by the crime and its consequences gave shape and substance to this article. It was published in the November 1986 issue of the Progressive.

In a decade of cataclysmic turmoil, 1968 was a year like no other. It began with the United States mired knee-deep in the Big Muddy of Vietnam and ended with Lyndon Johnson packing to leave the White House, Richard Nixon poised to move in, and the longest war in U.S. history still grinding ever deeper into the pit of disaster.

Events of the months in-between read now like a modern-day version of the biblical Revelation: violence in the universities, riots and burning in the cities, a poor people's march on the nation's capital, a splintering of the principal political parties, assassinations of a presidential candidate and of the spiritual leader of the nation's oldest and largest minority group. Even now, eighteen years later, it is hard to assimilate so much shock, hard to believe it all really happened.

Against a backdrop of looming defeat in Southeast Asia, racial unrest in the urban ghettos, strife on the campuses, and alienation among the poor, political factions in the United States grappled for control of the parties and the presidency. On the last day of March President Johnson announced that he would not seek reelection; Robert Kennedy, Eugene McCarthy, and Hubert Humphrey were the front-running Democrats who wanted to replace him, but on June 5 Kennedy was killed by an assassin in Los Angeles. George Wallace forged a right-wing third party; Richard Nixon won the Republican nomination over Nelson Rockefeller and Ronald Reagan in riot-torn Miami; and Humphrey got the ill-fated Democratic nomination in Chicago while police and demonstrators waged a bloody battle in the streets outside the convention hall.

Throughout five tumultuous spring and summer months, social upheaval shook the nation to its roots. And in those long days and weeks of sustained crisis, no single spark was more volatile than the one that flared in Memphis, Tennessee, on the afternoon of Thursday, April 4, 1968, when a sniper's bullet struck and killed Dr. Martin Luther King, Jr., the most visible and charismatic leader in the drive of twenty million black citizens for equality and justice under the law.

The crime set off an explosion of ghetto rage that ripped through dozens of American cities. An international manhunt to find the killer finally led, two months after the murder, to the arrest in London of James Earl Ray, an escaped convict from the Missouri State Penitentiary. He was taken to Memphis, where on March 10, 1969, nine months after his arrest, he entered a plea of guilty and was sentenced to ninety-nine years in prison.

But that was not the end of the Martin Luther King murder case, far from it. Since then, countless stories at odds with the prosecution's case have surfaced, at least a dozen books have been written about the crime, and a select committee of the U.S. House of Representatives has spent two years and more than five million dollars investigating this and other assassinations.

James Earl Ray, through a long line of attorneys, has attempted without success to get a jury trial based on a mountain of classified evidence in the case. He has also tried five times to escape his Tennessee confinement, once getting outside the walls for fifty-five hours before being caught.

As the years have passed, the recorded statements of James Earl Ray, his attorneys, the Tennessee officials who prosecuted and judged and incarcerated him, the Federal Bureau of Investigation and other federal officials, congressional committee members and their staffs, the press, private sleuths, authors, and others with a close interest in the crime have mounted into tens of millions of words. And yet, the state has never attempted to prove beyond a reasonable doubt to a jury of his peers that Ray was the one and only guilty party, and Ray himself has never testified under oath before a jury. In the minds of many, perhaps most, of the people who have followed the case closely, there is still more doubt than certainty that James Earl Ray, acting alone, planned and carried out the assassination of Martin Luther King.

There is little reason to believe that one more book or television inquiry, or yet another newspaper or magazine article, will erase the doubt and deliver the certainty. Even the House Select Committee on Assassinations, when it finished its investigation nearly eight years ago, expressed the belief that Ray killed King "as a result of a conspiracy"—that is, with help from unknown others—and that conclusion raised more questions than it answered.

But now, with the benefit of eight relatively quiet years to absorb and reflect upon the known facts, several principal figures in the case, including some doubters, some believers, and James Earl Ray himself, agreed to talk about it one more time. Ray, who has not granted press interviews in recent years, not only sat for questions but also allowed the conversation to be tape-recorded. His remarks and those of the others I talked to over a period of about two months in the summer of 1986 still don't solve any of the puzzles concerning what really happened in Memphis on April 4, 1968, but they do at least provide some historical perspective. They also hold out the hope, however faint, that someday the whole story will emerge.

∿

The place to begin this look back at the crime and the times is with a brief chronology of some pertinent and uncontested facts:

• Martin Luther King, Jr., was in Memphis on March 28, 1968, to lead a protest march in support of striking sanitation workers; he left for Atlanta the next day, vowing to come back for another demonstration the following week. His well-publicized return occurred on Wednesday, April 3. He and several members of his staff registered at the Lorraine Motel.

• James Earl Ray, using the alias Eric S. Galt, bought a 1966 white Mustang in Birmingham on August 29, 1967. On March 30, 1968, in the same city, he used the name Harvey Lowmeyer when he purchased a 30.06 Remington rifle, some ammunition, and a telescopic sight. On April 3, 1968, he registered under another alias, John Willard, at a rooming house on Main Street in Memphis. From his room and from the bathroom at the end of the hall, Ray had a view of the front of the Lorraine Motel.

• At 6:01 P.M. on Thursday, April 4, while the Reverend Dr. King was standing on the balcony of the Lorraine with members of his staff, a bullet struck him in the lower right jaw and penetrated into his trunk, killing him almost instantly.

• James Earl Ray was within a mile of the Lorraine Motel at 6:01 P.M., although his exact whereabouts is still in dispute. He left Memphis in his white Mustang within minutes of King's murder. The rifle he had bought in Birmingham and other items belonging to him were found wrapped in a bundle lying in a doorway near the entrance to the rooming house where he was registered.

• Piecing together some of the evidence, police and FBI investigators concluded that Ray was the prime suspect. His trail led to Atlanta, to Toronto, to London. Finally, on June 8, more than two months after the crime, Ray was apprehended at Heathrow Airport in London. He was extradited to Memphis on July 19 and jailed to await trial for the murder.

• Arthur J. Hanes, Sr., a former mayor of Birmingham, former FBI agent, and former defense attorney for Ku Klux Klansmen accused of murdering civil rights activist Viola Liuzzo in 1965, made arrangements with Ray to represent him in court. William Bradford Huie, a well-known Alabama author and an acquaintance of Hanes's, made a three-way arrangement with Hanes and Ray for exclusive rights to Ray's story.

• A trial date was set, then postponed, then set again for November 12, 1968 (shortly after the presidential election), only to be postponed again at the last minute when Ray dismissed Hanes in favor of Percy Foreman, a famed and flamboyant Texas criminal lawyer. All the money promised in the various agreements among Ray, Hanes, Huie, and Foreman was to come from sales of material written about the case by Huie.

• Foreman negotiated a plea-bargain agreement with District Attorney General Phil M. Canale, the state's chief prosecutor, giving Ray a ninety-nine-year sentence in return for a guilty plea. Ray opposed the agreement at first, saying he preferred to plead not guilty and testify in his own defense, but he relented. On March 10, 1969—James Earl Ray's forty-first birthday—criminal court judge W. Preston Battle read the charge in court ("that on April 4, 1968, at 6:01 P.M., the defendant fired a shot . . . and fatally wounded Martin Luther King"), and Ray pleaded guilty to the charge. A jury was selected, each member agreeing in advance to assess a ninety-nine-year sentence in return for the guilty plea. When the jury was seated, Ray asked for permission to speak. He said in part, "I am not bound to accept these theories of Mr. [Ramsey] Clark . . . Mr. [J. Edgar] Hoover . . . Mr. Canale, Mr. Foreman. . . . I mean on the conspiracy thing." (U.S. attorney general Clark, FBI director Hoover, prosecutor Canale, and defense attorney Foreman all subscribed to the belief that Ray had acted alone, and no conspiracy existed.) Prosecutors then called five people to testify, after which a narration of the state's case against Ray was read aloud without interruption. There was no cross-examination. The agreed-upon sentence was then handed down by Judge Battle, and James Earl Ray was led away. He was taken the next day to the Tennessee State Penitentiary in Nashville.

• Three days later, on March 13, Ray wrote to Judge Battle "to inform the honorable court that . . . famous Houston Att. Percy Fourflusher is no longer representing me in any capacity." Soon thereafter he filed for a new trial, claiming that he had been pressured and coerced into pleading guilty. Over the next eight years no fewer than eight attorneys, ranging from right-wing racist J. B. Stoner of Augusta, Georgia, to left-wing radical Mark Lane of New York City, represented Ray in various court proceedings. Attorneys Bernard Fensterwald, Jr., and James Lesar of Washington, D.C., spent six years attempting in federal court to get a new trial for Ray, but their efforts finally ended in failure in 1976.

• In a lengthy written statement and in further response to questions from the House Select Committee on Assassinations in Washington during August 1978, Ray denied that he killed Martin Luther King. The gist of his story was that he was involved with others in a conspiracy to commit a crime, that he didn't know until after it happened that the intended crime was Dr. King's murder, and that he could not positively identify any of the people in the conspiracy. The committee subsequently concluded that Ray did in fact shoot King, that he "knowingly, intelligently, and voluntarily pleaded guilty," and that even though other people may have helped him in some way, the burden of the crime correctly fell on him.

The eighteen years of his confinement as a convicted assassin have not been an uneventful period in James Earl Ray's life. He has been represented to one degree or another by at least twenty attorneys and has handled enough of his legal work personally to be considered a pretty fair "jailhouse lawyer." He has sued, among others, attorneys Arthur Hanes, Sr., and Percy Foreman, writers William Bradford Huie and George McMillan, *Playboy* and *Time* magazines, and the Federal Bureau of Investigation.

In June 1977 Ray escaped with six other convicts from Brushy Mountain, a maximum-security prison in the rugged backcountry of east Tennessee, and it took more than two tense and dramatic days and nights of searching for law enforcement officials with bloodhounds to finally track him down and return him to custody.

Through attorney Mark Lane, he addressed the nation's leading black public figures in 1978, stating flatly that "I did not kill Martin Luther King, Jr.," and asking them to help him get a new trial. Several of them, including Southern Christian Leadership Conference veterans Ralph David Abernathy, Jesse Jackson, Hosea Williams, and James Lawson, came to visit him, and all declared their belief that Ray did not act alone and that he deserved a new trial. On October 13, 1978, when Ray was married at Brushy Mountain to Anna Sallings Sandhu, a courtroom artist from nearby Knoxville, it was Lawson, an ordained minister, who conducted the ceremony.

On June 4, 1981, Ray was stabbed twenty-two times in the head, neck, and chest by four black inmates in the prison library at Brushy Mountain, and seventy-seven stitches were needed to close his wounds. He was then transferred to a cell on death row at the main prison in Nashville and segregated from other inmates—presumably both to protect him from others and to minimize his chance of escaping. He has remained there in isolation for the past five years, and his requests for transfer to less-restrictive quarters have been denied.

Many unanswered questions remain about the death of Martin Luther King, Jr., and the guilt of James Earl Ray, and as the years slip by and memories fade, the entire case drifts deeper into the blurred pages of history and legend as surely as Ray himself recedes into obscurity. Time has not changed many minds; those who were convinced in the late 1960s that a conspiracy was organized to take King's life still tend to hold that conviction, and those who felt then that Ray acted alone still tend to believe that he did. In the absence of a jury trial of the facts, the state has never had to submit its case to cross-examination, and Ray has not been able to testify under oath in his own defense. And as a consequence, the division of opinion on the basic questions of what really happened and who was involved are as unsettled now as they were in 1968.

∽

The Reverend James Bevel is one of many people whose beliefs and feelings remain unchanged. A close associate of King's, he was staying at the Lorraine Motel on the day of the assassination and was standing nearby when the fatal shot was fired. A few months later he visited Ray in the Memphis jail and then told reporters he was convinced that someone else pulled the trigger. "Ray didn't do it," Bevel said. "He might have been involved, but not at a conscious level, not with foreknowledge. . . . Ray was the fall guy. He was used."

The Reverend Mr. Bevel is pastor of a church in Chicago now. "My feelings haven't changed," he said. "I still believe as strongly as ever that James Earl Ray didn't pull the trigger. People said he was some great seething racist—that's bull. He's just an ordinary guy—not political, not ideological. He doesn't have the demeanor of a killer. All I wanted was for the man to get a fair trial, to get his day in court, and he never got it. If he did get it, even now, we might be surprised to find out what really happened, and who was involved."

Congressman Louis Stokes of Cleveland was the chairman (and one of four black Democratic members) of the House Select Committee on Assassinations. With the help of more than four dozen lawyers, investigators, and researchers, he came to a different conclusion than Bevel, ten years after the crime. (Stokes declines public comment now on the committee's 1978 findings, but its final report presumably reflects his views and those of a majority of the twelve members.) In his questioning of Ray, Stokes patiently attempted to draw out a full description of the mysterious "Raoul," the man Ray said was his principal conspiratorial partner for almost a year before the crime and the probable triggerman on April 4. In the end the committee concluded that no hard evidence could be found to prove that such a man as "Raoul" existed.

It was precisely that lack of alternative suspects that provided the most telling argument against Ray's contentions. In ten years of trying, scores of professional interrogators—prosecutors, defense attorneys, judges, congressional committee members, detectives, researchers, investigative journalists—had pored over the evidence, pursued the leads, and questioned witnesses, but no one had matched name and face to a single person who could be charged with conspiracy in the crime.

Nevertheless, the committee still could not come up with the hard evidence to show that Ray was the gunman. He had bought the gun, to be sure, and his fingerprints were on it—but no witnesses positively identified him, and no proof was presented that he fired the shot or even that the fatal bullet issued from the weapon in question. To this day it has not been determined absolutely that the rifle Ray bought in Birmingham was the murder weapon.

The committee did find abundant evidence that FBI director J. Edgar Hoover and his top aides had a deep and abiding hatred for Martin Luther King. They kept him under surveillance for years, and their internal memos in the 1960s talked of his "dependence on Communists," spoke of "neutralizing" and "isolating" him, and undertook to "mark him now . . . as the most dangerous Negro of the future in this nation." Hoover publicly called King "the most notorious liar" in the country.

From the political right as well as the left—from J. B. Stoner and elements of the Ku Klux Klan as much as from Mark Lane—came blunt accusations that the FBI "planned and carried out" the King assassination. Lane even asserted that black members of the House committee knew of such a plot but were afraid to divulge it. Committee members denied the claim, and the final report explicitly stated that "no federal, state, or local government agency was involved" in the crime.

The Reverend James Lawson, a Memphis minister in 1968 and now pastor of a United Methodist church in Los Angeles, was a disciplined practitioner of nonviolent resistance in the civil rights movement and as such was a faithful supporter of Dr. King's. His leader's death grieved him deeply, but Ray's conviction was troubling to Lawson—and still is.

"I'm one of those people who is persuaded we don't know the whole story," he said, "or Ray's connection with it. I didn't like the way he was pressured to plead guilty. It was a political decision. He may have been involved in some way, but I doubt very much that he acted alone, or that he masterminded the plot."

Lawson visited Ray at Brushy Mountain in 1978 and also saw him and spoke to him at the committee hearings in Washington. "I met Anna then, too," he recalled, "and later on, when they decided to get married, she called me in Los Angeles and asked me if I would conduct the ceremony. I agreed to do it, and I flew to Knoxville at my own expense. I felt kindly to both of them. It was not just that I doubted his guilt; it went far beyond that. I knew that if Martin were alive and in my position, he would have married them even if he knew Ray was guilty. As one of my sons said to me, 'If you believe all that stuff you've been preaching, you'll do it.' He was right, of course."

Ramsey Clark's perspective on Ray differs from that of Lawson, Bevel, and many other black civil rights activists. As the attorney general under President Johnson, Clark was responsible for the swift entry of the FBI into the murder investigation, even though the crime was technically not a federal but a state offense.

"Many blacks believe Ray had powerful help," said Clark, now a New York attorney. "I understand their torment and sympathize with it as a human matter. But I had a duty to make an independent, rational judgment based on all the evidence—and from the very beginning, the evidence indicated only one person acting. In practically everything he did—robberies, travel, everything—he was a loner, a man who didn't plan and carry out things with other people."

Ironically, the federal government had to downplay political and conspiratorial motives in the crime in order to extradite Ray from England—and then had to claim a probability of conspiracy in order to justify FBI intervention in the case. And since the FBI was already engaged in secret surveillance of King, it would have been doubly ironic—or, to state it bluntly, hypocritical—for the government to say, in effect, We're entitled to spy on him, but if he gets killed, we can't get involved. These contradictions caused Ramsey Clark much grief, and he is still bothered by them.

"It's clear from the record that J. Edgar Hoover hated Dr. King," he said. "That's not the most analytical word, perhaps, but it's a fair word. There's plenty of evidence in the files, much of it widely circulated, to show that the bureau considered King to be one of the most dangerous men in America. Furthermore, there were some types of investigations you couldn't depend on the FBI to conduct, because they were too cozy with local law enforcement officials. So I can understand why some people look suspiciously at the FBI's involvement in the effort to solve this murder.

"But the very fact of Hoover's hatred of King made it all the more necessary in his eyes for the investigation to be virtually flawless. In order to protect the bureau from attack by people who knew of his bias, he felt a unique self-interest in conducting the most intensive and thorough investigation. They did just that, in my view—and now, after all these years, the conclusion they came to still holds up: that Ray, acting alone, planned and carried out Dr. King's assassination. That may not mean that someone didn't put him up to it—but if they did, they kept their distance and covered their tracks so well that no one has ever found incriminating evidence of a conspiracy."

Washington attorneys Bernard Fensterwald, Jr., and James Lesar are totally unconvinced by Ramsey Clark's reasoning. Their extensive efforts in federal court to win a new trial for Ray finally failed in the U.S. Supreme Court in December 1976. Along the way, they became convinced that Ray was set up to be convicted of the crime—and that the government was perfectly willing, even eager, to let him pay for it.

"There was never any effort on the part of state or federal authorities to get to the bottom of the murder," said Fensterwald. "All they ever wanted was to nail one man: James Earl Ray. The FBI got into the case by alleging a conspiracy to violate King's civil rights and then did everything they possibly could to avoid pursuing it. The state's case, which was put together with massive help from the FBI, was a straight murder charge against Ray—no conspiracy. They could not have proved him guilty beyond a reasonable doubt, and they didn't want to risk losing. The state and federal government had to have somebody to convict, or the social upheaval would have been horrendous, so they pressured Percy Foreman to plea-bargain, and he gave away his client's chance to testify before a jury. Phil Canale even threatened to call William Bradford Huie as a witness against Ray."

Canale, the district attorney in Memphis at the time, denies that he engineered Ray's guilty plea. "Neither I nor anyone working for me put pressure on the defense to plea-bargain," he said. "In fact, they came to me with the idea. I don't recall saying anything to Foreman about calling Huie to testify. Looking back, I still think we handled it right. There was no conspiracy. No credible proof was ever presented to show that anyone else was involved but Ray. I feel just as strongly now as I did then that justice was done."

James Lesar scoffs at that notion. He and Fensterwald, in seeking a jury trial for Ray, contended that there had been a miscarriage of justice in the way the plea was obtained, in the financial arrangements between Huie and Foreman, and in the way the case was handled in court. And beyond all that, Lesar is convinced that someone other than Ray killed King. "I don't think he fired the shot," he said. "I don't even think the fatal shot came from the rooming house. That means there had to be another gun and another gunman. Ray was set up."

Phil Canale acknowledged that he and other Tennessee officials, including Governor Buford Ellington, welcomed the help of the FBI in the King murder probe, and he conceded that the state's case against Ray was largely based on investigative work done by agents of the bureau. But the FBI's credibility as an impartial agency had already been seriously eroded by its handling of other civil rights–related cases, and its reputation for right-wing bias lingered long after J. Edgar Hoover's death.

One person in an unusually good position to assess political attitudes and internal operations in the bureau was Arthur Murtagh, now retired after more than twenty years of service as a special agent. He was based in Atlanta from 1960 to 1971 and was one of a handful of men in the security section assigned to keep a secret watch on Martin Luther King.

"In his vendetta against King, Hoover became progressively more fanatical," said Murtagh. "He was a real bigot, so biased that he wanted to see King destroyed, and when the murder happened, he didn't want the bureau to get involved in the investigation. It was Ramsey Clark who insisted that we enter the case. But the FBI didn't look for a conspiracy. That would have given validity to the injured side, to the blacks. So if we had to be in it, Hoover wanted in and out as quickly as possible. He wanted to pin a criminal offense on somebody before it could be shown to be a conspiracy, a political crime."

Murtagh took care to avoid the direct assertion that FBI officials were knowingly and purposely involved in a plot to assassinate King. Instead, he said that many people in the bureau leaned to the right with Hoover and "worked within the informal network of right-wing groups to get and sometimes give information, and supported informers who committed serious crimes, including murder. I'm not saying that FBI agents murdered anyone, but I am saying that they created and arranged a climate in which death took place."

Murtagh said he had "no knowledge that any specific person in the bureau was a direct participant in this conspiracy—but I'm absolutely convinced in my own mind that there *was* a conspiracy, and that it included some people known to and even paid by the FBI. That means there are people out there walking around—unless they've since died—who took part in the King murder, who know what happened, and who believe what they did was right. That's a sad truth, but it is the truth. It's also J. Edgar Hoover's legacy."

Writers, no less than investigators and lawyers, have widely divergent perceptions of the King-Ray story. George McMillan, author of *The Making of an Assassin,* believes now, "more than ever, that Ray acted alone to commit this crime. I don't think anybody helped him, not in any important conspiratorial way. Hundreds of people have spent thousands of hours trying to demolish the facts, and they have all failed. Ray was the lone assassin; that's the indestructible fact."

William Bradford Huie, perhaps the best known of the King assassination authors, reached the same conclusion in *He Slew the Dreamer* and in numerous other public pronouncements on the case. His views and those of Harold Weisberg, author of *Frame-Up*, a private investigator's "defense of James Earl Ray," represent the poles of opposite opinion.

Huie made contact with Ray while he was still in jail in London and began the procedure by which the author and two attorneys—first Arthur Hanes, then Percy Foreman—came to control the legal rights to Ray's story. "Everyone wanted to believe there was a conspiracy," said Huie, a seventy-five-year-old writer whose work is widely appreciated. "I certainly believed it, and that's what I set out to prove." But sometime in the fall of 1968, just as Ray was about to drop Hanes and engage Foreman to defend him, Huie began to have doubts.

"I came to realize that Ray was just a small-time criminal," he said. "He wanted recognition, glory, so he planned this crime and carried it out on his own. He had no help, none whatsoever—he was just lucky, and he almost got away with it. Believe me, I'm an old reporter, and a damn good one—I didn't take anything for granted, and I even had Ray's cooperation through his attorneys, although I didn't talk to him personally until after he had pleaded guilty and gone to the penitentiary in Nashville. You have to understand that I had more interest than anyone in finding a conspiracy. It would have been a sensational story, and it would have made lots of money—magazines, books, movies, TV. I put up at least sixty thousand dollars to secure the cooperation of Ray and the lawyers, and the lawyers ended up with almost all of that money. What I ended up with was a story saying that one little insignificant man killed Dr. King. It was hard to believe, and it certainly wasn't the sensational story I thought I'd find, but it was the truth, and there was nothing to do but tell it just that way."

In an interview with a Nashville newspaper reporter in 1977, Huie said Foreman got Ray to plead guilty because "he simply saw that Ray was an unstable racist who could not be controlled" in a courtroom. In a recent telephone conversation from his Alabama home, Huie said, "Foreman was more interested in avoiding a trial than the government was. There was no conspiracy, so there would be no big money, and no drama, and he didn't want to get tied up in a long drawn-out case that he couldn't win. Foreman wanted to make a deal and get out. He called me from Houston just before the scheduled court appearance in March 1969. Ray had told him he didn't want to plead guilty, he wanted to testify, and Foreman was worried."

According to Huie, Foreman said, "We ought to leak a story to the press that Ray is going to go into court on Monday and plead guilty. It'll make Ray mad, and scared, and when he simmers down he'll be ready to do what I'm telling him to do."

And so, Huie recalled, "That's just what I did. I leaked the story to a reporter in Huntsville, Alabama, and it was big news all over the country. And sure enough, by the time Foreman got to Memphis, Ray was ready to cooperate. The deal had been made—a guilty plea in exchange for ninety-nine years—and Ray had to go through with it or he'd have been sent to the electric chair. Foreman knew Ray was guilty. What he was trying to do was save his life, and that's what he did."

The way eighty-four-year-old Percy Foreman recalled it, he didn't have any trouble convincing Ray to plead guilty. "Hell, it was Ray's idea," he said from his office in Houston. "Once I saw how strong the state's case was, I was sure they wouldn't settle for anything less than a death sentence. I might have been able to get a hung jury if I could have hired a prominent black lawyer or a white liberal like John Jay Hooker, Sr., of Nashville, but Ray wouldn't agree to that. He wanted me to try to make a deal to keep him out of the electric chair. Hugh Stanton, the public defender, was working with me, and he said he thought Phil Canale, the prosecutor, would consider a proposal from us. So I got Ray to write it out in his own handwriting that he would plead guilty, and I took that to Canale and the judge, and that's how the agreement was reached."

Foreman said he had no doubt at all that Ray was Martin Luther King's lone assassin. "He not only did it," the attorney asserted, "he wanted to be known as the one who did it. He wanted the boys back in the Missouri penitentiary to know he had made it to the big time. That was his motive. He did it without any help, except from his brothers, and he'd have gotten away if he hadn't thrown down the bundle that had his rifle and his belongings in it. I saved his life, and he practically got down on his knees to thank me—and then within a day or two, he repudiated everything and started trying to reverse it."

Author Harold Weisberg can draw upon tens of thousands of pages of data he has accumulated on the King assassination to contradict virtually every important assertion made by Foreman and Huie. The seventy-three-year-old Weisberg, a Maryland resident, is a former newspaperman and private investigator. He has studied and written about assassinations in this country since 1963, when President Kennedy was murdered in Dallas. In *Frame-Up,* his meticulously detailed account of the King-Ray murder case, he maintains that Ray was a decoy, not a knowing conspirator; that neither the FBI nor the state ever even looked for a conspiracy; that the state's case could have been destroyed under cross-examination; that Ray's guilty plea was coerced; and that the people who planned and carried out King's assassination are still at large.

"I've done more investigative work on this case than anyone else," he said. "I filed suit under the Freedom of Information Act to get over sixty thousand pages from the FBI's files. I've spent many hours with James Earl Ray, and I've talked to dozens of other people who have some knowledge of the story. All I've ever wanted is to bring out the truth, the whole truth, and let the chips fall where they may."

The truth as Weisberg sees it is that Ray was in a criminal association for more than a year with unknown others who set him up to be the unwitting decoy and the prime suspect in the King murder. "Ray didn't commit the crime, and the government knew it," Weisberg said. "I don't agree with those who say the FBI plotted the crime, but they never investigated it, either. By their own admission, they focused on Ray right from the start and carried out a full-scale fugitive hunt to find him, but they never conducted a conspiracy investigation to solve the murder. It suited everybody—the prosecution, the defense, the Memphis establishment, the FBI, and William Bradford Huie—to pin it on Ray and close the books, so that's what they did."

And who were the people who planned the crime and drew Ray into it? "I don't know," said Weisberg, "and I doubt if Ray does either. He might know enough to get a good investigation started, but I doubt if he knows any real names—and if he did know, he probably wouldn't tell. If he put the heat on somebody, he'd probably be killed."

Weisberg is firmly convinced that a vigorous defense would have saved James Earl Ray from the judgment that he plotted and carried out the King murder. "There are no dependable witnesses to testify that Ray was in the rooming house, gun in hand, when the fatal shot was fired," he declared. "There is no proof that he ever fired the rifle he bought in Birmingham, or even that it was the murder weapon. The FBI couldn't find his fingerprints on the white Mustang. He has been called a cold-blooded killer, a racist, a right-wing political nut, a criminal who yearned for notoriety—and yet, in his long history of crimes, he never once fired a shot, never physically hurt anyone, and no one has yet been able to expose him as a fire-breathing hater of blacks, a political fanatic, or a man who craves public exposure for any reason. He is an intelligent man, a cunning man, but nothing in his career indicates that he is capable of planning and carrying out a crime like this, and then making his escape."

Eleven locked doors separate James Earl Ray, Number 65477, from the world beyond the walls of the castlelike Victorian fortress known as the Tennessee State Prison. His windowless cell in Unit 6—death row—is the place where he has been isolated from other inmates since 1981. He can talk with prisoners in adjacent cells but cannot see them. Once a day he is led in handcuffs to a small interior yard where he can exercise for one hour. The only other times he leaves the cell are when he goes to the showers (taken to and from in handcuffs) and when he has visitors. Regular visitors—his wife, Anna, and his brother Jerry—can see him for an hour once a week. All others must have his permission and the approval of the warden to meet with him in the unit's visiting room.

That room is actually a cell within a room. Ray is brought there first and locked in the cell; then his visitor enters and is locked in the cell with him. They sit in hard plastic chairs at a formica-topped table. No one else is in the room, but guards look in frequently through a glass panel in the outer door.

At age fifty-eight, Ray looks much the same as he did when he was jailed in Memphis eighteen years ago. He is an inch or so under six feet tall and weighs slightly more than his former 170 pounds. His dark brown hair has turned gray at the temples, and he reads with the aid of a pair of gold-rimmed glasses. No wrinkles line his face, but there is a thin two-inch scar on his left cheek, a reminder of the time five years ago when he was attacked and stabbed. He dresses in a blue prison shirt with snaps for buttons, dark blue pants with vertical white stripes emblazoned DEPT. OF CORRECTIONS, and soft-soled slippers. He wears a plain gold wedding band on the ring finger of his left hand. On first meeting with a stranger, he seems indirect and distracted, somewhat ill at ease, even shy, but as the conversation progresses, he relaxes a bit. His pale blue eyes move quickly away from and back to his visitor as he speaks in rapid bursts in a voice that is slightly high-pitched and nasal.

On August 1, 1986, we talked for three hours.

"My health is pretty good, considering," he began. "I probably eat too much, but I'm interested in nutrition, and I try to take care of myself. I never have smoked, don't use drugs—not even caffeine—and I lift weights every other day out in the yard. Until about two months ago they wouldn't take me out there except at night, and I got pale as a sheet, but now I've got some color back. Actually, this death row unit is kind of unhealthy. I've been trying to get transferred back to the general population, but they won't do it. They say I'm here for my own protection. When anybody else gets stabbed in prison, they put the person that did it in segregation; with me, it's the other way around."

Ray spends most of his waking hours writing or reading ("law books, mostly, to help in the suits I'm involved in"), keeping some printed materials in his cell and having others brought to him from the prison library and from outside. He said he hasn't read most of the books about the King assassination, though he has scanned several of them—and sued some of the authors. "William Bradford Huie wrote a lot of vicious things about me," he said. "I have no really hard feelings toward him, though. He's just a mercenary type, just looking out for himself." As for current events, Ray said he doesn't pay much attention—seldom watches the television set in his cell, or listens to the radio, or reads newspapers or magazines—but it is apparent from his conversation that he is familiar with people and events in the news.

He reads and writes well, and quickly. Recently he turned over to an editor—someone he declines to identify—a book manuscript that he worked on for five years. "It shows the government's duplicity—all the classified records, the double standard," he explained. "I'd like to get it published overseas, so people there can see that the stuff American politicians and the media criticize in places like Nicaragua and Chile is the same stuff that's happening in the United States. The book deals with my confinement in segregation, the stabbings, how the prison system operates. We also go into who we think financed the King murder. It won't necessarily clear me—I can't prove too much from jail—but what you can show is the tactics the government used to convict you, and if the public reads that, it's going to raise some questions about whether the person is guilty."

Jerry Ray comes from Missouri to visit his brother once or twice a month, and Anna Ray, who lives in Tennessee, also visits about that frequently. "My wife used to come once a week," said James Earl Ray, "but she got assaulted by an inmate a year or two ago—he hit her with one of those big floor ashtrays—and it kind of scared her off. She doesn't come now as often as she used to."

Ray shrugs at how commonplace prison violence is. "I was in the general population at Brushy Mountain when I got stabbed," he said. "There was two rival gangs—one black and one white—and I just happened to be in the middle. I don't think it was anything personal toward me. It's no big deal getting stabbed—there's hundreds of people that gets stabbed in prison. The only big deal for me is, I'm the one that got locked up for it. I've never said who stabbed me. It wouldn't make no difference who it was anyway." (Three inmates were tried and convicted of the assault, and time was added to their sentences.)

After being represented over the years by so many lawyers he's lost count, Ray now handles most of his legal business by himself. "I've got a lawyer helping me in a civil case," he said, "but other than that, I'm not tied up with a lawyer now. I've never had any money to hire attorneys, so I've just had to get whoever I could. Mark Lane is probably the most effective lawyer I've had. He'll defend anybody. How many Jewish lawyers do you know who will defend Moslem and Arab revolutionaries? He'll go all out for you, too. If I got a new trial, Mark is probably the first one I'd ask to defend me."

Getting a new trial is a subject that James Earl Ray talks about often, even though previous failures now make the prospects dim. "If I get a new trial," he said, "the only thing the courts will consider is

205

whether I was denied my constitutional rights, such as being coerced into pleading guilty, or a conflict of interest among the attorneys. It's all very complicated, but those would be the grounds for granting a new trial, and then the state would have to prove that I'm guilty. I don't know what they'd argue in court, whether they'd say it was a lone nut that did the killing, or a conspiracy, or what. They've never committed themselves one way or the other. If I got a jury trial, I'm almost positive I'd get acquitted. They don't have no case against me. It's not so much that what's in there is enough to acquit me, but it's not enough to convict, not enough to support their case. We can't get access to their case because so much of the information has been classified—in the state courts, in the Justice Department, in the House assassinations committee; 185 cubic feet of classified material in the FBI alone. Everything that might be helpful to me has been classified. So I believe the government doesn't have enough evidence to convict me, and that's why I can't get a new trial."

Ray said he "wouldn't be surprised" if the FBI was indirectly involved in planning the King assassination: "They use informants to get inside and stir up trouble, and if they get into some heavy stuff, kill somebody or cause somebody to be killed, the FBI protects them and covers up for them. It's been proved that they had people inside the King organization, watching him, trying to discredit him. Then when he was killed, they wanted to pin it on a single person, someone like me, somebody who's expendable. They wanted to keep the lid on, keep blacks from burning up the cities. That's what Canale said, and what Governor Ellington said. He said if the case went to trial, there'd be widespread destruction in the U.S."

In Ray's eyes, it is the press as much as the government that should be blamed for the way the King murder investigation was handled. "When the media wanted everything to come out about Nixon, it came out," he said. "In the King case, it was just the opposite—the government wanted to keep the truth covered up, and the news media went right along with them. They're all tied up together—the government, the politicians, the news media. The public don't know what's going on. Public opinion is whatever the TV networks and news magazines say it is, and the politicians go on doing whatever they want to do anyway. There's no point in talking to the news media, no point in being in the public eye. I don't care anything about seeing myself on TV or reading stories about me in the press. It's just a waste of time. If I got out of here tomorrow, I'd go to another country and forget all about this stuff."

However much or little he pays heed to the pronouncements of politicians and the media, Ray does acknowledge the efforts of some black public figures to support his attempt to get a jury trial: "Most whites are uptight about what they say in public, but a lot of blacks in positions of power don't care what the media says. James Bevel came to see me when I was in jail in Memphis and then said he didn't think I killed King. People like James Lawson, Ralph Abernathy, Jesse Jackson, Hosea Williams, they all visited me, and they all spoke up for a trial. I thought a lot of them for having the nerve to come down here and do that. I don't recall any white politicians who ever did it. Percy Foreman told the papers that I didn't want any blacks coming around me, but I never said that. Those guys are more independent of the news media than whites are. A guy like Hosea Williams, he says what he thinks, he's not tied to the white establishment. I'd be a lot more comfortable with somebody like him than I would be with Phil Canale or the governor of Tennessee."

The invitation to James Lawson to conduct their wedding ceremony was his bride's idea, Ray said, but he had no objection. "Anna contacted him," he said. "It didn't matter to me who did it, as long as he was a preacher. I think she may have asked some local preachers, but they were afraid of what people would say. Reverend Lawson wasn't afraid. He seemed like a highly intelligent person, and a tough person mentally, and strong-willed. A lot of people have said I'm a racist. But you know, you can make a racist out of just about anybody. To me, a racist is somebody who commits hostile acts against a person of another race. I've never been involved in any of that. I just look at individuals—and I have a lot more respect for many blacks than I do for many whites."

Time is not on Ray's side in his efforts to obtain a jury trial. The courts have rejected all his appeals, leaving his original guilty plea and his testimony before the House Select Committee on Assassinations as his official response to the charges against him. They are a weak response, at best. He said he pleaded guilty because "I had been put in a position where I didn't have no other choice. I made a serious mistake there. I wasn't under oath. It was a narrow technical plea—I was saying that I was just as guilty under the law as other parties in the conspiracy, if there was a conspiracy. See, what I didn't know at the time was that Foreman had agreed to accept everything Canale said as truth—had agreed to ratify the state's case. I certainly didn't mean to plead guilty to that."

As for his House testimony, Ray maintained that the written statement he read at the Washington hearings in 1978 "was all I knew about what happened that day. There might be some small, insignificant errors, but in general, what I wrote down and read to the committee was my actions. Later on, we found out more about what other people did, but that was everything I knew about my actions, and I'd still tell it the same way.

"I had been to a service station and was on my way back to the rooming house when I saw the police had blocked off the road. One of them waved me off, said I couldn't go in there. I still didn't know what had happened. I turned south and drove through a predominantly black neighborhood, looking for a phone. I had this New Orleans number, and I was going to call to see if anything had happened on the gun deal I thought I was part of. But then, when I got toward the edge of town, I heard on the radio that King had been shot, and pretty soon I heard that the police were looking for a white man in a white Mustang. That's when I decided to head for Atlanta.

"The state claimed that I or whoever shot King ran from the rooming house and threw some items down on the street and got in a Mustang and drove off. But since then I've found out that there were two Mustangs there, and about twelve or fourteen policemen within a hundred feet. But their testimony is classified. So is the information on the rifle. I never fired it, and I doubt very much if anyone did. Harold Weisberg said in his book that it never had been sighted in, zeroed in. CBS filed suit in 1975 to get the rifle for a ballistics test, but the court refused to let it be fired. I told the House committee that somebody else killed King, and I don't know who they were."

In the final analysis, it is not knowing "who they were" that has sealed James Earl Ray's fate. He has maintained that if he could get a new trial, he could present evidence to indicate who financed the King assassination, but he adds that "we don't have the actual person's name or anything like that." He has said he would testify in his own behalf, but he admits that his testimony would not include anything about his own actions that he hasn't already told; apparently, only the government's classified materials on what others said and did could possibly clear Ray or prove the existence of a conspiracy.

His primary interest, he said, is not in clearing his name or seeing someone else brought to justice, but simply in getting out of jail: "Of course, it would be real satisfying to have this all cleared up, but I don't ever expect that, and I don't think they'll ever find the person who killed King. It was a professional killing. We might be able to show who the bag man was, and who he represented, but it would be very hard to do. I don't think there was ever more than four or five people that knew all the details of this case—and if they're still living, they'll probably never tell.

"So I'm just interested in getting out of jail. I'd like to have a trial so I could show how devious and repressive the power structure is. That's more important to me than what people think—most of them are going to believe whatever they read or see on TV anyway. I'd just like to be able to say I outlived the prosecutors and judges that put me here, because I know what a big thrill they'll get if I die in solitary confinement."

The pattern in Tennessee and most other states is that prisoners with ninety-nine-year sentences get parole consideration after serving about thirty years. Even with one or two years added to his sentence for his escape in 1977, Ray thus might conceivably be allowed to go free in the year 2001, when he will be seventy-three years old.

"I don't think they'd let me go unless it served their purposes," he said. "If I was eighty-five or ninety years old and wanted to make a big confession, they might release me and call it a humanitarian act—but I'm not counting on it. The only way I'm going to get out is through a new trial, and I still have hope of that. I'm not making plans to stay in some rat-hole like this for the rest of my life. I might be here, but I just don't make no plans about it—that would be a depressing thought. You've got to figure you're going to get out one way or the other. I never have gone into a jail figuring that it would be my home for the rest of my life.

"They say if you stay in long enough, you get into a frame of mind where you're satisfied. I think that's really what the state wants. That's why drugs are the best friend a warden ever had. People get on drugs and they're not thinking about escaping or getting a new trial or anything else—they're just thinking about getting their fix.

"I can't see that. Drugs take all your money, your time, your thought. I'd rather have hope, and keep on trying to get out of jail."

When his sixty-third birthday passed in March 1991, James Earl Ray remained in maximum-security detention at Brushy Mountain State Prison in east Tennessee, where he was transferred in the late 1980s. His birthdate also marked the beginning of his twenty-third year of imprisonment for the murder of Martin Luther King, Jr.

MORRIS DEES AND THE SOUTHERN POVERTY LAW CENTER

This article on the Alabama-based Southern Poverty Law Center and its founder Morris Dees was researched and written as an assignment for Foundation News, *a bimonthly journal based in Washington, and was published in the May–June 1988 issue. The* Progressive *also published a version of it in July 1988. Because of space limitations, neither magazine was able to use more than about half of the lengthy story. All of it—some ten thousand words—is printed here for the first time.*

The scene was like something straight out of Perry Mason: a hushed courtroom, a tearful defendant, a stunning climax to an emotional trial. With the judge's permission, the defendant, a twenty-three-year-old white man, stood in front of the jury box and poured out his heart.

"Everything I said is true," he declared. "I was acting as a Klansman when I done this. I hope that people learn from my mistake." Turning to the mother of his murder victim, he pleaded in a tremulous voice for her forgiveness. Then, to the jury he sobbed, "I do hope you decide a judgment against me and everyone involved, because we are guilty."

In his seat at the plaintiff's table, Morris Dees, Jr., chief trial counsel for the Southern Poverty Law Center of Montgomery, Alabama, felt the hair rise on the back of his neck. It was, he said later, "the most emotional moment I've ever experienced in a courtroom."

That 1987 drama in federal court in Mobile came to an almost anticlimactic end four hours later when the all-white jury returned a seven-million-dollar damage judgment against the United Klans of

America, a secret cell of white supremacists once reputed to be the oldest and largest Ku Klux Klan organization in the nation.

The defendant and another man had already been convicted in an earlier criminal trial for the brutal murder and lynching of their randomly chosen victim, a nineteen-year-old black youth. The legal strategy that led to the civil case and resulted in such a crushing economic blow (albeit largely symbolic) to the financially strapped Klan unit was conceived and executed by Dees and his legal associates.

More than a century after Jefferson Davis made Montgomery the cradle of the Confederacy and fifteen years after the Reverend Martin Luther King, Jr., made it the birthplace of the civil rights movement, Dees used his skill as an attorney and his talent as a salesman to establish the Southern Poverty Law Center there. In the nearly two decades since then, attorneys for the center have built an impressive record of courtroom victories in a diversity of cases affecting minorities and low-income citizens in the South.

Even more remarkable than the Southern Poverty Law Center's rise to prominence in the "New South" of the post–civil rights era is the success story of Morris Dees himself. Born into a family of moderate means in the rural south Alabama black belt during the Great Depression, he turned imagination and hard work into agricultural profits while still in high school. Then, during five years as an undergraduate and law student at the University of Alabama, Dees sharpened his sales and marketing skills to a fine edge. He and a partner, fellow student Millard Fuller, sold everything from holly wreaths to birthday cakes, and by the time they moved to Montgomery in 1960 to start a law practice and a mail-order sales business, they had assets in excess of a quarter of a million dollars.

The business quickly overshadowed the law practice, with cookbook publishing being the most lucrative of a variety of ventures. The company grossed a million dollars in 1963, and the two men were millionaires before they turned thirty. Fuller sold his interest to Dees in 1965 for one million dollars; Dees in turn sold the enterprise to the Times-Mirror Company of Los Angeles at the end of the decade for a reported six million dollars.

In the meantime, Dees had turned again to his law practice, and he showed a growing interest in civil liberties and civil rights cases. In

1970 he formed a partnership with attorney Joseph J. Levin, Jr., and the following year they incorporated the Southern Poverty Law Center to focus on social activist litigation. For capital, Dees relied not on his own fortune but on the same sort of direct-mail appeals he had mastered in his business, and soon the SPLC was a well-financed enterprise, a liberal and independent presence in the midst of a Southern citadel of conservatism.

Dees's golden touch as a money-maker was not limited to business and the law. In 1972 he signed on as a volunteer fund-raiser for presidential candidate George McGovern, and his efforts reportedly netted the campaign more than twenty million dollars. For Jimmy Carter in 1976, Ted Kennedy in 1980, and Gary Hart in 1984, he also raised multimillion-dollar sums.

At the law center in Montgomery, Dees and Levin and a small staff of attorneys tackled such issues as legislative redistricting, employment discrimination, capital punishment, workplace safety, and numerous inequities based on race, class, sex, and age. In 1980 they began Klanwatch, a monitoring and reporting project to expose terrorist activities of Ku Klux Klan groups and other racist organizations.

In the improving social and economic environment that is one of the legacies of the civil rights movement in the South, the SPLC has done quite well for itself while doing good for others. Up from poverty, so to speak, it has achieved institutional permanence and respectability—has, in fact, become a sturdy pillar of the local economy. The center now has a staff of about thirty-five people, a million-dollar headquarters building, an annual budget of close to $2.5 million, and a permanent endowment estimated to be valued at more than $22 million.

Morris Dees, still boyish-looking at fifty-one years of age, has remained the moving force behind the Southern Poverty Law Center. He has been honored for his efforts by such groups as the American Bar Association, Common Cause, the National Association for the Advancement of Colored People, and Ralph Nader's Trial Lawyers for Public Justice. His accomplishments as a lawyer, businessman, and fund-raiser are the stuff of legend. His personal wealth and that of his organization have made him an object of envy. Not surprisingly, he is a figure of some notoriety and controversy—greatly respected by some, disliked and distrusted by others.

Defenders as well as critics often speak of him ambivalently as an unpredictable character, a bundle of contradictions. Dees, they say, is a crafty hustler with a social conscience, an outgoing man and a moody loner, a fearless but thin-skinned combatant, a poor country boy turned wealthy urban adult, a Baptist in transition to Judaism. For all his public exposure, he remains a very private man, seldom written about in any depth and not well understood even by those closest to him.

Looking back on his colorful career and listening to a host of Dees watchers, pro and con, helps to bring the man and his work into focus.

When he was born in rural Macon County, east of Montgomery, in 1936, Morris Seligman Dees, Jr., became the second-generation bearer of a name his grandfather had chosen to honor a prominent south Alabama Jewish merchant who had befriended him. The Deeses were devoted Baptists and farm dwellers (Morris, Sr., was an overseer and gin operator on another man's cotton farm), and had it not been for the ravages of the Depression, they would have lived a comfortable cut above the poverty level.

As the first of five children, Morris, Jr. ("Bubba," the family called him), grew to maturity with few amenities and lots of responsibility. When he reached his teens, he began to raise and sell farm products (watermelons, chickens, cattle); by the time he graduated from Montgomery's Sidney Lanier High School in 1955, he had transcended his "farm boy" image and salted away more than enough to put himself through college. "I was making more profit than my daddy," Dees recalls. "He had debts, a family, other demands on his money. Most of mine was clear."

Soon after Dees entered the University of Alabama as a freshman that fall, black citizens back in Montgomery launched a boycott of the segregated city buses, and twenty-seven-year-old Martin Luther King, Jr., emerged from the pastorate of the Dexter Avenue Baptist Church there to become the central figure in the Southern-born, black-led civil rights movement. And at the university in Tuscaloosa the following February, Dees watched from a safe distance as a young black woman, Autherine Lucy, accompanied by a priest, walked past scores of angry white protesters to be admitted under a federal court order. (Miss Lucy was expelled a few days later, after the demonstrators had become a riotous mob and she had accused state and university officials of complicity with them.)

Segregation was not an issue that Dees was ready to jump into—on either side. "I remember feeling some sympathy for the girl," he says. "I've always pulled for the underdog. But I had a traditional white Southerner's feelings for segregation. I did make some comments in Sunday school that weekend to the effect that we ought not to hate people we don't even know, and right after that the preacher removed me from the leadership post I held because he said I was 'too immature' to serve."

What seized the young freshman's attention then—and held it through five undergraduate and law school years—was not civil rights or academics, but selling. "I got married right out of high school," he says, "and I was strongly motivated to make a lot of money. I had a mail-order business going pretty soon after I enrolled at Alabama. A couple of years later I met Millard Fuller, who had come from Auburn University to enter law school, and pretty soon we became partners."

They were a pair of earnest strivers—Southern country white boys, church-raised, married, ambitious, eager to get rich and maybe to get into politics, the ultimate salesman's challenge. (Both of them worked as student organizers for political candidates, Dees in 1958 for a self-styled populist gubernatorial dark horse by the name of George Corley Wallace.) Business was too good, though, for either the political siren or the lure of the law to entice them away.

With a devotion that seemed almost religious in its intensity, they made money hand over fist—and, indeed, they sometimes linked their material success to sacred roots. "I learned everything I know about hustling from the Baptist Church," Morris Dees once told a reporter. "Spending Sundays sitting on those hard benches, listening to the preacher pitch salvation . . . why, it was like getting a Ph.D. in selling."

Practically every idea they came up with turned a profit. They sold a quarter of a million holly wreaths, published a student telephone directory, even ventured into real estate. One of their most imaginative schemes was pitched to the average of sixteen University of Alabama students celebrating birthdays each day. Through postcards to their parents, the entrepreneurs sold personalized and campus-delivered birthday cakes to an average of four correspondents a day for three years, at a profit of two dollars a cake.

By the time they moved to Montgomery in 1960 to start a law practice and a mail-order sales business, they had a six-figure reserve fund at their disposal. Fuller remembers their initial ventures into legal work as being "little more than ambulance-chasing." It was the direct-mail selling that brought them attention and wealth. They sold door-mats, toothbrushes, tractor seat cushions; they published cookbooks and directories. At one point their book company, Famous Recipes Press, was said to be the largest cookbook publisher in the nation. The volume of their incoming and outgoing mail reportedly exceeded that of the entire Alabama state government—the other major enterprise in Montgomery.

While the South was locked in the throes of social upheaval in the 1960s, Dees and Fuller were single-mindedly in hot pursuit of their first million, a pinnacle each man reached in 1964. "Morris and I were able to go downtown together, pick out a Lincoln Continental with all the luxury options for each of us . . . and pay cash for both cars on the spot," wrote Fuller in a book some years later. He added: "Morris Dees and I, from the first day of our partnership, shared one overriding purpose: to make a pile of money. We were not particular about *how* we did it; we just wanted to be independently rich. During the eight years that we worked together, we never wavered in that resolve."

When the "freedom riders" demonstrated against segregation on interstate buses in 1961, they suffered severe beatings by white mobs in the Birmingham and Montgomery bus terminals. Fuller recalls agonizing privately with Dees over that shameful spectacle, but they concluded that "it would be bad for business if rising young lawyers and businessmen spoke out for social justice and equality." One of the men charged in connection with the beating of the freedom riders in Montgomery asked Dees and Fuller to defend him—and, wrote

Fuller, "we took the case. Our fee was paid by the Klan and the White Citizens' Council. We expressed openly our sympathies and support for what happened at the bus station."

Nothing seemed to slow the growth of the Fuller and Dees marketing enterprises, but Fuller grew increasingly unhappy with the path his life was taking, and when his marriage almost went on the rocks in late 1965, he decided on a drastic course of action. He sold his share of the business to Dees, and he and his wife also divested themselves of "our land and houses and boats and cars and cattle and horses." Without a backward glance, they took the money—something over two million dollars—and gave it away. Soon thereafter, they left Montgomery to take up missionary work in Africa. Millard Fuller is now the founding director of Habitat for Humanity, a Georgia-based international housing venture serving low-income families.

The continually expanding company that Morris Dees found himself the sole owner of at the beginning of 1966 was no longer challenging enough to hold his undivided attention, and as the decade wore on, he looked restlessly for new fields to conquer. (Politics, he says, was never a serious option; though he had once harbored an ambition to be governor of Alabama, the thought never carried over into active pursuit.) The U.S. Jaycees honored him as one of ten outstanding young men in America in 1967, but by then Dees was on the verge of leaving the commercial arena.

He and his wife, Beverly, were divorced in 1968 after thirteen years of marriage and two children. Easing gradually back into the practice of law, Dees began for the first time to take cases of a civil rights–civil liberties nature, and the challenge rekindled some of his lost enthusiasm.

As the decade drew to a close, he decided to make major changes in his life. He married again; he formed a law partnership with Joe Levin, Jr., a young attorney whose father was a prominent member of the Montgomery bar; and he accepted an offer of about six million dollars (some close observers say more) from the company that published the Los Angeles *Times* for the marketing firm that he and Millard Fuller had built out of imagination, cleverness, and relentless pursuit.

The year was 1970. Morris Dees had passed his thirty-third birthday, had attained the independent wealth of his dreams, had taken a new wife and a giant step in the direction of remodeling his career. He was ready for the next phase of his life to begin.

～

Jay Murphy, once the Mister Chips of the University of Alabama Law School faculty, well remembers when Dees and Fuller were there, and he has followed their careers with satisfaction and pride. "They've made a lot of money," he says, "and they've done a lot of good with it. Millard gave all of his to the Lord. Morris used his to do what the Lord would do if he was a lawyer."

What Morris has done as a lawyer, beginning in the late 1960s, is to take unpopular cases representing blacks and poor people suing for justice under recently passed civil rights laws. First through the Alabama branch of the American Civil Liberties Union and then with Joe Levin, Dees began to disengage himself from the attitude of "businesslike assent" to segregation that he and Fuller had maintained.

In 1968, the year of Martin Luther King's martyrdom in Memphis—three years after the dramatic Selma-to-Montgomery civil rights march, five years after Governor George Wallace's defiant stand against another attempt to desegregate the University of Alabama— Dees emerged as a hard-hitting lawyer for long-suffering victims of discrimination. With the same energy and intensity that he had applied to the pursuit of profits, he now sought equal justice under the law—and within a short time, he met with a similar degree of success.

He tried to stop Auburn University from building a branch campus in Montgomery and thus delaying the biracial expansion of historically black Alabama State University there (the effort failed). He and Levin brought pressure upon the city's YMCA to force open its recreational facilities to children of all races (that effort succeeded). They joined Birmingham lawyer Chuck Morgan and the American Civil Liberties Union in compelling the Alabama legislature to divide itself into single-member districts, thus assuring the election of the first black lawmakers since Reconstruction. They helped to force open the ranks of the Alabama state troopers to blacks.

"At first," recalls Wayne Greenhaw, a Montgomery journalist, "Morris shook everybody up. He took cases nobody else would touch. He's been responsible for bringing much change to this community, improving the lot of blacks and hitting the whites where it hurt—at the Y, in sports, in law enforcement. They couldn't ignore the man—he was rich, independent, successful, and he wasn't scared of anybody. He wasn't diplomatic about it, either—that's not his style. He had his big house, his fancy cars, his good-old-boy manner, and if folks didn't like it, he just thumbed his nose at them."

From his perspective, Dees no doubt found the experience satisfying, to say the least. Rising as he had from rather humble circumstances, he could identify and sympathize with poor people, white and black. He had grown up understanding that those who had no money were at the mercy of the well-to-do. Pulling for the underdog seemed to come naturally to him. The independence that only wealth could bring was finally his—and when he relied on the security of that wealth to snub the rich and serve the poor, everybody noticed.

With a half-million dollars of the profit from the sale of his company, Dees had collaborated with a former law professor to establish the James Madison Constitutional Law Foundation in New York. It was to be his vehicle for addressing basic legal and social issues in American society, but it never really got off the ground. "I was here, it was there, it didn't work," says Dees without elaboration. "I left the money and got out of it."

He wanted to stay in Montgomery and to keep living in the spacious ranch house he had built in 1963 on a two-thousand-acre farm in the fertile countryside some twenty-five miles outside the city. He also wanted to combine his direct-mail business experience with the practice of public-interest law. When the victories began to pile up in his crusade for the underclass in Alabama courtrooms, Dees concluded that he had a winning combination: poor people in need of representation, privileged people in need of humility, new laws to effect both, and a fund-raising strategy for paying the bills.

Morris Dees and Joe Levin set up the Southern Poverty Law Center on paper in 1970 and incorporated it as a nonprofit, tax-exempt organization the following year. "We borrowed twenty-five hundred dollars from the bank," Levin recalls, "and used it to start a direct-mail fund-raising program. Morris worked without pay, but he didn't put any of his own money into the operation. We both felt that if it couldn't be self-sustaining, it wasn't worth doing." (Dees says he did provide some of the start-up money but declines to say how much.)

Levin was the legal director, and Dees was the direct-mail specialist and idea man. They persuaded Julian Bond, the well-known black civil rights activist and Georgia state senator, to serve as president of the center, a largely honorary position, and a board of directors and an advisory council were named to add further visibility to the enterprise. The council never took an active part in the center, and the board, though it did meet at more or less regular intervals, was not a policy-making body; Dees and Levin were the real decision-makers, and Bond helped to draw attention and support to their activities.

Michael Fidlow, a direct-mail specialist, was hired away from the former Fuller and Dees marketing firm in Montgomery to become chief operations officer for the SPLC. He and Dees devised a fund-raising strategy that focused mainly on liberal donors outside the South, and they enjoyed great success in attracting support for the lawsuits that Levin and Dees were filing. "The timing was perfect for litigation in the civil rights field," says Fidlow, now a California executive. "Our focus was on groundbreaking cases that had the potential of defining new directions in the law, and when we started winning, we soon had more money than we could spend."

Fidlow stayed at the law center from 1971 to 1978, during which time the staff grew from four or five to about twenty. "By then," he recalls, "we had built up a donor base of about nine thousand people giving monthly, and we had a healthy reserve invested at 11 or 12 percent. Morris was a genius at direct-mail fund-raising—he still is, of course—and we all thought the center had reached the point where it no longer needed to raise funds. The job was done, and that seemed like a good time for me to leave, so I did."

It was Dees, with Fidlow's help, who found the donors and captured their interest and their continuing support with persuasive letters of appeal. Good prospect lists are essential to any direct-mail endeavor, and Dees knew how to get them. He built the SPLC's master list to big-league proportions with an astute early move: in late 1971, he volunteered to help raise funds for presidential candidate George McGovern, specifically offering to write the campaign-opening solicitation letter.

"I wrote a six-page letter," he recalls, "and they didn't know what to do with it. McGovern's advisers passed it around and edited it, and finally they asked me to send out a two-page version of it to their list of forty thousand names. I went ahead and printed the whole thing as I had written it, and got other lists from such organizations as the American Civil Liberties Union and Americans for Democratic Action, and we mailed the big letter to about 250,000 people. I used my own money to do it—in effect, I loaned the money to the campaign— because I was confident we'd do well, and I would get my loan back."

The response was dramatic. "Some people sent us their Social Security checks," says Dees. "One woman sent us her son's ten-thousand-dollar government insurance check after he was killed in Vietnam. The money just poured in. We got about a 15 percent response. During the course of the campaign, we mailed 15 million pieces and raised twenty-four million dollars, of which probably twenty-two million was net."

After the 1972 election Dees returned to the law center with high visibility and acclaim as a fund-raiser—and more important, with the campaign mailing list that he and others had compiled. "McGovern let me use it," he says. "It had grown to about 700,000 names, and they were the same kinds of people we looked to for support of the center." In a literal sense, the list was worth its weight in gold.

It was also in 1972 that the Southern Poverty Law Center won important victories in two pivotal lawsuits: the state trooper racial exclusion case and the legislative redistricting case. In just two years the center had become a major public-interest legal organization in the South. Three new attorneys—Howard Mandell, Charles Abernathy, and Pamela Horowitz—joined Dees and Levin on the legal team, and soon the caseload expanded into new areas: criminal justice, economic discrimination, occupational health and safety, the rights of children and the handicapped. Capital punishment also became a major law center interest after the U.S. Supreme Court reinstated the death penalty in 1976.

In 1975 Dees and his associates were involved in several highly publicized trials, including that of Joan Little, a black jail inmate in North Carolina who stabbed a white jailer to death when he allegedly tried to rape her. Dees raised major sums for the defense, and his handling of that and two other racially complicated murder cases at about the same time made him an object of white hostility in his hometown and elsewhere in the South.

Time magazine called him "the second most hated man in Alabama" (after federal judge Frank M. Johnson, Jr., who was handling desegregation cases). Dees seemed almost to thrive on the notoriety. White conservatives reviled him as a traitor to their way of life, but he also managed at times to draw wounded cries of injury from liberal whites and occasionally even from blacks.

After the Joan Little case, Dees and a Georgia attorney named Millard Farmer, an activist in capital punishment cases, were brought together by a mutual friend who wanted to see the two of them join forces. They subsequently formed Team Defense, an Atlanta-based project funded in the main by the SPLC and aimed at combatting the death penalty in the South.

The two lawyers quickly found themselves in a duel of wills and egos, and their alliance lasted only a year. "I asked him to take four or five cases and then produce some trial manuals for lawyers who would be working in the field," says Dees, "but he ended up taking twenty-some cases, and then wanted to hold us responsible for financing them. So we cut off his funds, and he tried to force us to pay for all his cases. We ended up paying enough to handle about four."

Farmer's version of the dispute is that Dees "funded the project for a year and then just suddenly quit cold turkey, without warning, and walked away from his commitment. I was naïve at first. I thought he was sincere. I thought the Southern Poverty Law Center raised money to do good for poor people, not simply to accumulate wealth. We had to subpoena him to appear in court and show cause why he should not be required to fund the defense. He countersued, and we settled. He paid us about the equivalent of a year's budget." (The actual settlement amount was about fifty thousand dollars.)

Bad feeling lingers between the two men. "Morris Dees is a skillful but deceptive lawyer who's running a basically dishonest operation," Millard Farmer declares. Says Dees tersely of Farmer: "He's a fool."

Farmer still handles a substantial number of capital punishment cases. Dees says the SPLC "has never been interested in going into the death penalty trial business" but rather in developing trial tactics and teaching them to other lawyers. In the mid-1970s, however, the law center was reported to have failed only once in twenty-five tries to save clients from death sentences, and in 1980 Dees told an interviewer that the SPLC was still representing twenty-four people on death row. It was not, however, an attractive cause around which large sums of money could be raised through the mail, and his realization of that may have dampened Dees's interest in the subject.

The success of his fund-raising efforts for McGovern inevitably sent Morris Dees's reputation soaring. His services were sought by several presidential candidates in 1976 before he finally agreed to serve as finance director of Jimmy Carter's campaign. It was a reluctant choice, Dees says, partly for philosophical reasons ("Jimmy's a political animal—he backs down on the issues"), but mainly because Dees was convinced that direct-mail appeals on Carter's behalf wouldn't work.

"You can't raise money through the mail for just any candidate," he explains. "You've got to have a candidate who's way out on the extremes—a Reagan, a Wallace, a McGovern, a Goldwater. The people who will give big money through the mail are either on the far right or the far left. They're true believers. You can't fire them up with a middle-of-the-road cause or candidate. You've got to have someone who can arouse people."

George Wallace is such a person—or was, in the stormy midcentury decades—and had he and Dees been on the same wavelength ideologically, they might have made an unbeatable combination, working as they were a stone's throw from each other for more than a quarter of a century. But the two men have had little to do with each other since Dees was a student campaigner for Wallace back in 1958. Lacking any apparent mutual affinity or respect, they have coexisted in Montgomery—not so much as mortal foes but rather as competitors whose strategy has been to ignore each other's presence.

There was an occasion in 1968, though, when Dees and the Wallace fund-raisers were thought to be collaborating. Ray Jenkins, then an editor for one of Montgomery's daily papers, recalls "coming upon Dees in Wallace's outer office during the heat of the governor's third-party campaign for president. Morris was taken aback to be found there. By way of explanation, he told me he was just talking shop, sharing some advice on direct-mail techniques. I remember writing a critical editorial about their exchange—a sort of 'politics makes strange bedfellows' piece."

As the Carter campaign rolled into high gear in 1976, Dees was widely hailed as the fund-raising genius of the political left, an opposite-poles version of the right wing's Richard Viguerie (who, incidentally, raised large sums for Wallace that same year and exchanged public compliments with Dees). In impressive substantiation of his reputation, Dees managed, in spite of new campaign finance restrictions and Carter's lack of extremism or charisma, to raise the maximum amount allowable under the law.

In the opinion of press secretary Jody Powell and other members of Carter's White House staff, Dees attracted significant numbers of volunteers, contributors, and dollars to the campaign—enough to earn him Carter's thanks and praise. They also say that Dees wanted Carter to reward him with a cabinet post—specifically, attorney general—and when he failed to get it, he left in a huff for Alabama.

Dees emphatically denies that he ever had such ambitions. "I had no interest whatsoever in working for the Carter administration," he says. "I wouldn't have moved to Washington for anything. When the campaign was over, I was ready to go back home, and I did."

Four years later Dees went to the White House to tell Carter he was going to work for Ted Kennedy in the 1980 campaign. "Jimmy had told me he would take a stand for abortion and against the death penalty—two of my main interests—but he didn't," says Dees. "We talked about those things when I went to see him, and then I told him I was joining Kennedy."

Powell's recollection of the meeting is altogether different: "Dees got around the appointment process somehow and got on Carter's calendar under false pretenses. He could have told any of us he was raising money for Kennedy, but I think he just wanted whatever satisfaction he could get from telling the president to his face. Morris is that kind of guy."

During the last years of the 1970s the Southern Poverty Law Center continued to expand and change. Joe Levin, the founding partner, took a post in the Carter administration in 1977, and he was replaced as legal director of the SPLC by John Carroll, a Harvard Law School master's graduate with an earlier background in Alabama. Others who had served in the small cadre of staff attorneys also moved on, and new ones came aboard, but the center never had more than five lawyers at a time, even though its caseload and operating budget grew steadily.

"Morris created a wonderful place for lawyers to work in public-interest law," says Ira Burnim, who joined the center in the late 1970s. "It was ideal, really, because you always knew you had the money and the resources to do litigation the way it ought to be done. Once the choices had been made about what cases to pursue, we were completely free to go wherever they led."

Deciding what cases to pursue was the only real sticking point. Says Carroll: "There were always lots of questions about mission and method—disagreements, it's fair to say—but Morris is very persuasive, and incredibly creative. I wouldn't call him a good personnel manager, but he's a great trial lawyer, and working with him has always been a stimulating experience."

It was also in the late 1970s that Julian Bond resigned as president of the law center. "It was by mutual agreement," he recalls. "I had been fairly active in making appearances for the center, but they wanted someone who could be more closely involved, and I just didn't have the time to do it. Also, I had been quoted on some issues concerning Jews and Arabs, and Morris was afraid my name was hindering fund-raising efforts with Jewish donors. I didn't agree with that, but I did think it was time for a change, so I stepped aside. I'm proud of my association with Morris and the center. They've done a lot of good."

That overriding sense of things accomplished, of victories won and goals achieved, colors many people's assessment of Dees and the SPLC. Chuck Morgan, who made his own indelible mark as an Alabama civil rights lawyer two decades ago and now is an attorney in Washington, praises Dees as "a good trial lawyer and a good low-key salesman. He's a genius at direct-mail fund-raising. Of course, he oversells; that's the nature of the fund-raising game. He's turned his capacity to raise funds into a real force for good."

Just as the law center attracted increasing public attention and a certain controversial image during its first decade, so too did Morris Dees himself. In his professional life, he sported a creative and unorthodox style that was not only colorful but effective—explicitly measurable in terms of dollars raised and cases won. In his personal life, numerous examples of behavior that many people found surprising and unconventional added weight to his reputation as a complex and unpredictable character. The more money he accumulated, the less he let it show. The manifestations of personal wealth that he had delighted in flashing when he and Millard Fuller were partners seldom resurfaced; instead, Dees often wore blue jeans, drove an old-model Mercedes, took up cross-country motorcycle riding and calf roping on the rodeo circuit, and hung out with nonlawyer types in a country juke joint–pool hall on the outskirts of Montgomery.

In the summer of 1980 he and his second wife, Maureene, fought through a sensational closed-door divorce trial that was the talk of the town. In his middle-aged prime, Dees showed no outward concern about his notorious image; some, including newspapermen Ray Jenkins and Wayne Greenhaw, got the impression that he took a perverse delight in the public clamor. Indeed, he later told a Washington interviewer, "nothing that came out of that trial bothered me."

Says Dees now of his hometown image: "Acceptance of eccentricity is an old Southern virtue. A lot of people have seen me in just that way—good and bad, and always unpredictable. They couldn't be sure what I'd do next."

Around the city, few people are passive or indifferent in their opinions of the man—but some are ambivalent. "I have the most deeply mixed feelings about Morris," says Virginia Durr, long one of Alabama's most progressive and outspoken citizens. "He's been immensely effective in the fight against racism and inequality, but I can't reconcile his good deeds with the way he treats people. His behavior detracts from the great things the law center has done."

Pamela Horowitz, an attorney at the center for three years in the mid-1970s and a close observer of it in the years since, offers this reflection on the institution and Dees's stamp upon it:

"I arrived at SPLC when it was still on its initial mission—litigating pathfinding class-action cases that had a major impact on poor people in the South. The times and the issues were simpler then, and we were young lawyers with messianic urges, trying to bring about social change. As new issues arose—capital punishment, occupational health and safety, the environment—we tried to address them. Morris always starts off on new missions with great enthusiasm, and then he loses interest and fades. He's so creative, so full of ideas, that he leaves people behind to do the grunt work while he speeds on to the next visionary goal. That's the real story of the center. It's ridiculous to question his moral commitment to the larger ideals; after all, he's chosen to make the law center his life mission, and he's backed up his commitment with hard work, lots of impressive legal victories, and an enormous amount of money.

"He has a tendency to do things by his own rules, to ignore others, and that has hurt him. But you have to remember—it's his ball, his court, his game. His main objective since his days at the University of Alabama has been to be totally independent, so he can do his own thing and not have to answer to anyone. That's exactly what he's created in the law center. I might disagree at times with his agenda or his behavior, but I don't question his right to run the place the way he wants to—and as long as he's not breaking the law himself, I say more power to him."

Some of the other lawyers who have worked with Dees disagree that he is or should be the only authority within the center. They point out that the SPLC is a public-interest organization and a non-profit corporation and thus has both legal and moral obligations to account for its funds. But, says one of them, echoing others, "Morris appoints the board and hires the lawyers, and he can ignore them or fire them if he wants to. As long as the Internal Revenue Service and the people who send him money are satisfied with his performance, he has no one else to answer to. What it comes down to is this: Morris Dees *is* the Southern Poverty Law Center."

The SPLC had reached a hiatus in 1979 when an outbreak of Ku Klux Klan violence in north Alabama opened the door to a new mission for Dees and his ten-year-old institution. All his fundamental interests—trial law, social justice, salesmanship, financial independence, personal ambition—could be seen as coming together in the vision he glimpsed of a direction and a goal for the 1980s.

"Too many people who get caught up in social movements and causes stagnate themselves," says Daphne Dwyer, a former member of the law center staff. "Morris has never had that problem. He's always thinking ahead, planning future moves." In 1980, he moved.

Since it was founded on the Tennessee-Alabama border in 1866 by a band of former Confederates, the Ku Klux Klan has flared and faded and flared again like a recurring nightmare in the South. As a loosely connected network of underground vigilante groups, the Klan has used secrecy, terrorism, and violence to convey its message of Anglo-Saxon Protestant supremacy. In the classic historical pattern, rich and powerful rulers—in this case, white racists bent on maintaining control—have sent men and boys from the underclass to carry on the fight for them. Sporadically, assaults on blacks, Jews, Catholics, and foreigners have brought grief to the minorities and shame to Southern whites.

Alabama has borne its full share of the grief and shame. In a period of relative inactivity that followed the civil rights successes of the mid-1960s, many Alabamians assumed that the Klan was fading into oblivion. But on a May morning in 1979 violence erupted when Klansmen attacked a group of black demonstrators in the north Alabama city of Decatur, and another resurgent "new Klan" was back on the troubled minds of Southerners once again.

Ten people were injured in that melee—blacks, Klansmen, and police officers—but the only man charged with a crime was Curtis Robinson, a black demonstrator who pulled a gun and shot a Klansman who had assaulted him. Robinson was arrested and accused of assault with intent to commit murder; Morris Dees and the Southern Poverty Law Center came to his defense.

That was the beginning of the SPLC's most publicized and successful venture to date, a two-pronged program of anti-Klan litigation and education backed by a national fund-raising campaign that has more than doubled the center's budget and endowment in just eight years.

Other civil rights litigation groups, including the NAACP Legal Defense Fund, the American Civil Liberties Union, and the Center for Constitutional Rights, were also handling Klan-related cases at that time, and in August 1979 the New York–based Center for Constitutional Rights had founded the National Anti-Klan Network to monitor white supremacist groups of all kinds. But none of these civil rights groups were based in the South, and none had the budgetary latitude to address Klan issues in a big way. The SPLC, on the other hand, was on the scene, flush with funds, and poised to shift its focus from capital punishment to a new social issue.

The reviving Klan loomed in Dees's vision as a perfect target. It was, in the eyes of millions of people, black and white, a menace to society. From his closer perspective, however, Dees could see chinks in the armor: poverty and poor education in the ranks, competitive squabbling among the leaders, scattered and disunited factions, undisciplined behavior, limited funds, few if any good lawyers. Estimates of Klan membership in the South in 1980 generally were below ten thousand, compared with more than sixty thousand in the 1960s and several million in the 1920s.

Looking ahead, Dees was confident that the SPLC had the resources to mount a legal offensive against this fragmented enemy and that ample funds could be raised through the mail to support the effort. The four other lawyers on the center's staff at the time—John Carroll, Ira Burnim, Steve Ellmann, and Dennis Balske—had other cases on their agendas, and the elevation of the Ku Klux Klan to the top of the list of Southern social problems was not a choice they might have made individually. But Dees was effectively a majority of one, and the center, without altogether abandoning its other public-interest cases, moved nonetheless into a new phase of activity.

Randall Williams, a journalist who had worked as an editor and paralegal staff member at the center in the mid-to-late 1970s, was brought back in 1981 to direct the formation of Klanwatch, a region-wide monitoring and research unit providing public exposure and public education on terrorist groups. An Alabama native raised in rural white poverty, Williams was proud of the center's track record ("a worthy cause being pursued by good people, with good effect"), and he approached the new venture with much enthusiasm.

Through research, publications, publicity, videotapes, and eventually a half-hour documentary movie, Klanwatch mounted a relentless campaign of exposure and attack on Klan units and other paramilitary organizations throughout the South. The legal wing of the center, meanwhile, turned more slowly to the attack, partly out of a lack of specific cases to prosecute and partly out of a lingering reluctance among most of the lawyers to shift focus.

"From the day I returned to work at the center," says Williams, "I found the debate over allocation of resources raging, and it had been going on before I got there. Most of the lawyers argued that the Klan was more bark than bite, and that there were certainly bigger problems facing blacks and the poor. My own view was that while there were more important issues to be faced, the Klan was still a threat to peace and safety and racial equality, and I liked the prospect of taking them on. I didn't see it as an either/or choice, but as a question of emphasis and priorities."

For Dees, though, the Klan project was a choice and in time an obsession. With characteristic intensity and energy, he pushed Klanwatch, case development, and direct-mail solicitations to the limit. "The fund-raising was incredibly successful," Williams recalls. "The money poured in; everyone, it seemed, was against the Klan. We developed a whole new donor base, anchored by wealthy Jewish contributors on the East and West coasts, and they gave big bucks. Our budget soared—and still, we raised millions more than we could spend."

The harder Dees pressed in pursuit of the scattered and disorganized remnants of the Klan, the more he must have sensed the cleverness of his strategy. America's image of the Klan as a large and menacing threat bore little resemblance to the reality of pitiful little clusters of desperate men full of hate and bravado and ineptitude. To be sure, they were capable of violence, and sometimes they lashed out with deadly results. There were other white supremacist groups, too, and sometimes they committed acts of terrorism. But unlike the Klans of earlier times, none of these extremist cells had enough power to control even a small fragment of political or social or economic life, or to hold large segments of the population in a grip of terror.

In fact, the ragtag gangs of violent Klansmen proved not even to be a match for Morris Dees alone. He tormented them. They cursed him in print and on television, made threats on his life, branded him a traitor and a Communist and worse—and Dees used the threats in his fund-raising letters and in Klanwatch publications to further his advantage over them. With relentless and sometimes reckless abandon, he kept after them, and the more his campaign succeeded in public and in the courts, the more it prospered financially. The hapless and divided Klan units, on the other hand, seemed unable to retaliate. It was almost as if the only attention they could get was from their most hated enemies—Dees and Klanwatch.

In July 1983 the law center's Montgomery offices were firebombed, causing minor damage. Contributions to the center skyrocketed again. In short order, informers helped the SPLC and law enforcement officials to identify three suspects in the bombing, including a former candidate for county sheriff. A year and a half after the incident the three pleaded guilty to the bombing and drew fifteen-year prison sentences. Such victories had become all but routine for Dees and his associates. Beating the Klan in court, said one SPLC lawyer, "is sort of like shooting fish in a barrel."

Dees was by then driving an old Chevrolet with armor plating and bulletproof glass, and on occasions he wore protective clothing and took bodyguards along when he appeared in public. Such precautions seemed out of character for a man of his customary daring and fearlessness, and some of his colleagues interpreted the actions as part of the psychological strategy against the Klan, rather than a concern for safety.

In place of its old office, the SPLC constructed a modern headquarters featuring state-of-the-art electronic security; it cost about one million dollars, and it was immediately controversial. "The building design establishes a corporate image to reflect the national importance of the Southern Poverty Law Center," read a folder describing the structure. Others, less charitable, called it "the poverty palace" and "the home of the Southern Affluent Law Center." Even among its occupants there was disagreement, some expressing pride and others embarrassment at the substance and symbolism of the building.

Numerous changes took place in the law center's staff during the years of the anti-Klan build-up. Attorney Steve Ellmann resigned, as did legal director John Carroll, and two new lawyers, Deborah Ellis and Dennis Sweet, were added to the professional staff. Sweet was the first black lawyer at the SPLC in its fourteen-year history, and Ellis was the second female; Dees remained the only lawyer with exclusively Southern legal training, all the others having taken one or more of their degrees from schools in the North.

Founding partner Joe Levin, by then a Washington attorney, took Julian Bond's place as president, and former SPLC attorneys Howard Mandell and John Carroll were named to the board. As the Klan project continued to expand, several earlier legal interests—capital punishment, affirmative action, voting rights—were pushed to the back burner. In the spring of 1985 William Stanton, a researcher and investigator on the staff, replaced Randall Williams as Klanwatch director; Williams remained as head of publications and education.

Change also continued to mark the personal life of Morris Dees. He was married and divorced for the third time; he became a grandfather; he raised funds in 1984 for Gary Hart's presidential campaign; he turned fifty in 1986; he had a face-lift; his personal fortune reached double-digit millions; and he moved closer to a spiritual tie to Judaism. "I shed my fundamentalist beliefs long ago," he says. "I go to synagogue now, and my daughter has been confirmed there. I have a Jewish heritage of sorts, with my middle name and all, and I'm very comfortable with that."

By 1986, says Randall Williams, "the center had changed drastically. We were sharing information with the FBI, the police, undercover agents. Instead of defending clients and victims, we were more of a super snoop outfit, an arm of the law enforcement people. And the Klan was changing too, from an active, growing, openly defiant, unchallenged force in the 1970s to a much smaller and shrinking—though still violent and extreme—remnant in the mid-1980s. I thought we had done what we set out to do, but Morris was still firing away with all the guns and still writing to donors about the Klan menace—and the money was still flowing in."

The fund-raising letters are a study in the art of persuasion. Most are signed by Dees, and a few bear the names of prominent friends of the center. All are emotion-tugging appeals to action. "Frankly," declared one of the latter, "Morris and his colleagues at the Center and in the Klanwatch project are embattled. They need and deserve our immediate help. . . . I know you share my abhorrence of the Klan and other hate groups. I also know you value courage. [But] as much as we might praise this heroic work, admiration is simply not enough. . . . Won't you help them carry on the struggle?" It was signed by George McGovern.

Another letter, mailed in 1985 over the signature of Rabbi David A. Baylinson of Montgomery, asked for funds to protect the law center and staff, "who are suffering under a siege of Ku Klux Klan and neo-Nazi terrorism unparalleled in this decade." Rabbi Baylinson went on to identify the founders of the SPLC as "Morris Seligman Dees and Joe Levin Jr., two young Montgomery lawyers."

The use of Dees's full name was uncommon. "Morris used his middle name in mailings to Jewish zip codes," says attorney Ira Burnim. "The intent, I assume, was to boost returns." The SPLC's annual income from fund-raising letters such as these is in the five-million-dollar range—about twice as much as the center manages to spend each year. Regular surpluses and income from investments managed by a New York financial firm have swelled the law center's permanent endowment to more than twenty-two million dollars.

Another fund appeal signed by Dees and addressed to Jody Powell was returned by the former aide to President Carter with a note saying the letter was a deliberate attempt to exploit the sensibilities of Northern liberals, and therefore offensive. "I'm sure the implied linking of Jefferson Davis to Klan lynchings will stir the juices of ignorant Yankee contributors," Powell wrote, "but it pisses me off."

In connection with another fund-raising mailing, attorneys for the New York *Times* complained that the SPLC had edited a story from the newspaper, thus changing its meaning, and reproduced it on newsprint to appear as though it had been clipped from the paper.

As the Klan project came more and more to dominate the work of the law center, heated philosophical debates raged among the lawyers. "Things got really bad after we moved into the new building in the fall of 1985," says attorney Deborah Ellis. "We argued about the Klan, the fund-raising letters, the building. I came to believe that Morris was on the Klan kick because he saw them as such an easy target—easy to beat in court, easy to raise big money on. We were ignoring the more serious issues. The Klan is no longer one of the

South's biggest problems—not because racism has disappeared, but because the racists simply can't get away with violence and terrorism any more."

Dennis Sweet agrees. "There's not much left to the Klan," he says. "You ask most Southern blacks what worries them the most and they'll name a lot of things before they think of the Klan—if they think of it at all."

Montgomery city councilman Joe Reed, one of Alabama's most influential black politicians, asserts that Dees "has done a lot of good in this state—some of it when he didn't have to—and I respect him for it. But I don't share his view that the Klan is our biggest worry. It's not a serious problem now. Blacks are not afraid of the Klan like they used to be, and neither are whites. The Klan is weaker now, and the law is stronger—thanks in part to Dees."

Dees's insistence that the law center's main thrust should be aimed at the Klan finally brought him to a showdown with his four attorneys and with Randall Williams. In 1986, after a dispute that Dees climaxed by threatening to fire attorney Ira Burnim, the others responded by resigning in protest.

Reflecting on that turn of events, Joe Levin now offers his "objective view" that "honest people were having strong disagreements over direction." He adds: "If I were being unobjective, I'd say that Morris waited too long to get rid of some Eastern liberals he should have fired long before."

The four lawyers continued to work on their individual cases until the projects could be turned over to new staff attorneys. Three of the lawyers—Dennis Balske, Dennis Sweet, and Deborah Ellis—then ended their ties to the center. Ironically, Ira Burnim—the only one facing dismissal—later worked out an accommodation with Dees and still has a continuing relationship with the SPLC.

Two years after the breakup, Dees maintains a resolute conviction that the five staff members had drifted away from the center's mission and thus no longer belonged there. Not surprisingly, the resignees— those willing to discuss the matter, at any rate—see the root of the problem in Dees himself and conclude that it was he, not they, whose loyalty to the SPLC's mission and history proved lacking.

Sweet says Dees's "lack of respect, courtesy, honesty, and forthrightness with me constituted my main complaint. I have respect for some of the things he has accomplished, but we didn't work well together, and I felt it better that I resign."

Ellis calls Dees "a genius in many ways, but a very flawed genius with many bad personal qualities." And Randall Williams, while remembering "many hours spent in pleasant and productive work with Morris," nevertheless concludes that "he had hunkered down, he wouldn't yield on any of these issues, and finally he wanted us all to leave. He can be charming and persuasive, as long as that works for him—but the main thing is, Morris has to have control, and to maintain it, he can be manipulative, ruthless, autocratic. Nobody accused anybody of anything criminal—it was all a matter of personality and philosophy, of what the center stands for and how it presents itself. He had his vision, and we had ours, and in the end they were just too different to hold together."

Dees himself shows little interest in discussing the internal problems of the law center. "I didn't fire anybody, not really," he says. "They just didn't have the same vision as I did, as our board did. We're not a public-interest law firm, not a legal aid society taking any case that comes in off the street. We only want the precedent-setting cases, the models for new directions in the law. Maybe our name is part of the problem. Poverty law was a useful term in 1970, but I'm not sure it has much meaning now. We're interested in a lot more than poverty.

"A lot of groups we work with in litigation on social issues are poor themselves, living from hand to mouth. Sometimes they're a little envious of us. I'm sorry they feel that way, but I can't do anything about it. We just run our business like a business. Whether you're selling cakes or causes, it's all the same thing, the same basic process—just good, sound business practices."

Morris Dees is not looking back; as always, he's planning ahead. "What I really enjoy doing more than anything is practicing law," he says, "and that's what I hope to keep doing. There are times when I wonder if our work at the law center is finished, but something unexpected always comes along. If there's one talent I think I have, it's not getting stuck. I seem to have enough creativity to keep moving to something new. Now that the Klan thing is winding down, we're looking at some new areas, especially in education. Who knows what the Southern Poverty Law Center will be doing a year from now?"

Morris Dees has continued to pile up victories in the courtroom and through the mail and to gain wider recognition for his exploits. In 1989 he unveiled a multi-million-dollar Civil Rights Memorial in front of the Southern Poverty Law Center's headquarters in Montgomery, honoring forty citizens who died during the midcentury struggle for racial equality in the South. On the day the memorial was dedicated, Dees publicly proposed a major Civil War–Civil Rights complex for downtown Montgomery that would link the memorial, the state capitol, the first White House of the Confederacy, and Martin Luther King's Dexter Avenue Baptist Church to create "a single big attraction that no other city offers." The SPLC's review of hate crimes in the United States in the 1980s recorded 242 incidents (from murder, bombing, and arson to assaults, cross-burnings, and threats) in 1989 alone; about one-fourth of those were in the South, and another 20 percent were in California. In October 1990 the SPLC won a jury award of $12.5 million against white supremacist Tom Metzger in a Portland, Oregon, trial, but the American Civil Liberties Union said afterward that the overall conduct of the case by Dees and his colleagues may have weakened and eroded the framework of civil liberties. A made-for-television movie about Dees and the law center was aired on NBC in 1991, and his "as told to" autobiography, A Season for Justice, *co-authored by Steve Fiffer, was also published in 1991. Meanwhile, as fund-raising letters continue to bring in large sums of money through the mail, the Southern Poverty Law Center's endowment has grown to more than thirty million dollars.*

∾ HAMMOND ACADEMY: A REBEL YELL, FADING

Thirteen years separated the start of this article from the finish of it. I wrote it the first time in 1976, on assignment for the New York Times Magazine. *Due to numerous complications beyond my control, it was never published. In 1988 I went back to Hammond Academy to update the piece for* Southern Magazine, *and the following year, just before its scheduled publication, I made changes reflecting further developments at the school. The article was once again left in limbo when* Southern *ceased publication with the September 1989 issue. This is the first time this piece has been published.*

They were the Rebels, a reactionary remnant of latter-day devotees to the Lost Cause. They flew the Confederate flag above their newly built or borrowed classrooms, and sang "Dixie" with fierce pride, and made the soldier's gray and gold or the red and blue of the flag their school colors. They invoked the memory of their Confederate ancestors, praising them as American revolutionaries. Their response to the new American social revolution for racial equality was a rebel yell and a defiant cry of "Never!" In truth, though, they were not in rebellion at all but once again in retreat, fleeing from the ghosts of history—and long before the real revolution ever reached them, they had already decided they'd rather switch than fight.

The all-white private schools that suddenly burst upon the scene in the mid-1960s were primarily a Southern phenomenon arising from the imminent prospect of desegregation in the public schools of the region. Except in a relatively small number of elite prep schools and military academies and some Catholic schools in a few cities, the South had never claimed a strong private school tradition. In the absence of such a pattern—and in contrast with a general decline in private education nationwide at the time—the so-called seg academies spread like kudzu through the eleven states of the Old Confederacy (soon to be followed by a wave of new Christian academies driven more by religious zeal than racial segregation).

Though they varied considerably in size and quality, the segregated academies belonged to a common class and shared a common philosophy. The white parents, teachers, administrators, and community leaders who organized them in church basements and prefab buildings and modern new facilities spoke of preserving "Southern traditions" and "neighborhood schools" and "quality education"—all of which they equated with the maintenance and perpetuation of segregation. Believing as they did that pervasive white supremacy was essential to the preservation of Southern society, they readily abandoned the public schools and developed these new institutions, as much to show the depth and sincerity of their convictions as to demonstrate their economic power.

By 1970 the number of seg academies in the region had soared to well over a thousand, and their combined enrollment reportedly exceeded a half-million students. As a writer covering education in the South at that time and as a strong believer in public schools, I was intrigued and troubled by the emergence of these new institutions. It was as if a significant percentage of white Southerners had decided, without discussion or debate, to secede from the Union all over again. As hundreds of communities adjusted to the new reality of private schools for whites and public schools for blacks, this neosegregationist turn of events seemed blindly self-delusive and self-destructive to me.

I was convinced that the South had languished for generations partly because it had insisted on maintaining two separate public school systems, when in truth it could not even afford to support one. Then, just as the states were being compelled by Congress and the courts to combine those two systems, a large segment of the white majority was taking extreme measures to establish a new and costlier kind of segregation.

I followed the private school movement closely in those years. One of the schools that especially interested me was organized in 1966 by a group of influential white citizens in the South Carolina capital city of Columbia. They named it James H. Hammond Academy in honor of an antebellum congressman and governor best remembered for his ardent advocacy of slavery and secession.

South Carolina was fairly typical of the South at large in its rapid spawning of such schools, and Hammond Academy was a prime example of the biggest and strongest of them. In its first year of operation the school enrolled 265 students; within a decade it had expanded to a full twelve-grade program, and classrooms seemingly couldn't be built fast enough to keep up with the demand.

In 1976, on assignment for a magazine, I went to South Carolina to interview some private school officials and to get a closer look at several of the academies. Hammond, the flagship, was first on my list.

The six-building facility on a wooded twenty-five-acre campus in the Columbia suburbs was bulging at the seams with thirteen hundred students. A Confederate battle banner hung from one of the flagpoles at the main entrance. The school's tax-exempt status had been revoked by the Internal Revenue Service because its leaders refused to sign a pledge of nondiscrimination. Indeed, Hammond was so unabashedly segregationist that it wouldn't even compete in sports with other private schools whose teams included black players.

The administrators and board members I interviewed on that visit confidently told me they had caught the wave of the future. "I'd guess that at least 90 percent of our parents are in agreement about the race question," said one of them. "We're far better off without Negroes here. We like the way we are, and we intend to stay that way. If it means we can't have tax exemption, so be it. Eventually, that'll change. Segregation is coming back in this country. It's a more natural condition. In time, we'll be vindicated."

As the South has continued through the 1980s to grapple with its multitude of education problems, I've often thought about that visit I made to Hammond. A fair amount of change has taken place since 1976, and both public and private schools have been affected, for better and worse. What, I wondered, has happened to Hammond? In the spring of 1988 I went back to Columbia to see.

The campus was still there, tucked away in a shady cul de sac on the southeastern edge of the city. A few yellow buses, private replicas of the public school fleet, waited in the drive for the afternoon dismissal bell. My first impression was that Hammond looked pretty much as it had in 1976.

But when I glanced up at the flagpoles near the main entrance, I knew immediately that something was different. Hanging there on the three poles were the flags of the United States, South Carolina, and Hammond Academy. The Rebel flag was nowhere to be seen. It had been quietly and unceremoniously retired in about 1984, I was told later, and replaced by the Hammond Academy banner.

As an act of symbolism, the removal of the Stars and Bars was a significant event in Hammond's history, but it paled in comparison with the more substantive changes I found there:

• Tuition had soared from a maximum of $800 in 1976–1977 to an announced maximum of $3,780 in 1988–1989, and mandatory one-time contributions to the school's capital building fund had been raised to $2,000.

• Enrollment had fallen by about 40 percent (from 1,300 to 800) between 1976 and 1987, and a further drop to 650 was being anticipated.

• Tax exemption from the IRS had been restored, paving the way for two capital fund drives that had netted more than two million dollars.

• A new headmaster, the third of this decade—and, of all things, a Yankee—had restructured the board of directors, replaced some teachers, expanded the curriculum, and generally taken steps to thrust Hammond into the competitive mainstream of independent schools nationwide.

• And perhaps most surprising of all, about a dozen black students had been enrolled, and others were being sought, with scholarships as an inducement.

"A lot of people who were here when Hammond started in the 1960s wouldn't recognize the place now," J. V. Morrison, the director of development, told me on that return visit. "We're working on a different image, so different that in some ways it's almost like starting over."

It had taken the retirement of one headmaster, the dismissal of another, and the high-risk recruitment from afar of a third to turn

Hammond onto its new course. Along the way, most of the original twelve-member board had stepped down, making way for a larger and more active governing body of twenty-one. And in 1987–1988 alone, a combination of firings, resignations, and expansion had brought sixteen new faculty members to the campus to join about fifty returning teachers.

At the time of my visit Nicholas M. Hagerman was just completing his second year in command of the Hammond conversion, and though the process had at times been filled with tension and frenzy, the forty-eight-year-old headmaster seemed calmly unaffected by the pace or the pressure. A straight-talking New York native who had studied and worked in the South before moving to Columbia, Hagerman had earned an enviable reputation as a troubleshooter during ten years of short-term rescue missions at several private schools around the country.

He was recommended to Hammond's headmaster search committee by a Boston-based consulting firm. However improbable the match may have seemed at first glance, it quickly developed into a firm union. Hammond's rapidly evolving board and family of patrons apparently were ready to gamble the school's future on a series of transforming changes; Hagerman, a gambler at heart, jumped at the challenge.

Following his prescription for change step by step, the board raised the tuition and capital-fund requirements, pushed external fund-raising, reduced the school's growing indebtedness, and implemented a financial aid program for needy students (about $100,000 was budgeted for 1988–1989). A kindergarten program was added, the middle school was reorganized, and new courses in music, drama, art, and speech were introduced. Teacher salaries were raised to the norm for independent schools in the Southeast (though they remained slightly below the average for Columbia's public schools), and an employee retirement plan was started. The sixteen new teachers recruited by Hagerman included seven from South Carolina, six from cities as widely scattered as Pittsburgh and Phoenix, and three from overseas.

Hammond's recruitment efforts, its scholarship fund, and its general emergence from segregationist isolation drew favor from the

Southern Association of Colleges and Schools (the regional accrediting agency) and the National Association of Independent Schools. If the reorganized academy could diversify its student body, stabilize its enrollment, erase its debt, build an endowment, and continue to turn out college-ready graduates, Hagerman declared, it should have a long and productive future in Columbia.

But without the segregationist impulse, was all that possible? Nick Hagerman and his colleagues confidently believed that it was, though they acknowledged the difficulty of the task. They would have to keep costs from rising too high and enrollment from falling too low; they would have to make needed personnel changes without alienating too many employees, board members, and parents; they would have to summon the means and the will to avoid being an exclusive school for rich white children; and they would have to deliver education of such caliber that those who paid for it would consider it well worth the price.

"The cost is great, but you get so much for it," said Julia Moore, president of Hammond's association of parents, when I met her in 1988. "I've had children in school here for eleven years, and I can tell you we were ready for the positive, progressive changes that are taking place. Many of us came here in the first place because of the solid academic foundation that existed, and we have worked hard for the other things we felt Hammond needed—social, cultural changes that are necessary to the development of the whole child. We wanted minorities, we wanted more emphasis on the creative arts, we wanted a broader curriculum and a more diverse student body—not a parking lot full of MGs and Mercedes Benzes. We wanted some continuity, but we also wanted change—and so far, I think we're getting both. We're on the right track."

Board chairman Bill Barksdale, like most of the other parents in leadership positions, had been present through Hammond's transition from seg academy to prep school. "The first generation of parents and teachers," he said, "was preoccupied with the race issue. Now the second generation is here, and we're more concerned with building a good reputation as an outstanding college prep school. We want people who can thrive in a high-quality educational environment, and to that end, we're recruiting good students wherever we can find them—whites, blacks, Jews, foreigners. We're competing with other private schools, and with the public schools. Our only worries are economic, not social."

Concerns about continuously rising costs and their adverse effect on enrollment crept into the conversation of virtually every parent, teacher, and policy-maker I talked to at Hammond—and almost in the same breath, they spoke of Nick Hagerman as the central figure in their deliverance.

When I interviewed him in his office on an April afternoon in 1988, Hagerman clearly seemed to understand the school's history and the challenge it presented. "In the period from the midsixties to the late seventies," he said, "the whites who led the academy movement were motivated by their fear of racial integration. They saw the public schools in disarray, and they were able to generate the money and the energy to establish alternative institutions ranging in quality from good to awful.

"Then, as the seventies drew to a close, the first generation of academy founders and teachers and parents retired, and at about the same time, the public schools began to turn the corner toward improvement. Necessary program changes, higher salaries for new teachers, and inflation forced tuition sharply higher, and race had become a less-emotional factor. Parents began to question whether private education was worth the cost."

Hagerman paused to reflect on the dilemma he had just summarized. So many questions hung suspended, unanswered. He knew them all too well. They had to do with attitudes and perceptions, with mission, with money. Rhetorically, he cited them one by one: "Why do we exist? Do we need to continue? What is our basic philosophy? Are we meeting it? How are we different from the public schools? What do we have to offer our students that is worth the cost to them and their parents? What will we be like in twenty years? Can we survive?"

His conclusion was strongly affirmative: "We've got to be competitive in every way—in costs, resources, salaries, and most of all in the educational quality we deliver. We want to be cooperative, too—with other independent schools and with the public schools of this city. We're on schedule, and headed in the right direction. This is going to be *the* academic address in Columbia."

~

That was the state of Hammond Academy in the spring of 1988. But four months later, just before the beginning of the fall term, Nicholas Hagerman abruptly resigned as headmaster. His top assistant, Adeline Lundy, head guidance counselor at the school for seventeen years, was named to replace him in an interim capacity for the 1988–1989 term.

Neither Hagerman nor Lundy nor members of the board and administration at Hammond will elaborate on the terse and cryptic official statement that the headmaster stepped down "for personal reasons." Within the larger family of patrons, this lack of public comment has inevitably created whispering camps of Hagerman critics and defenders. From all that can be gleaned in off-the-record conversations with the various factions, the probable cause for his departure appears to boil down to the looming crisis of numbers: declining enrollment, rising costs, and ever-increasing tuition.

The fall 1988 enrollment skidded below the projected 650 to 630 and seemed almost certain to go still lower. Another 4 percent across-the-board tuition increase has already been announced for 1989–1990. The scholarship fund, the principal instrument in the attempt to diversify the student body, has been drastically reduced. "The baseline issue for Hammond Academy," said one informed participant-observer, "is not social or academic—it's fiscal. This is the question: Can a former seg academy that wants to be a mainline college prep school attract enough students to pay the cost?"

Adeline Lundy believes it can; she is devoted above all to Hammond's survival. "We're still headed in the same direction that Nick pointed us in," she declares. "It's basically his plan. We aren't here just to serve wealthy whites, and we aren't an adversary of the public schools. We're an independent college prep school—smaller than before, but better—and we're determined to stand for the very best in academic achievement.

"Our goal is to hold enrollment at the present level of 630, and I'm sure we'll be within fifty of that number, plus or minus, when we open next fall. We're having a very successful year, maybe the best we've ever had. I feel a lot more positive and confident about our future now than I did when I agreed last August to be the interim head."

Most educators probably would argue that in a city the size of Columbia, with a metropolitan population of close to a half-million,
there ought to be room for a few good private schools. At the high
school level, Columbia has only two major ones besides Hammond:
Cardinal Newman, a Catholic school with about four hundred students, perhaps 5 percent of whom are black, and Heathwood Hall,
an Episcopal school with about eight hundred students, including a
black minority of 5 or 6 percent. Neither was ever tagged as a seg
academy, but their black enrollments have always been quite small.

"We confidently believe that ours is the best independent school in
the state," said Jim Shirley, headmaster of Heathwood Hall, in a telephone interview in the spring of 1988. The school was founded in
1951 and grew slowly over its first twenty-five years, reaching an enrollment of 725 (including about 40 blacks) in 1976. The thirteen-
grade school (kindergarten through senior high) had a tuition of
about one thousand dollars a year at that time, and its leaders pre-
dicted that enrollment would soon climb to 925 and be frozen there.
But it took ten more years to reach a plateau of 840 students, and
since then there has been a slight decline.

Cost is the governing factor, says Shirley. Tuition in 1988 was in the
four-thousand-dollar range, and while scholarships averaging two
thousand dollars each were available to about 150 students, the hard
truth is that Heathwood, like Hammond, is simply beyond the financial reach of low- and moderate-income families. "The economic reality," said the headmaster, "is that we're going to be smaller, though
I hope we can hold the line at about eight hundred. Many independent schools are in financial trouble now, and more will be. The public schools are improving, and as the cost of private education keeps
going up, it's inevitable that changes in enrollment patterns will
follow."

Of the dozen or so private schools that sprang up in Columbia in
the 1960s and 1970s, about half have since gone out of business; the
segregationist impulse, by itself, was simply not enough to sustain
them. Most of the ones that remain have, like Hammond Academy,
adopted a public policy of nondiscrimination. Larry Watt, executive
director of the South Carolina Independent School Association, once

a haven for seg academies, says "the great majority" of his group's seventy member schools now have open admissions and tax-exempt status. "This is not the group of white-flight schools it once was," he adds. "We don't require them to sign a nondiscrimination pledge, but almost all of them have come to realize that it's imperative."

The rival Palmetto Association of Independent Schools, to which both Hammond and Heathwood Hall belong, does require its members not to practice discrimination in enrollment or employment. Under segregation, says Executive Director Dallon Weathers, "the white public schools got all the advantages, but both white and black schools were far below the national average. Now there's just one public system, and we see it as part of our role in private education to work side by side with them for the general betterment of all. The only justification for private schools is to achieve excellence, not to further segregation."

Without the old segregationist appeal, independent schools such as Hammond Academy must promote themselves in the way traditional private schools always have—as places that offer to those who can afford it (and a few others on scholarship) some advantages that are generally unavailable in public schools: a low student-teacher ratio (about twelve to one at Hammond); a single-campus setting for thirteen years of schooling; a hand-picked faculty with diverse and sometimes unconventional training and experience; lots of parental involvement in school programs and activities; a selective admission process that culls applicants who might pose academic or disciplinary problems; and a sense of internal control that is a consequence of paying tuition and electing a governing board from within the community of patrons. For these privileges, and for a high degree of social and economic homogeneity and the high level of achievement that so often results, parents in Columbia are now paying close to fifty thousand dollars to put a child through private school from kindergarten to senior high graduation.

Following a trend that can be seen in some other Southern states, enrollment in the private schools of South Carolina peaked at fifty-four thousand in 1978 and has since fallen to about forty-six thousand, a drop of 15 percent. Also since the late 1970s small numbers of black students have desegregated many of the previously all-white academies, particularly in urban areas.

In the public schools, meanwhile, the steady out-migration of whites that accompanied desegregation appears to have ended across much of the South—and in some places, a reversal of the exodus has begun. Even as public school systems begin to show signs of recovery and improvement, the private institutions are increasingly preoccupied with rising costs, falling enrollment, and the specter of budget deficits that could eventually put them out of business.

Obviously, public schools don't have the luxury of selective admissions and small classes and direct parental control of individual schools. Bound as they are to receive and to try to help all the pupils who come to them—the well prepared, the middle class, minorities, new immigrants, the poor, the handicapped, the troubled—it's no wonder that they manifest a higher degree of friction and failure than private schools that, in Nick Hagerman's candid phrase, "don't want other people's problems."

It is stimulating to speculate what might have happened if the money and energy that white Southerners have put into segregated education during the past twenty-five years or more had been spent instead on the needs and problems of the public schools. Could the South have spared itself any of the painful consequences it has suffered and still suffers because of the historical inadequacies and inequities of its educational systems? We will never know the answer.

In the public schools of Columbia now, a degree of stability and upward mobility has gradually taken hold since the traumatic years when desegregation was in its infancy. (There are actually five public school systems within the Columbia metropolitan area, and they range in racial makeup from about 75 percent white to 75 percent black.) Across South Carolina, a substantial new state-initiated program known as the Education Improvement Act is gradually being implemented, and with it is emerging an attitude of hope and anticipation. The road ahead, though, is certain to be long and torturous.

As taxpayers, parents who send their children to public schools have become more articulate and insistent about their expectations, and South Carolina's governmental and educational leaders, like those in other states of the region, have finally begun to respond to their demands. They also see the correlation between educational quality and economic health, and that is another strong motivation for seeking broad-based school improvement.

By the same token, parents who send their children to private schools (and, of course, pay their share of public school taxes as well) are equally as determined to get their money's worth. Most of them, apparently—even some of the more conservative whites—no longer consider segregation a sufficient justification for such expenditures; for many, in fact, it is now seen as a negative characteristic of a school.

The seg academies in the South—those typified by Hammond Academy, at least—appear in the past quarter-century to have come full circle to the same position as that of the traditional private schools that predate them. Like most of those established institutions, Hammond aspires to offer stability, security, and quality for a price, and the price more or less assures a high degree of economic, social, and racial homogeneity. These are the privileges of affluence, the advantages and rewards of upper-class status, in what we like to call our class-free society.

The more things change, the more they stay the same.

A new headmaster, the third in three years, took office at Hammond Academy in the fall of 1990. Enrollment has continued to decline (from 630 in 1988 to 540 the following year to below 500 in 1990), and tuition has been increased by about one-third since 1988.

∾ THE ENIGMA OF THE SOUTH

*In a lifetime—fifty-six years—of Southern resi-
dency, over half of it spent as a practicing journalist
and nonfiction writer, I have never come close to
solving the puzzle of the South, nor have I ever lost
interest in the mystery of it. Half a dozen times in
the 1980s, in magazine and newspaper articles,
speeches, and longer essays, I tried to bring the region and its culture into focus. Those repeated approaches to the same complex subject are combined
and condensed in the essay below.*

In the mid-1960s, when I was writing
for a Southern-based magazine reporting on race relations in education, I sometimes visited schools and communities in the North to
learn as much as I could, for comparative purposes, about desegregation there. On one such assignment, I spent a couple of days in
Grosse Pointe, Michigan, an old and elegant suburb of Detroit that is
the home of the Fords—the motorcar Fords—and there I met a lady
of liberal persuasion who graciously volunteered to invite some of her
friends over for coffee so I could interview them.

She called up all the people she knew who had voted for Lyndon
Johnson and Hubert Humphrey—there were, as I recall, about
fifteen of them—and asked them to come and meet "a young man
from the South who wants to talk about desegregation and race relations."

They all came, and when I arrived a few minutes past the appointed hour, conversation in the living room suddenly ceased. I was
puzzled by the uneasy hush. Finally I said, "Is something wrong?"

After a long pause, one member of the group found her voice and
said with some astonishment, "You're white!"

How swiftly the times change. In those days, when legalized segregation was collapsing under the pressure of civil rights litigation, legislation, and activism, the conventional wisdom held that while racial discrimination was the nation's number one domestic problem, the affliction was more or less confined to white people living in the Southern states. There was a lot of talk then about Alabama and Mississippi, about George Wallace and Ross Barnett, about police dogs and fire hoses, about white terrorists in the Ku Klux Klan. In such an atmosphere, it must have seemed logical for Northerners to assume that any Southerner visiting Grosse Pointe to ask questions about race relations would have to be black.

But that was before a series of explosive riots swept like wildfire through Detroit, Los Angeles, Newark, Cleveland, and other Northern cities and before the prospects of housing desegregation in Chicago and school desegregation in Boston met with angry and violent resistance from whites. By the 1970s white self-righteousness and complacency concerning racial issues had ceased to be a commonplace attitude in the North.

Meanwhile, some rather miraculous things were happening in the South. Blacks were not only gaining the franchise but also experiencing the joys of election, some becoming mayors of major cities and even members of Congress. The public schools of the region were becoming more racially mixed than those in all but a few communities elsewhere. And most astonishing of all, a descendant of slaveholding white planters was elected president of the United States in 1976, in part on the strength of his firm commitment to racial equality and the subsequent support he received from an overwhelming majority of black voters.

Who in his wildest dreams could have imagined in 1968, after the Reverend Martin Luther King, Jr., was assassinated, that eight years later the slain martyr's father, the Reverend Martin Luther King, Sr., would stand before the Democratic National Convention and a television audience of millions and pray God's blessings upon the head of a white planter from south Georgia? Who could have imagined that the elder King and Jimmy Carter and the assembled throng in New York's Madison Square Garden—among them George Wallace and the son of Ross Barnett—would join arms and lift the rafters with a rousing chorus of "We Shall Overcome," the battle hymn of the civil rights movement?

The euphoric beginning of the Carter presidency was truly a time to remember. There we were, riding along in the back of the national bus—and then, all of a sudden, we were in the driver's seat. Within a matter of months, we moved from stoop labor on the back forty to juleps and cheese straws in the parlor. Southerners were being wined and dined, sought out, listened to. As any waltzing former wallflower can tell you, it's nice to be wanted, and the attention-starved South quickly learned to savor the pleasure. The word soon spread that Cinderella had a Southern drawl, and this time she was dancing barefoot by choice, ready to boogie on through the night.

We had been told for generations that the South would rise again—and suddenly, in marvelous and unexpected ways, it happened. The South was catapulted to favor. The press explored and extolled it; bankers and other investors gravitated to it, bringing money; expatriates and outlanders alike came to visit or take up residence. Books were written about this latest of many "New South" revivals, and about the "power shift to the Sunbelt."

Long-suffering Southerners who had endured the dark decades of colonial dependency struggled to contain their vindictive impulses. They recalled the familiar highway signs, tucked away in the kudzu thickets and posted on the fencerows, proclaiming a message of hope: J.C. IS COMING AGAIN—BE READY. And with the roguish, irreverent sense of humor that is so prevalent among Southerners, they celebrated wildly when J. C. turned out to be Jimmy Carter, the triumphant peanut farmer, returning to his humble origin in Plains, Georgia. There were doubters and infidels, in and out of the region, but they were dismissed by the faithful as jealous scolds, sore losers—afflicted, said one disdainful wag, with peanuts envy.

Americans of all persuasions seem to have a weakness for such erratic behavior, and Southerners have it in spades. The South can be feared and hated by non-Southerners one day and uncritically imitated the next; as for us Southerners, we seem to have no trouble hating and imitating Yankees simultaneously. I knew Northern liberals in those days who viewed Jimmy Carter with fear and loathing. They heard his Southern drawl and his Baptist piety and started foaming at the mouth. "Some of my best friends are Southerners," one New Yorker of my acquaintance told me unwittingly—and I discovered that in his heart of hearts, he was firmly convinced that all Southerners were alike, and he certainly didn't want his daughter to marry one.

Even within the South, in the midst of what should have been the Carter years of reconciliation and unity, we remained divided and unable to agree among ourselves on the principles that defined us, on what was truly important to us or what made us alike and different.

There were many Southerners—who knows how many of the white ones—whose ardor and loyalty were for the Old South of the distant past, a South of dependence on slavery, of devotion to Anglo-Saxon Protestant purity and to automatic privilege for whites of the upper class, the upper station. These latter-day rebels harbored an abiding hatred of Yankees, integrationists, federal judges, liberals. When they spoke of loyalty, tradition, history, family, heritage, they looked away to a distant time and place when a handful of older white men controlled the land, the people, the power. Those were the men who looked upon blacks as disposable chattel, who kept one set of moral codes for their women and another for themselves, and who, for the honor and glory of the South, sent other men's sons to fight and die for them. Given the opportunity—even given the chance to seize the opportunity—the contemporary Southerners who identified themselves openly or secretly with those sentiments in the 1970s would gladly have returned to that antebellum past and tried again to fashion from it the birth of a nation.

At the same time, there were many others—most blacks, and many whites—who had no love in their hearts whatsoever for such a racist and inequitable society but who nonetheless looked upon their homeland with affection and even defended it against upcountry critics from the North. They too spoke of loyalty, tradition, history, family, heritage. They cherished the same land as their conservative fellows, but it was an altogether different set of values and virtues they extolled.

Those conservative and liberal factions of Southerners were no longer at war with each other, not in any direct way—they had, in effect, agreed to disagree—but the differences and the distances be-

tween them remained wide and deep. Even the terms themselves—
liberal, conservative—had lost their meaning. Time was when conservatives were enemies of change, defenders of the status quo, preserv-
ers of the past, while liberals were deeply committed to growth and
change. But by the mid-1970s it was liberals who were trying to preserve and protect such threatened Southern assets as the environment, the black heritage, natural resources, and old buildings—and
it was conservatives who led the drive for development and change,
which they called progress.

In that conflicting jumble of skewed perceptions and wrung-out
emotions, there was ample evidence to support just about any conclusion you wanted to draw. Was this the heralded "New South" we had
been promised perennially since Atlanta's Henry Grady coined the
phrase in the late nineteenth century? Perhaps. Or was it another
mirage, a fleeting image that would soon be gone with the wind? That
was also possible.

Certainly it was in many respects a New South, and as a lifelong
Southerner, I was pleased and proud to see the positive changes it
brought. I was delighted to see Jimmy Carter in the White House, the
more so because he so unequivocally rejected the doctrine of white
supremacy upon which much of the Old South was based. I was also
proud to see the South becoming healthier, better educated, less
poverty-stricken, and more self-sufficient than it had ever been in the
past. I took special delight in the stories I heard about Washington
bureaucrats trying to imitate the Southern tongue and New York society matrons serving cornbread and turnip greens and sweet potato
pie to their guests.

But all the while I kept remembering a conversation I had in New
York while Carter was accepting the nomination at the Democrats'
love feast. An old friend whose roots are in North Carolina had invited me for a drink to celebrate this national victory of a Southern
native son. We were filled to overflowing with pride and hope, but as
we talked, he gradually began to articulate a nagging worry that lay
dark and unexpressed in my own breast. I think of his words now as
prophetic.

"If Carter pulls this off," he said, "he'll go down in history as one
of our greatest presidents, and the South will be back in the national
fold at last, and on equal terms. But if he fails, Southerners up here

won't be able to find a rock big enough to hide behind, and the South will still be seen as a separate and unequal backwater region, a stepchild of the superior North."

Jimmy Carter lost his bid for reelection four years later, a victim of the energy crisis, the Iran hostage seizure, and the television persona of Ronald Reagan. Intellectually, Carter may have been the best-equipped president we ever had, but he was unable to put his ideas and plans into compelling words powerful enough to galvanize the nation. It was an irony of classic dimensions. For over a century the South had been sending waves of silver-tongued demagogues into public life, white men who had almost nothing going for them except rhetoric. Then, finally, we sent a good man all the way to the White House—and he turned out to have almost everything on his side except rhetoric. If Carter had been as good on his feet as Huey Long or George Wallace or Jesse Jackson, he probably would have trounced Reagan in 1980 and perhaps even have changed the course of history for the South and the nation.

Not all that has happened in the 1980s is a consequence of that political struggle, of course; in fact, the Carter victory in 1976 may have blinded us to some already-surging currents of change that were making the newest New South look suspiciously like the Old North warmed over. We had made great strides in eliminating racism, but the disease was still in us, buried deep and discreetly masked by code phrases such as *reverse discrimination* and *neighborhood schools*. We had built glittering cities of steel and glass, but they looked for all the world like the cities of the North, and they emptied out at night as our commuters retreated to the suburban Grosse Pointes we had built beyond the moated loops of our freeways. We had supplemented our agricultural economy with modern industry, but in the process had made farming impossible for all but the corporate giants of agribusiness. We had sought and welcomed and even given tax breaks to Northern industrial corporations—and often averted our eyes from such subsequent problems as increased environmental pollution and the exploitation of nonunion labor.

Our freeways have come to look like extensions of the Pennsylvania Turnpike. Our airports are indistinguishable from those in the North, except that they're generally bigger (the Dallas–Fort Worth jetport is larger than the island of Manhattan). Even when we pioneer in the development of new facilities, such as the air-conditioned As- trodome in Houston, we can't seem to resist overplaying the game of one-upmanship—so now we have the Louisiana Superdome in New Orleans, which looks like an earthbound mushroom cloud and cost ten times more than Thomas Jefferson paid for the Louisiana Pur- chase.

On top of all that, we have outfitted and lacquered these monu- ments of the latest New South with the same plastic and styrofoam, the same computerized systems, the same processed fast foods, the same televised trivia, the same neon, the same theme parks and tape decks and double knit suits that symbolize America to the world. What is worse, many of those emblems of our rapidly amalgamating nation are Southern originals. The New South creed is becoming the New South greed, and the South, having been exploited to a fare- thee-well for more than a century, now seems intent on mindlessly exploiting itself.

To be ambivalent about the direction and pace of change in the South is to run the risk of being misunderstood on all sides. I do not long nostalgically for the "good old days" of the bygone South; more than that, I don't believe they were ever really all that good, even for the white males of wealth and property who dominated life in the region. I am not an elitist, a racist, a radical, a neoagrarian, a neocon- servative, or a hopelessly blinded romantic. I am not an opponent of industrialization, a skeptic of cities, or an enemy of growth. I am simply a believer in and an advocate of some qualities and character- istics that I think are uniquely and distinctively Southern—and very much in danger of extinction.

I like Southern speech, in all its rich diversity and expressiveness, and Southern food, which is equally as varied. I like the pace of life here, and the people—most of them—and the ease of personal rela- tionships. I like the old architecture and much of the music, old and new. I love the natural beauty of the South, and the reverent attach- ment so many people have to the land. I like the independence and eccentricity of Southerners, and their sense of continuity with the past, and their sense of humor.

But it is these very qualities of grace and space and soul that seem most susceptible to erosion in the modern South. The miraculous vessels of the contemporary age—television, computers, and all the other forms of high technology—have brought us variety and latitude and convenience, and we like that and accept it. But they also bring us uniformity and impersonal detachment and a confused and weakened sense of values, and those things we are compelled to accept in the bargain, whether we like it or not.

In my most pessimistic moments, I am persuaded that the South has already surrendered whatever virtues it has left and that its total loss of identity is only a matter of time. In that view, Atlanta will soon become the Manhattan of the Southern plains, Birmingham will be asphyxiated in a pall like Pittsburgh's, Nashville's dream of rivaling Hollywood will turn out to be a nightmare of reality, Charleston's segregation will match that of Chicago, and the Mississippi River from Baton Rouge to New Orleans will burn as foully as the Cayahoga in Cleveland.

Perhaps all these negative consequences of rapid change in the twilight of the twentieth century are inevitable. Maybe all the possible ways in which growth and industrialization and urbanization can take place are so limited that we are bound to follow the patterns of Northern cities, bound to repeat their mistakes. But I'm not entirely convinced of it. I may be a little bit schizophrenic, but as a Southerner, I come by my schizophrenia naturally. I can be both fatalistic and hopeful, resigned and defiant, and see no contradiction in that at all. I am not a pessimist at heart. There still lives in me the irrational notion that human beings, though they are the only species that foul their own nests, are also the only ones who plant flowers and paint pictures and write songs, and that those attempts at creativity, however tenuous and fragile, will finally be enough to save us. If we are reduced to nothing but our vocal chords, I keep thinking, we will still find a way to talk ourselves out of the mess we're in.

The people of the South have been hearing voices for centuries, for as long as men and women have congregated here and tried to put their thoughts and feelings into words. Aboriginal voices of great eloquence, such as that of the Seminole Osceola, a Floridian, or the Cherokee Sequoyah, a Tennessean. Voices of white explorers and pioneers whose words we found carved in tree trunks on Roanoke Island

and at Cumberland Gap. Voices of black heroes courageously defiant of slavery, people like Frederick Douglass and Harriet Tubman, Nat Turner and Sojourner Truth. Voices of war and peace, and of reconciliation—Henry Clay, Jefferson Davis, Abraham Lincoln, Robert E. Lee. Voices of the Old South and the New, of statesmen and demagogues, orators and professors, preachers and lawyers, novelists and poets. Voices of the uncounted legions of master storytellers and scribes—men and women, white and black, old and young, rich and poor, learned and unlettered. People blessed with natural and effortless and even unconscious eloquence, with an innate ability to describe and relate. William Faulkner, I am persuaded, was not a geographical aberration, not a Southern accident; on the contrary, he was a product of the native voices that resonated all around him, and had he been a Californian or a New Yorker, he would have been a very different writer.

Southern voices, old and new, are as much a part of who we are as any other feature of our existence. We are so steeped in porch talk, table talk, hearth talk, and pillow talk, so engrossed in history and family, so much a part of the land around us, that it is hard to imagine a South not filled with a babble, a cacophony of voices. We even hear voices when they're not there, and out of the imagination and mystery of those haunting echoes have come great volumes of myth and romance and gothic wonder.

There is also much irony and paradox in the voices of the South. Many outsiders have concluded that we are speaking with a single voice, a monolithic drawl, when in fact the voices of Southerners have been and are astonishingly diverse and varied—in content as well as in accent. And there is the abiding contradiction of a South blessed with an abundance of gifted writers and speakers—and cursed with an even greater abundance of citizens who can't read or write, who don't buy books or use libraries, and who generally don't place a high value on the ability to use words.

Strange it is that such a combination of mute and eloquent people should come up together, side by side, but such is the contradictory nature of Southern life and history. In his remembrance of a boyhood in Kentucky and Tennessee, Robert Penn Warren holds especially dear the ones who loved words; to him, they had no equal.

257

"I have learned," he said in 1979, "that in the North they tell jokes, they even make joke books, but in the South, at least in the South of that pre-television time, they told tales—elaborate, winding, wandering creations that might never wear out, stories full of human perception and subtlety, told with a richness of language and expression. They told tales that were the essence of Southern fiction—not idle gossip, not diversions, mind you, but tales of wit and character, of pathos, of scope. Yankees—except in back-country Vermont—don't really know about tales. What I'm getting at is a regional difference, a Southern gift that springs from the pores of the society. It's a classless gift, as apt to be heard in the conversation of a Tennessee tenant farmer or an Alabama plantation lady or a Louisiana fisherman as in the eloquence and art of Eudora Welty or William Faulkner or Katherine Anne Porter."

Thinking of that classless gift and its perilous future, Robert Penn Warren concluded with an observation that could become an epitaph for Southern voices. "Television," he said, "may be the death of the tale."

All our strengths—of family and history and tradition, of geography and climate, of music and food, of spoken and written language—are endangered treasures. For every Southern family bonded by cross-generational remembrance, a dozen have split and scattered beyond recall. For every friendly store clerk or helpful stranger, there are scores of automatic tellers and electronic answering devices. Our sultry atmosphere has been neutralized by air-conditioned malls and all-weather controls—while outdoors, atmospheric haze and acid rain and poisonous effluent are destroying our sparkling waters and golden sunsets.

For every kettle of black-eyed peas or pan of scratch biscuits or platter of country ham emanating from a Southern kitchen, there are now a blue million Kentucky Fried drumsticks and Big Macs. And the land, the family farm? Suffice it to say that the largest farm in North Carolina today is half the size of the state of Rhode Island—and its owner is an investor in New York or Germany or Saudi Arabia or someplace light years removed from the sandy loam of Carolina.

For Southerners under the age of thirty, it becomes harder and harder to understand what all this introspection and hand-wringing were about in the first place. They are the first generation not to be defined by the experiences that shaped their elders—and their children and their children's children will be even less affected by the accident of being born and raised in the southern region of the United States.

The experience of black Americans—black Southerners in particular—is a prism through which we can see clearly what is happening to the South just now. Since the end of World War II blacks have acted with courage and determination to throw off the mantle of segregation and inequality that had been unfairly placed upon them. They have demanded to be recognized as complete and equal citizens of this region and this nation. Many whites incorrectly perceived that what the blacks wanted was simply to be like us. But in recent years they have taught us a different lesson. They wanted the same rights and privileges and opportunities that all citizens are supposed to enjoy, of course—but they also wanted to retain their identity as African-Americans, to nourish and strengthen their own cultural identity, to celebrate themselves and their forebears with pride and dignity, just as every other American is free to do.

Think what a parallel that experience suggests for all of us, black and white, who are Southerners. For well over a century we have been trying to recover from the ravages of a lost cause, trying to prove to a smugly superior and self-righteous nation that we are deserving of their respect. We have wanted to be fully accepted into the national community. Many people in other parts of the nation have mistakenly concluded that we wanted more than anything to have what they had, do what they did, be who they were. If we have absorbed at all the lesson offered to us by the black teachers in our midst, we will insist not only on having our full rights as Americans but also on retaining our character and our identity as Southerners.

What we are witnessing now is the integration of the South with the rest of the nation. In the literal meaning of the word *integration*— "to make whole"—lies our hope for the future. If we do it right, we will make the United States truly one nation, indivisible, with liberty and justice for all. In that best of all worlds, the South would spread its strengths throughout the land, and the best qualities of the rest of the nation would permeate the South, and we could retain and perpetuate our regional identity and our Southern heritage within the larger context of the united country. In the same manner, the real integration of black and white cultures in this society would bring about not the erasing of one for the sake of the other, but a fusion of the two in such a way that we could each be both singular and plural, multicultural brothers and sisters.

If we could accomplish such an equitable union of the races and of the regions of this nation, we would at last have a society worthy of the great ideals that Thomas Jefferson, one of the first in a long line of eloquent Southern phrasemakers, put into the Declaration of Independence more than two hundred years ago.

Surely that is a dream worth nourishing, a goal worth seeking—to forge a nation that is the sum of its distinct parts, rather than an amalgamation of them. In such a society, there would always be a South and a multitude of voices to tell its tales. For the sake of us all, I hope and pray that such will be the future of the South.

⚖ Index

Lippmann, Walter, 152
Little, Joan, 221, 222
Liuzzo, Viola, 191
Long, Huey, 254
Longwood College, 119–20, 122
Lucy, Autherine, 8, 215
Lundy, Adeline, 244
Lunn, Edith, 53
Lynchings, 164–65, 166, 212
Lyons, Georgia Ann, 136

McCampbell, Vera, 64–65
McCarthy, Eugene, 188
McCarthy, Joe, 152, 157
McCoy, William, 86–87
McDade, George, Jr., 178
McDougal, Luther, 20
McGill, Ralph, 156
McGovern, George, 158, 213, 220–21, 223, 233
McMillan, George, 193, 199
McMillan, John E., 167, 174, 177, 185
Malcolm X, 2, 52
Malone, Vivian, 8
Mandell, Howard, 221, 232
MAPCO, 83, 86, 95–96
Marcum, Homer, 91, 94
Martin, Burke, 71
Martin County, Ky., 77–104
Massey (A. T.) Company, 95
Maynard, Gladys, 99–100, 104
Maynard, Ronnie, 88
Maynard, Vernal, 99, 100–101
Mays, Frances, 169, 184
Mays, Maurice F., 165, 169–70, 172, 173–83, 185
Mays, William, 169, 182, 183
Meeks, Colleen, 69–70
Mendil, Mack, 184, 185, 186, 187
Mendil, Sadie, 184–87
Meredith, James, 8, 13, 17
Metzger, Tom, 236
Mining. See Coal mining
Mississippi: race and class in, 8, 13–22
Montgomery, Eddie, 40

Montgomery, Ernestine, 48–49, 55
Montgomery, Fred, Jr., 39–40, 42, 47, 48–49, 50, 51, 55, 56, 57
Moore, Alice, 24–25, 26, 30, 35–37, 38
Moore, Darrell, 36
Moore, Julia, 242
Morehead, Armstead, 138, 140
Morehead, Armstead S., 140–41
Morehead, Charles, 138, 140
Morehead, Charles S., 140
Morehead, Elizabeth, 140–41
Morehead, James T., 140
Morehead, James W., 140–41, 143, 144
Morehead, Lizzie Bibb, 132, 136, 137, 141, 142
Morehead, Presley, 138, 140
Morehead, Sam, 140
Morehead, Tom, 132, 136, 137, 139, 140–44, 145
Morehead, Virgil, 136
Morehead State University, 97
Morgan, Chuck, 73, 218, 225
Morris, Kizzie, 46
Morrison, J. V., 240
Morse, Joshua, III, 17–20, 21, 22
Moss, Gordon, 113, 122–23, 129
Muncy, Betty, 93
Murphy, Jay, 218
Murphy, William P., 17
Murray, Donald, 7
Murray, Irene, 41, 46, 56
Murray, Thomas, 41, 46, 56
Murtagh, Arthur, 198–99
Mynatt, R. A., 173, 174, 179–80

National Anti-Klan Network, 229
National Association for the Advancement of Colored People, 25, 58, 66, 67, 108, 110, 111, 113, 115, 123, 124, 167–68, 173, 228
National Conference of Negro Women, 115
National Education Association, 37
National Science Foundation, 160
Nelson, T. A. R., 173, 178, 179–80